Zen Teachings in Challenging Times

Introduction by
Patricia Dai-En Bennage

with

Myoan Grace Schireson, Shosan Victoria Austin, Myosho Ann Kyle-Brown, Melissa Myozen Blacker, Zenki Mary Mocine, Byakuren Judith Ragir, Shunzan Jill Kaplan, Sosan Theresa Flynn, Ganman Cathy Toldi, Myokaku Jane Schneider, Josho Pat Phelan, Isshin Havens, Hobu Beata Chapman, Joan Hogetsu Hoeberichts, Carolyn Joshin Atkinson, Enkyo Pat O'Hara, Konin Cardenas, Diane Shoshin Fitzgerald, Myoshin Kate McCandless, Tenku Ruff, Myo-O Marilyn Habermas-Scher, Shodo Spring, Sarah Dojin Emerson, Heiku Jaime McLeod, Eido Frances Carney

Temple Ground Press

Temple Ground Press
3248 39th Way NE
Olympia, WA 98506

Copyright 2018 Temple Ground Press

All rights reserved. No part of this publication may be reproduced, stored in a retrieval system, or transmitted, in any form or by any means, electronic, mechanical, photocopying, recording, or otherwise, without the prior permission of Temple Ground Press.

Cover and interior design and photography by Fletcher Ward,
Set in Minion Pro 8/17

ISBN 978-1723235634

Temple Ground Press, Olympia, WA

Dedication

… hearing the name or seeing the form of
Kanzeon, Avalokiteshvara, Kuan Yin,
the embodiment of compassionate loving kindness
with mindful remembrance is not in vain,
for the woes of existence can thus be relieved.

Enmei Jikku Kannon Gyo

Kanzeon! Namu Butsu
Kanzeon! At one with Buddha
Yo Butsu u in, Yo Butsu u en
Related to all Buddhas in cause and effect
Buppo so en
Our true nature is
Jo raku ga jo
Eternal, joyous, selfless, pure
Cho nen Kanzeon
Morning mind is Kanzeon
Bo nen Kanzeon
Evening mind is Kanzeon
Nen nen ju shin ki
This very moment arises from Mind
Nen nen fu ri shin
This very moment itself is Mind

Contents

Introduction 11
    Patricia Dai-En Bennage

I
Kanzeon! Namu Butsu
Kanzeon! At one with Buddha

Blowing in the Wind: Facing Challenges with Zen Practice 21
    Myoan Grace Schireson

Impact: Accidental Zen—How the Three Pure Precepts Trained Me to Heal Self and Others 35
    Shosan Victoria Austin

The Four Noble Truths of Practice in Times of Challenge and Struggle . 47
    Myosho Ann Kyle-Brown

Cutting the World in Two 59
    Melissa Myozen Blacker

I Hate Donald Trump 67
    Zenki Mary Mocine

II
Yo Butsu u in, Yo Butsu u en
Related to all Buddhas in cause and effect

Emergency Spirituality 77
    Byakuren Judith Ragir

Deep Connection to the Dharma 87
    Shunzan Jill Kaplan

Disillusionment 95
    Sosan Theresa Flynn

Feeling Our Way to Embodied Wisdom 107
    Ganman Cathy Toldi

Breath Is Life 117
    Myokaku Jane Schneider

III
Buppo so en, Jo raku ga jo
Our true nature is eternal, joyous, selfless, pure

Friendliness to the Self 127
   Josho Pat Phelan

A Bumpy Ride with Dukkha 139
   Isshin Havens

Taking Refuge in Sangha: How Wide Can This Buddha Field Be? 147
   Hobu Beata Chapman

Love and Fear 159
   Joan Hogetsu Hoeberichts

Accepting Our Lives in Difficult Times 167
   Carolyn Joshin Atkinson

IV
Cho nen Kanzeon, Bo nen Kanzeon
Morning Mind is Kanzeon; evening Mind, is Kanzeon

Showing Up in Troubled Times 179
   Enkyo Pat O'Hara

Grappling with the Green-Eyed Monster 187
   Konin Cardenas

Finding Peace 197
   Diane Shoshin Fitzgerald

Beings are Numberless: When Bodhisattvas Get Discouraged 205
   Myoshin Kate McCandless

Karkinos: The True Crab 219
   Tenku Ruff

V
Nen nen ju shin ki, Nen nen fu ri shin
This very moment arises from Mind, this very moment itself is Mind

In Which This 231
   Myo-O Marilyn Habermas-Scher

When the World Is On Fire: Reflections on These Times 241
   Shodo Spring

Birth and Death 253
    Sarah Dojin Emerson

Picking and Choosing.. 263
    Heiku Jaime McLeod

Can Kanzeon Bodhisattva Laugh? 273
    Eido Frances Carney

Chants 283

Glossary 287

Acknowledgments 297

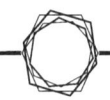

Patricia Dai-En Bennage, abbess emerita, Mt. Equity Zendo, Jihoji, formerly in Muncy, Pennsylvania, trained in Japan at the Aichi Semmon Nisodo in Nagoya for eleven years, with *angos* later at Hosshinji, Hokyoji, and Koshoji. She is the translator of *Zen Seeds* written by the Abbess Shundo Aoyama of the Aichi Semmon Nisodo. Dai-En graduated from Sophia University, Tokyo, in 1972. She trained with the Rinzai master Omori Sogen Roshi for three years. On the Shikoku eighty-eight-temple pilgrimage, she met her teacher, Noda Daito Roshi, and after ordination in 1979, she was sent to the Aichi Semmon Nisodo. She graduated from Shike training in Kyoto in 1989, and returned to Pennsylvania to pioneer Mt. Equity Zendo. She also led zazen at Bucknell University and at six federal prisons. Dai-En was recognized by the International Women's Day Outstanding Women in Buddhism Awards given in Bangkok in 2008 for Outstanding Contribution to Buddhism.

Introduction

Patricia Dai-En Bennage

This book of essays comes from priests who are my sister teachers in the Dharma, and whose spiritual perspectives rise out of the foundational teachings of Soto Zen Buddhism. All the writers stand in the lineage of Zen masters from Shakyamuni Buddha to the present day. Their teachings resonate in the long history and ancient wisdom of Zen as it evolved from India, China, Korea, and Japan, and now is blooming in North America, South America, Europe, Africa, Australia, and New Zealand.

In the twenty-first century we are faced with past actions coming forward to confront us with difficult intensity and calamity. At the same time, humankind has produced profound inventions, particularly in medicine and science that have benefited so many of us. But although a great number of people around the world are living in relative comfort, many others are not. Any person awake to the movement of our cultures and societies and the difficult interactions of our governments must consider whether we have evolved in wisdom in our global relationships and choices. Are we using our resources and abilities in the best possible way toward a more humane and inclusive approach to life? No doubt, Mother Earth has always experienced critical times and this era holds no less profound concern.

What period in history has not seen challenges? Every era has had its sufferings. Throughout the years, people have confronted troubles and been tested in courage. Those who face famine, war, disease, poverty, inequality, slavery, migration, turbulence—any kind of grave threat—must summon courage if they are to survive.

This book of essays by Buddhist women teachers looks at a range of personal or public challenges and draws on the teachings—the Dharma—to offer ways to view those challenges and respond to them with courage. No doubt, calling on Kanzeon, the Bodhisattva of Compassion, is a point of reliance. This volume of essays is organized around our presencing in the Bodhisattva's act of hearing the cries of suffering and responding with compassion. It is through this act of compassion that we find our ability to stand with courage in a world of suffering, bringing the Bodhisattva alive and present in our midst.

As a Soto Zen teacher, I can offer the example of Dogen Zenji, the thirteenth-century founder of Soto Zen in Japan, whose own life was beset with difficulties. He lived in a time fraught with turbulence, and his response to those difficulties is instructive for us in our own challenging times. Soto Zen teachers like myself, bestowed with the mantle of leadership, follow in Dogen's footsteps as he models composure and resolve, demonstrating the vow of lived Dharma in the face of challenge. His story is to be honored as we model our teachings on the example of his life.

The heavens arched over Dogen, and Saint Francis, and Rumi in the late twelfth and thirteenth centuries; their lives overlapped. What was in the stars at that time! Dogen was born into a good family, but when he was just two years old, a toddler learning to read kanji (Chinese-derived characters), his father died. Who taught him to read during his tender years, alone without a father, when his mother, too, died, when he was seven, asking him on her deathbed to help this fleeting world? Dogen's uncle took him under his wing, no doubt with high hopes for this small genius. The broken family must have felt happy to see the quickness of Dogen's young mind; it boded well for his future. But whatever his uncle's plans may have been for the boy to carry on the family name, Dogen was determined not to live the life of a noble but to adopt the tonsure. The dying request of his mother that he be there for the needs of others—how could he have known what it was? But it was a direction he needed to go—away from sorrow and loss, from *dukkha*, but with dignity and learning, learning more to obtain the buddha dharma to help all beings.

Introduction

The top of Hiei-zan, the highest mountain in the area northeast of Kyoto, is reached in these modern times by car or bus via forty-seven hairpin turns; the weather up there quite different from what it is below. The great and grand Enryaku-ji is located there, and it was to this temple that Dogen climbed, quite possibly on his own, with great determination, to be tonsured at the age of thirteen. But no satisfying answer came to Dogen there, and in 1215, aged fifteen, he left to find the new Buddhist master Eisai, trained in far-off China, who had brought back to Japan the new Lin'chi or Rinzai Zen teaching. Did Dogen and Eisai ever meet? It is not known for certain, the master having died the year that Dogen made this decision. But Eisai Zenji had just transmitted his teaching to his disciple Myozen, at a new temple in the center of Kyoto called Kennin-ji, which had a magnificent vividly painted dragon high above on the ceiling. Dogen spent seven years there, absorbing the koans and practice of Rinzai Zen with Myozen. Still, Dogen remained unsatisfied, and determined to go to China for himself, even convincing Myozen to go with him. One might wonder who took care of Kennin-ji when both Dogen and Myozen left for China. The temple had to fare on its own, in this fresh new style of Buddhism, with the other disciples of Eisai Zenji. Surely Myozen would never have left had he felt that to do so would jeopardize the future of his master's teachings.

Myozen, through Eisai Zenji's lineage, had legal passage into China and its temples, but Dogen did not, and had to wait for entry to the country on the boat at harbor. But he had the good fortune to meet a tenzo, a monk in charge of a monastery kitchen, who proved to be one of his great teachers. The tenzo had come on board to purchase mushrooms for the temple meal. In their conversation, which had to have included sign language and gestures, it is said that Dogen "sweated" to try to understand him, not being able to depend on words and letters. This "sweating" is important. The tenzo had confounded the brilliant intellect of Dogen. Something changed in Dogen, something transpired—learning of the Way, not just through writing, but by kan—the sixth sense. Something new was cracking open in Dogen as they met in that small ship, which prepared him for his long wanderings on foot through China.

It was fortunate that Dogen knew the writing. Spoken Chinese and Japanese, so very different from each other, can be understood by speakers of the other language if the kanji or Chinese characters are traced on the palm of a hand, or drawn with a stick in dirt. In this way, Dogen could communicate with others in the beginning and then, as he acquired more language, at Tendo-zan, the temple of his new teacher, Juching. The Chinese monk Jakuen, whom Dogen met at Tendo-zan, communicated in the same way when he went to Japan. Before his teacher, Juching, died, Jakuen asked Juching for permission to follow Dogen to Japan, provided it was after his passing. Jakuen would have taken a small ship, then walked alone, in his Chinese robes, from the port of entry in southern Japan, all the way north, to where Dogen's temple was. Wending his way, inquiring from the Japanese, perhaps by showing them an address in kanji, he familiarized himself with his new land. Years later, when Dogen died, Jakuen left Eihei-ji and after some years, found a sponsor to build Hokyo-ji, even deeper in the mountains. He lived on into his nineties, going on the alms round with his cow and his dog, deeply knowing sufficiency.

These teachers knew courage. When words do not suffice, something else more intuitive must take its place. How refreshing and challenging this must have felt to the Chinese Juching, instructing Dogen, who had walked his way to Tendo-zan. Think, too, of how challenging it was in recent decades for ordained women from three continents to communicate with the abbess of the Nisodo, or with other Japanese Soto Zen masters. One challenge to modern-day Zen masters in temples throughout Japan has been to take in those from around the world who arrived with *hotsubodaishin*, the "heart for the Way"—in most cases without any language fluency except their "heart for the Way." The masters in present-day Japan recognized this *hotsubodaishin* and made *gassho*, bowing with both hands together, recognizing this attribute in their hearts. Think of the courage of the ones who step forward, and the trust of those who receive the earnest appeal of the pilgrim. This was the experience of both Dogen and Juching. Dogen and Myozen had come to China together but because Dogen was detained in port, each of them had to search for the Dharma throughout China on his own. In the fullness of time, after he had met Juching, Dogen learned that Myozen had died. Dogen took Myozen's cremated remains and returned with them to Kennin-ji in Kyoto. Myozen's name plaque is visible there today. Dogen remained resolute, however heart-stricken and alone. And when he realized that Kennin-ji had changed during his long absence, and was no longer the place of practice he had envisioned, he fearlessly set out alone.

Dogen was still in his twenties when he founded his small An'yo-in at Fukaku-za, "the seat of the deep grass." We can contemplate how it has been for North American teachers, and for the European and South American followers of Zen Buddhism that came after them, to found Zen temples based on ancient teachings so far away from Japan. Who first came to Dogen? Who left and who stayed on with him? Was it like what we're doing in the West? Juching had advised, "Stay clear of the capital and go into the mountains," and with the unrest that had roiled the temple on Mount Heiei, Dogen understood this necessity. He had spent sixteen years in Kyoto, and was ready to move far away.

Dogen left Kyoto with Ejo and several other monks, some from the main Rinzai tradition and some from the defunct but well-trained Daruma sect. They had come to Dogen to challenge him, but stayed on with Dogen; among these was Ejo, who became Dogen's disciple. Ejo realized that although he was two years older than Dogen, Dogen was deeper in understanding. He became Dogen's strongest support, and then his successor. Ejo's *Shobogenzo Zuimonki*, his account of Dogen's teaching, provides an easier entryway for beginners into parts of Dogen's great masterpiece, *Shobogenzo*.

Dogen's monks and followers must have walked to Fukui prefecture—its ancient name was Echizen—but who else came with them and banded with them? Besides the monks of the Daruma sect, could there have been others? Dogen writes about proper manners and comportment that his trained monks would have already known. Did Dogen find new followers on his way to Echizen? Who else, frightened and alone, perhaps unschooled, was looking for refuge, for safe harbor? Was there not safety in numbers? Who did Dogen take in? Who stayed? Who left? Who were sent away? Mention is made in the *Shobogenzo* of a monk who was sent away because he showed glee when the temple received generous alms. Stripped of his robes, he was made to exit via the east gate, the doorway used only for banishment. At Kosho-ji when it is *samu*, time to clean the zendo, even though the east gate is slid open for airing, and to this day no one crosses over the threshold, but walks around it. Every monk knows that story.

A wealthy sponsor named Hadano Yoshishige encouraged Dogen to move to where Daibutsu-ji, "the Great Buddha Temple" would be built, deep in the mountains. The temple's name later changed to Eihei-ji, "the Temple of Eternal Peace," and remains as such today. How did women, perhaps bringing donations of flowers and food, come to be Dogen's congregants, his students, and then, perhaps his disciples?

After Daibutsu-ji was complete and his fame grew, Dogen undertook the long journey to Kamakura to deliver his treatise to the shogun there. He derived little benefit from his effort. The country's political leaders invited him repeatedly to their courts, but fame and fortune were not what he was seeking. When the emperor asked him three times to accept the highly prestigious gift of a purple robe, Dogen did so at last, with the greatest reluctance, perhaps recalling again the admonition of Juching, to steer clear of the capital.

There can be suffering from not having certain things. There can be suffering from having too few as well as too many robes. Life is suffering, or as the Buddha called it, *dukkha*. I once received a *shikishi* from my teacher, a white square of stiff paper edged in gold, with calligraphy reading "*Kishu, Busshin*," meaning "Devil's Hand, Buddha's Heart/Mind." Because we have the one, we have the other; or, despite the one, there is the other. In the East, Sawaki Roshi proclaimed, "Loss is gain and gain is loss." In the West, Shakespeare Roshi proclaimed, "Faire is foul and foul is faire." The Buddha's core teaching is that "life is suffering," but he taught us the way out of suffering. And we carry on his tradition of the teaching, embracing it all, leaving nothing out. It is said that there are Three Great Gifts: the gift of material goods, the gift of the spiritual, and the gift of no fear. With the gift of sufficient material goods to keep body and mind together, we can partake of the spiritual. The gift of fear stands at the portal, and thanks to its presence, and our dealing with it, we come to no fear, ample enough to spread in all directions and to all beings.

In Burton Watson's translation of *Cold Mountain*, two couriers offer the two sages Han Shan and Shih-te fine gifts from an official of the Tang dynasty, because he had heard they were two worthy teachers. The two sages laughed and hooted, then ran away up the mountain, calling over their shoulders, "Thieves! Thieves!" Who was robbing them of what? The poet Gary Snyder venerated Han Shan. One day, he met a visiting American government official, Daniel Ellsberg, in a Kyoto bar. After a night of talking, Ellsberg left, deeply impressed—he had never before met a man who could not be bought. Some time down the road, his own conscience irretrievably awakened, he exposed the scandal of Watergate. These are the things that can happen when the Dharma grabs us and we go forward with courage. The sky becomes the limit. Losing too many loved ones to wars like Vietnam and now the Middle East can do that, too.

What arouses our courage? The teachers standing strong in these essays, endowed with the heart/mind of Kanzeon, show us the way to embody the Dharma, to bring integrity to all our activities, to bring courage to the table of life no matter what we face. To bring Dharma to life because buddha nature is what we are. As students of the Buddha, this is the Way we walk, on the pathway to help all beings. We must not be fickle in our steadfastness to alleviate suffering nor can we turn from the challenges ahead. It is a time for great courage and spiritual resilience. I cannot adequately express my gratitude to all of the teachers here who speak their deepest truths of the Dharma in order to benefit us all. To read this book, let it fall open to any page and find deep spiritual stability embedded here through the inspiration of Dogen and proffered by my sister priest/teachers with "the heart for the Way." We are all teachers of each other. Because the essays in this book are so deeply rooted in and dedicated to the heart of Kanzeon, I feel certain that the readers will put to work the teachings in this powerful volume.

I

Kanzeon! Namu Butsu

Kanzeon! At one with Buddha

Myoan Grace Schireson, Ph.D., is a Zen abbess, and a clinical psychologist. She received dharma transmission from Sojun Mel Weitsman Roshi of the Suzuki Roshi Zen lineage. The late Fukushima Keido Roshi of Tofukuji Monastery, Kyoto, asked her to teach the koan that she studied with him during her practice there. She founded two Zen practice centers and a retreat center, has empowered seven actively teaching dharma heirs, and offers meditation groups at Stanford University. She is the author of *Zen Women: Beyond Tea Ladies, Iron Maidens and Macho Masters* (Wisdom, 2009), and coedited *Zen Bridge: The Teachings of Keido Fukushima* (Wisdom, 2017).

Blowing in the Wind: Facing Challenges with Zen Practice

Myoan Grace Schireson

For Buddhist practitioners, challenge is like the wind. Challenge can turn you around, it can blow you away. Some challenges are distant, some more personal. This essay focuses on ways Zen practice can help us meet challenges that confront us on a personal level—challenges that trigger past traumas, upset our sense of stability, and test our resources for recovery. Suffering is inevitable in this life. Zen Buddhist practice offers insight into how when we experience challenges through the filter of personal losses, we increase our suffering. Zen also offers practices to help us recognize our suffering and release it. Using our own self-knowledge and peering through the eyes of Zen, then, let us explore how, despite our intentions, we may increase our suffering. More important, how do we learn to relieve it. Self-knowledge is key to making use of Zen resources. There are no formulas or magic solutions to personal suffering. We must honestly explore our own mind state, and then consider the resources available.

Life may have gone well when we were in utero, but it has been downhill ever since. Most human beings have the experience of being perfectly cared for in the womb—nourished without having to make any effort, never lacking for contact and company. Our skin is neither bruised nor itchy, the water temperature is perfect, and we are not expected to prove anything to anyone. In short, in utero we have no need to avoid pain or to seek pleasure or the attention of others. Perhaps our time in utero is the source of our craving for a steady state of satisfaction. Unfortunately, everything changed when we were born, and ever since we have been bombarded by discomfort. In Buddhist practice, we may work to identify just where we get caught by challenge and just which practice leads us to untangle the suffering.

In Buddhist terms, seeking pleasure is called seeking gain, and chasing after the positive regard of others is the pursuit of fame. These are two compelling ways that we long for happiness and create a cycle of suffering. According to an ancient Chinese proverb,[1] the emperor, viewing crowds walking below him, wondered aloud to his prime minister how many people passed through the city gates each day. The prime minister replied that there are only two people—Fame and Gain—pointing to the two vehicles humans attempt to ride to happiness. In a sense, our search for fame and gain are extreme expressions of a yearning to return to the perfect condition we experienced in the womb.

The concept of impermanence, the notion of no separate self, and the truth of suffering are at the core of Zen teaching, but however much we study and practice with these ideas, it seems our primitive human instincts to crave the physical security and positive regard we once knew in utero persist. And when we face challenges, our instinctive yearning for security is activated, as though material satisfaction or favorable recognition will return us to a safe and comfortable place.

Among many Buddhist teachings on the particular nature of suffering is a metaphorical construct called the Eight Winds. Considering the Eight Winds through the lens of developmental psychology yields insights into how, at various stages of human development, our cravings for gain and fame arise and express themselves differently, enabling us to identify our cravings for fame and gain over the course of a lifetime.

The Eight Winds

In Buddhist teaching, the Eight Winds are organized in four sets of pairs:

    1. Pleasure and pain

    2. Gain and loss

3. Praise and blame

4. Fame and shame

We can see these Eight Winds as ways we attempt to find security and comfort under difficult circumstances throughout our lives. When we are children, we seek security differently than when we are adults; and in old age, we seek comfort in ways different from our efforts in young adulthood. We have an opportunity through Zen practice to recognize in any given moment both which wind is blowing and how we can remain upright and find equanimity in the face of it. We will first explore the developmental aspects of the Eight Winds, then prescribe eight Zen practices for awakened beings to help meet the Eight Winds with equanimity. To be human is to be blown by the Eight Winds; to practice Zen is to recognize and face the prevailing wind.

Human Development and the Eight Winds: From Infancy to Old Age

From infancy through old age, the Eight Winds blow with differing velocity and spin. Infants protest the wind of pain and seek the wind of pleasure. Does anyone blame an infant for howling at hunger, for whining at a wet, stinging diaper, for protesting sleep interrupted? The infant's responses are preprogrammed and instinctive. The infant objects to physical pain. For the infant, pleasure elicits grabbing, cooing, and smiling. These are unrefined physical reactions; the baby doesn't think about why she dislikes pain, or why she likes feeding and cuddling. Cuddle in, cooing out. Hunger in, screaming out. Correcting discomfort through infantile mechanisms is natural, but trouble brews when we retain these instinctive reactions beyond infancy.

As we develop, things change. Thought enters the picture. Unlike infants, older children think of ways to maximize pleasure and avoid its loss. Crying and cooing are mostly sidelined as children learn to reason and plan for increased satisfaction. In terms of the Eight Winds, this is called the stage of gain and loss. Begging or stealing cookies from the jar, explaining and denying guilt to avoid spanking or other punishment—these are examples of thinking and planning how to extend pleasure and avoid pain. The older child craves and gains pleasure through toys, sweets, and affection, and tries to avoid loss of pleasure through performance (being good), distractions (toys, electronic devices, and cartoons) and play.

The push and pull of gain and loss continue into adulthood, transformed into conceptual gains of profession, possessions, and place. When gain and loss move in this direction, gain includes approval and status as much as the acquisition of desired objects and pleasurable sensations. Loss includes loss of status, criticism, and lack of future security. This wind blows on the developing self as we create a personal identity through degrees, awards, activities, popularity, likes on social media, or publications. In adulthood, our pursuit of security through seeking gain and avoiding loss can become unconscious, almost second nature. And this brings us face to face with the next wind—pursuing praise and avoiding blame.

In adulthood, pursuing praise and avoiding blame can become automatic. We retain our attachment to physical pleasure, but we have created a personal self that seeks pleasure in the form of praise. This self shuns disagreement, criticism, loss of status, and blame. For the personal self, criticism can feel like physical pain. The adult develops a notion of self-worth—of worthiness that seeks praise for reassurance and avoids blame. Seeking praise can pervade a wide range of adult tasks and circumstances, including job, university, church and state responsibilities, partnering, and parenting. Our bodily cravings for pleasure, comfort, and security are joined by desire that our illusive, created self-image be promoted and prized.

As we come to face mortality and the limitations of old age, we may become more concerned with achieving fame and avoiding shame. In old age, the pace of our daily activity tends to slow down, and we have time to recount and remember our life goals, relationships, and accomplishments. With a little luck we are aware of our mortality, and of our diminished ability to gather comfort and avoid pain. Besides an inevitable return to physical pain during aging, a lifetime of effort comes under scrutiny. Did I do enough, what were my mistakes, how will I be remembered? What will my reputation be when I am dead? What are my regrets? Our concepts of gain and loss, and our experience of praise and blame, are reviewed through the lens of personal values we've acquired during the course of our lives.

In the Face of the Eight Winds

When an experience astounds or unsettles us—something outside our expectations—we say we are "blown away." Even if the astonishment is pleasing, when change falls outside our expectation, our sense of security is threatened. "Blown away" can likewise describe a sense of groundlessness—a moment in which we've lost our place, lost the sense of balance we rely on. This sense of disorientation doesn't usually last very long. When we are surprised, our brain activates an automatic correction device to right the ship of mind. We reach for security, comfort or validation that will restore our balance. Without having to think, we attempt to return to a feeling of safety, a kind of stasis. But while a sense of groundlessness may be uncomfortable, it offers an opportunity to realize freedom through acceptance, rather than worsening suffering through craving.

Wherever we may be in our lives, we have astounding or unsettling experiences, for there is no escaping the Eight Winds. Our instinctive pursuit of gain and fame makes us especially vulnerable to groundlessness and suffering during challenging times. Specific Buddhist practices can help us to recognize which wind is moving us, and how our urges to seek comfort and security against the force of the wind create more conflict. Fortunately, Zen practice addresses each of these winds and our developing vulnerability to fame and gain in their various guises.

Eight Practices for Awakening

There are eight practices for awakening to help us to recognize when we are facing one of the Eight Winds. If we recognize which wind we face, we're better able to recognize the arising of our instinctive drive to seek pleasure and avoid loss. Zen Master Dogen labels these practices for awakening as remedies for "people who seek fame and gain." Challenging events and the Eight Winds will blow throughout our lifetimes, but recognizing how and when they are disturbing us can guide a return to practice. We cannot eliminate the suffering of this human life, but we do not need to make the suffering worse. Understanding the eight practices for awakening can help us recognize and face rather than fight with our suffering. While all eight practices are included in a mature meditation practice, individual practices are specifically useful under particular circumstances.

The eight practices are

1. Developing stability in meditation

2. Realizing impermanence

3. Seeing that more desires increase suffering

4. Understanding that all humans have cravings

5. Not looking outside ourselves for affirmation

6. Finding time for secluded contemplation

7. Making sincere effort

8. Cultivating wisdom, seeing the world as always on fire (in crisis).

Stability in Meditation

We don't expect babies or children to practice Zen, but as their caregivers, parents, grandparents, we have the means to help them face their difficulties, to respond with understanding and compassion instead of going into panic and crisis mode. Often it is more painful for a parent to watch a child or a friend suffer than it is for the child or friend who is suffering. How do we settle our minds at such times? How do we find equanimity? It is not possible simply to leap into mindful equanimity in the face of a challenge. A calm mind must be cultivated, developed, and strengthened through meditation practice. This takes time and continued practice, returning to stability, both on the cushion and throughout the day. We need to experience and establish stability in meditation during quieter moments in order to call forth equanimity in the midst of challenge and the strong wind of pain. Thus, stability in meditation is the first, essential practice. With a calm and stable mind, we can communicate calm and acceptance rather than panic and avoidance.

Realizing Impermanence

By studying the mind's capriciousness in meditation, we become familiar with how painful, disturbing thoughts come and go. We realize that experiences of pain and pleasure are impermanent—both for ourselves and for our children. Pain and suffering do not exist in a vacuum; when the mind is more stable and spacious, there is a place for the storm to rage and subside. Pain occurs, but how we work with it—through acceptance and spaciousness—affects its severity and duration. This realization of impermanence is the second essential practice. The impulse to seek pleasure and avoid pain is automatic. It requires diligent effort to recognize its arising. Watching in meditation how the mind reaches for relief, we develop the ability to realize impermanence in the midst of craving pleasure and avoiding pain. In the quiet laboratory of zazen, seeing how our mind reaches for pleasure, we understand how the same tendency arises off the cushion.

Seeing That More Desires Increase Suffering

In "Enlightenment Unfolds," Dogen said, "Monks, know that people who have many desires intensely seek for fame and gain; therefore, they suffer a great deal. Those who have few desires do not seek for fame and gain and are free from them, so they are without such troubles. Having few desires is itself worthwhile."(2) How do we determine whether this equation of Dogen's—More desires = More suffering—is true? The first step is to notice how desire feels in our own body. Where in the body do we feel our desire for things, our desire to be noticed, our desire to be liked? How strong is the desire and how long does it last? Does it go away when we achieve the object of the desire? Does it return? If the desire is more frequent, repetitive, and demanding does it also feel more intense? Does the desire feel good or is it in fact uncomfortable or painful? Does it ever go away completely? By investigating our own desire thoroughly, in our own body and mind, we can determine the truth of Dogen's equation. We may discover that some desires are like addictions, while others may be wholesome—like a desire for peace on earth, for peaceful relationships, and for meaningful work.

Understanding That All Humans Have Cravings

Most of us are unable to or uninterested in finding a means of support through monkhood or just engaging in meditation. We need to work and find our places in the world, we need to engage in the social milieu. Can we differentiate between desires that serve wholesome adult survival and development from impulsive desires to satisfy our habitual insecurity? Can we lessen the insatiable desire to be recognized in favor of working to help others?

Dogen taught that the Buddha said, "Monks, if you want to be free from suffering, you should contemplate knowing how much is enough. By knowing it, you are in the place of enjoyment and peacefulness. If you know how much is enough, you are content even when you sleep on the ground. If you don't know it, you are discontented even when you are in heaven. You can feel poor even if you have much wealth."(3)

Finding "enough," means finding it in our own experience. By noticing our thoughts, desires, cessation of desires, or perpetual desire we can compare our sense of ease with our personal experience of unease. It is only through observing and knowing our own mind that we may come into contact with what is enough and a constant desire for gain. We cannot simply cease craving—each of us needs to know what craving feels like personally and whether our longing is pleasurable or painful. Only then can we cultivate a realistic understanding of how much is enough.

Buddha's second Noble Truth says suffering is caused by craving. Dogen taught that all humans have cravings. He included this recognition as one of the eight practices of awakened beings. Nobody is exempt, so there is no reason to add to our burden blaming ourselves or blaming others for our cravings. We don't need to go down the path of "Why me?" When we experience cravings within our own bodies, we recognize we are no different from all other humans; we may feel less alone and become more open to accepting our suffering and that of others. Recognizing the universal quality of craving can help us to develop compassion for ourselves and for the suffering of others.

Not Looking Outside Ourselves for Affirmation

Part of understanding our craving for praise and aversion to blame is recognizing our tendency to look outside of ourselves for affirmation. How do we practice "Settling the self on the self" as recommended by Uchiyama Roshi? To settle the self on the self is to turn toward our own experience. What are we thinking, what are we doing? In order to cultivate wisdom and equanimity, we need to start with ourselves, to be open and honest when we notice our own desire for affirmation from others. What brought us to this moment of insecurity, and how do we return to watching our own mind or finding peace in our breath? Craving praise and affirmation can be endless; when will we be assured that we are OK? By settling on your own breath, you may place your center there, place your acceptance there. If you find yourself craving the affirmation of others, and avoiding their criticism, how can you return to feeling your own presence?

Finding Time for Secluded Contemplation

Buddhists recommend finding a secluded place to learn to enjoy meditation and noble silence. Balancing social activity with secluded time in nature is often the antidote for stressing over the perceived slights and disappointments we experience with others. Dogen taught, "Awakening is to enjoy serenity. This is to be away from the crowds and stay alone in a quiet place. Thus it is called 'to enjoy serenity in seclusion.'"(4) How do you balance your activity so you can return to the center of your serenity? Within each life there needs to be a time and place to return.

We cannot solely base our time for secluded contemplation as a faraway place. We need to find quiet and peace on a daily basis in meditation and contemplation in addition to making time for retreat. Wherever you are, can you find your breath? Can you allow your breath to dominate your experience in the moment. Can we "take the backward step" that Dogen recommended even in the midst of a crowded space? We can develop an unwholesome craving for seclusion if we don't balance our silent retreat time with our ability to step back and breathe mindfully in everyday activity.

Making Sincere Effort

Finally, as we approach old age and mortality, we need to remember to keep pulling the mind's weeds of craving for fame and fearing shame. At this point in the life cycle, it's essential to be realistic about our tendencies. Where do we get stuck, what are the familiar stressors? As we face age limits, and our own energy limits, do we find peace within ourselves or a sense of disappointment? When is enough accomplishment enough? We may find the mind's demands do not match our own situation.

Effortful practice continues to be necessary in order to face the challenges of old age. Can we do any part of a formal Zen retreat? Can we meditate daily in a chair or in bed? How do we come to terms with facing the limitations of old age? Dogen taught: "Awakening is diligent effort. It is to engage ceaselessly in wholesome practices. That is why it is called 'diligent effort.' You keep going forward without turning back."(5) Continuous effort is likened to water dripping on a stone—the water will wear away the stone. We may face regret and shame in old age—all the woulda, coulda, shouldas, but we need to remember to turn toward diligent and realistic practice effort.

As we age, we may question our accomplishments and regret our infirmities and our diminished energy. However, we need to understand that the world has always been in crisis. We need to continue to cultivate wisdom to practice in old age. We cannot rely on earlier practice accomplishments. Dogen said: "Indeed, wisdom is a reliable vessel to bring you across the ocean of old age, sickness, and death. It is a bright lamp that brings light into the darkness of ignorance. It is an excellent medicine for all of you who are sick."(6)

Cultivating Wisdom, Seeing the World as Always on Fire (in Crisis)

One antidote to despair and regret in old age is to accept our difficult circumstances as an eternal truth. We wish the world were more loving and peaceful—but it has never been so. There are peaceful moments, but human existence is impermanent. Old age may mean pain, loss of functionality, financial stress and disappointment in ourselves or others. As we age, if we are craving fame and believing in shame, we only add to the volume of our suffering. We may have hoped that inequities and injustice would be solved by our lifetime of efforts, but as we look around, we realize that the social justice for which we have worked, has not been achieved as we'd hoped.

As we face the challenges of injustice and cruelty in old age, it is helpful to recognize that we must combine our personal struggle and effort with the recognition that the world is always on fire with turmoil. Our efforts matter, our collective efforts matter. The results of our efforts, in a world on fire, can be directional and long term—perhaps even beyond this lifetime. A demand that things improve right now, before our eyes is unrealistic. Demanding that our efforts result in visible accomplishments adds to our disappointment, despair, and suffering. Experiencing the human world as it is, rather than how we demand it to be, helps us to continue our efforts with greater equanimity and less suffering.

We face challenges throughout our entire lives; our role in Buddhist practice is to recognize our own unique challenges and which practices lead us to clarity. We are blown about by the Eight Winds. When we try to overcome the challenges by satisfying our cravings for fame and gain, we sink more deeply into our suffering. However, if we understand our tendencies, experience our cravings, understand the nature of this human world, and practice meditation, we are empowered to work more peacefully with challenges. At various stages in the life cycle, we can apply the antidotes of practice. We can learn to skillfully utilize the Eight Practices for Awakening with each challenge we encounter.

While we cannot change the nature of human life—our craving and our suffering—we can work sincerely to meet challenges with steady practice every step of the way. Because of Buddhism's clear view of our human tendencies, we may consider each of our unique challenges in every stage of life. We can also choose exactly the trainings that help us when we face our suffering. There are as many ways of practicing as there are individuals—it is only through sincere effort that we can find our way negotiating personal challenge with Zen trainings.

Notes

1. *Proverbs and Common Sayings from the Chinese*, trans. Alfred H. Smith (1902) 121–22. Cited at http://db.wingluke.org/document.php?cat=library&id=2003.500.1809 (Seattle, WA).
2. Dogen Zenji, "Eight Awakenings of Great Beings," in *Enlightenment Unfolds: The Essential Teachings of Zen Master Dogen*, ed. Kazuaki Tanahashi (Boston, MA: Shambhala, 1999), 270.
3. Dogen, "Eight Awakenings," 271.
4. Dogen, "Eight Awakenings," 271.
5. Dogen, "Eight Awakenings," 271.
6. Dogen, "Eight Awakenings," 272.

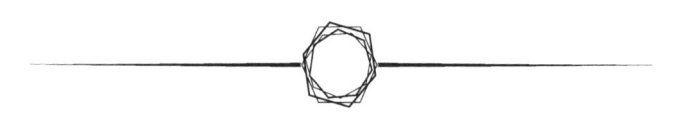

Shosan Victoria Austin has been practicing Zen meditation and yoga since 1971. A Soto Zen *kokusaifukyoshi* and a senior certified Iyengar yoga teacher, she offers yoga for sitters to Buddhist practitioners, as well as Zen teachings and ceremonies, public Iyengar yoga classes, and teacher training for practitioners in both disciplines. You can find her at victoriaaustin.org, the Facebook page Yoga and Zen with Victoria Austin, or at the websites of Iyengar Yoga Institute of San Francisco and San Francisco Zen Center.

Impact: Accidental Zen—How the Three Pure Precepts Trained Me to Heal Self and Others

Shosan Victoria Austin

> Refrain from all ill
> Cultivate all good
> Benefit all beings
> —The Three Pure Precepts,
> from my Soto Zen ordination

One day last year, one of my doctors said to me, "Your healing is very unusual." When I asked how, he thought for a bit. "Most people with your level of injury will do anything to escape the pain—drugs, surgery, avoidance behavior. If they decide to treat the pain, they might sign up for twelve sessions. You face the pain, and you continue to do the work. It is a creative process. You keep learning." When I asked what might make the difference, he responded, "Your practice."

Ten years ago, although I had been practicing for decades, my mind was on accomplishing good in the world, not on continuous therapeutic work. On September 16, 2008, things changed. I had completed my morning zazen (seated meditation) practice and a personal service of gratitude for my teachers. I'd done asanas (yoga poses)—handstand, arm balances from headstand, a few back extensions, and a resting pose. After morning work meeting, I went to City Hall to complete the paperwork for a series of Buddhist same-sex wedding ceremonies I was intending to perform before the vote on Proposition 8 in November. Now I was on my way to lunch at a popular restaurant on Valencia Street, with a group of yoga teachers welcoming a senior teacher to town.

As I reached to put a quarter into a parking meter near our lunch spot, though, a temporary wall from a construction site fell on my head and back. My forehead hit the parking meter, and the side of my head hit the curb. I was told I fell into the gutter and lay still.

It is a truism in Zen that unpleasant surprises can happen to anyone at any time, and that the main problem is that we suffer rather than rolling with the punches. Though I knew this, I had not expected to wake up in a hospital emergency room, surrounded by concerned and crying faces. I was shocked by brain fog, dizziness, and language issues over the next few days and weeks. My capable self-image took a sharp hit as I struggled for words and lost the ability to make sense of my experience. I discovered I could not read, nor drive. I spoke at a pace too slow for people to comprehend. I forgot my education, including many of the Buddhist and yogic teachings necessary to my occupation. Nor could I work, or practice most asanas, or sit to do zazen—I would fall down. I developed tinnitus and a twitch in my eye. I was later told that my social affect had become like that of an untrained autistic. Like many people with traumatic brain injuries, I experienced increasing hopelessness and despair, as I struggled to accomplish formerly routine parts of daily life.

To deal with the feelings as well as to recover as much ability as possible, I decided to take action. I sought out therapies: speech, vision, occupational, physical. The therapies were difficult, and I learned what it felt to be impaired, disabled, handicapped. I had been perfectionist in my previous life. Over the next few months, I became a model patient. I returned to zazen practice and to instructing others in Zen. At the advice of my yoga teacher, Manouso Manos, I returned to teaching my public classes. I explored Project Read at San Francisco Public Library and studied English as a second language to renew my fluency in reading and speaking. I studied math, starting with first-grade arithmetic. With the help of my Zen community, I completed a mature drivers' course and practiced all the lessons on the road. I developed therapeutic relationships with neuropsychologists who could assess the damage and help me see the big picture.

But being a model patient was not satisfying. Several times during the first year, the psychological armor I had constructed got dinged. I was upset when both the eye and orthopedic surgeons diagnosed permanent damage. I felt violated and expressed anger when they predicted that whatever didn't heal in the first few months, probably never would. I found that recovering each new skill came with its own risks and pains. Because my ability to distinguish between constructive and damaging pain was too impaired to parse the recovery needs of brain and spinal injury, I kept making mistakes that each took time to resolve. And I was frustrated that my desire to stop being handicapped so I could be myself in my community would not come true. My community was now habituated to believing I was permanently damaged, and I was constantly comparing my current abilities with those of the past. Though being a model student had always worked for me in learning situations, being a model patient first became less helpful, then actively harmful. Being a model patient would not make me a functioning citizen; its practices were not conducive to awakening.

The need to find a way of practice newly grounded in the present, dawned on me.

Refrain from all ill. The first of the pure precepts echoed in my mind. Perhaps my vow could free me through the healing process. Perhaps it could free me from the limitations of functioning as a patient, and help me function as a whole person. How could I *refrain* and cultivate, when not only did I not know enough, and the fluency of my thinking and planning mind was ruined?

One day the thought arose: *Ill is harmful action.* I needed to equip my mind and attention for knowledge and direct experience. Using an attention-training model suggested by my literacy counselor, I reorganized my files and tasks by color. I began brain training to learn to distinguish difficult sounds, increase memory, and relearn executive and strategic thinking. Then a further thought: *Unintended harmful actions come from ignorance and misperception.* I realized that state-of-the-art diagnostics could support my ability to distinguish harmful action. Painstakingly, I reconstructed my ability to associate what I was feeling in my body with the thoughts that described it and the strategies to resolve it. I sought health professionals who were willing to see me as an injured athlete rather than a perpetual patient. Gradually I learned how to refrain from unintentionally reinjuring myself, and I learned how to distinguish the workings of the healing power of nature in my own body and mind. And by the winter of 2010, my functional recovery was well on its way.

I expressed gratitude to the sangha for their support as we ate breakfast together on April 10, 2010. Over tea, one of my students requested that I consult with her about a practice issue that she had not been able to resolve. I said, "Sure, if you walk with me to my eye appointment." We discussed her question for several blocks. At one large corner, the green walk light came on. I started across, my student a step behind.

Later, my student said I had tried to run, but the SUV was going too fast. Apparently I had been struck in the gut, and had taken a full stunt roll over the vehicle. Then it seems that my toe had caught in some part of the front of the car, dragging me sixteen feet along the street on my face. Once again I was hospital-bound, awaiting a slew of tests, treatment for breaks and wounds, and orbital reconstruction. The unexpected had landed another punch.

I am told that I woke up in a hospital bed, half my face broken, my head the size of a pumpkin, weeping tears of blood. I remember being physically miserable despite a high level of pain management. Despite medication, there was constant breakthrough nausea and vomiting and very little sleep. In the night, both before and after tests and surgery, questions and doubts would come up: "Is my life pretty much over?" "I don't think I can make it for another hour unless I can find a comfortable position—and there isn't one." "How can I help anyone, if I am like this?" In short, I was physically, physiologically, and psychologically flattened, and this time was even worse than the time before.

Then, one night after midnight, something new happened. Suddenly the intuition arose that if my lifetime practice was true, it was true right now. When could a practice be tested more thoroughly than in a catastrophe? Though I could not yet sit, I decided to do zazen.

I asked the night nurse to raise the head of the bed and to arrange my pillow "spinewise," with a rolled towel for my neck and a folded towel for my head. In the next hour, the despair began to clear and my mind to settle. The next few days, I did zazen meditation in my hospital bed every night. Gradually the nurses began to come and sit with me. Though drugged, I was able to instruct them in chair zazen and to request a series of new pillow arrangements to help me breathe through the pain of my cracked, bone-bruised ribs. One nurse said, "I love coming here. There is light in this room." The companionship and support of the nurses had reminded me of my deep intention to live and to heal. And then my lifetime practice took over. If one's intention is settled, isn't there also a path? I determined to realize my intention through the path of studying the Three Pure Precepts, body and mind.

Though I don't mix zazen and yoga practice, both practices simultaneously began to improve. About a month after the second accident, Dr. Geeta Iyengar came to Portland to offer a yoga teachers' therapeutics course. My colleagues strapped me up, packed for me, and got me to the conference. At that time, Geetaji was wearing a neck brace for cervical stenosis. She took one look at my hard casts and said, "Now we are alike." Though it hurt me to laugh, her greeting and therapeutic adjustments communicated directly, from body to brain, that there are forces in human life greater than the tendency to add suffering onto pain. Her approach reinforced my vow and my two practices.

The practices were exponentially more difficult, though, than they had been after the first accident. Over the next few weeks, I had plenty of time to think, as I was too dizzy to walk even to the bathroom. The new titanium plate under my eye wept fluid and became uncomfortably hot or cold, depending on the temperature and air movement in the room. To leave the apartment even for the ever-increasing series of medical tests, scans, reviews, and therapies was a major task requiring the assistance of several people. Plus I had to deal with protective equipment such as braces, boots, masks, and slings. With damage to five teeth, nerve damage in my throat, and a new hiatal hernia, I could not eat solid food. As time went on, I heard more and more advice that the chances of returning to my old life were now almost nil. The tests in those months would confirm thirty-two medical conditions, including increases to the previous damages plus many new ones: cerebellar injuries, damage to the cranial nerves controlling the movements of the eyes, trigeminal neuralgia, spinal spurs, internal injuries, and wrist and foot damage among them.

Multiple traumatic brain injury is cumulative in impact. From the first accident. I was still relearning fluency in reading, general knowledge, and executive function. Though I had slowly developed the ability to stay present for a very short conversation by phone, FaceTime, or Skype, I was still relearning social skills. The new injuries put me at risk for seizures, which my neurologist recommended that I address with psychoactive drugs, plus high-level opioids and heavy-duty systemic medication. He said, "The pain is permanent. You have to learn how to manage it. There are very few side effects for these medications, compared to the potential further damage you will cause by enduring chronic pain."

When I tried this approach, though, the medications did not cure the pain. Instead, they changed it to a dull pervasive malaise. My personality became flat and irritable, and I lost any sense of connection between body, speech, and mind. I was afraid I was doing ill no matter which approach—yoga and zazen, or medication—I took. I could not yet identify what cultivating good might entail. I had no confidence that my choices in this situation were benefiting even myself, let alone all beings. I returned to the neurologist to ask if it was possible to reduce the pain without decreasing my sensitivity. He said, "No." Despair returned, growing deeper. How could I heal without the support of sensitivity directing my efforts?

This time the turning point came when I realized that I was going to have to respond deeply to these pains as a spiritual issue. I must open up to pain to shine a light on how to heal. If pain was to be a given, I must allow myself to be sensitive in each injured area, and I must use this sensitivity to differentiate pain from suffering. *Refraining from all ill* was going to have to mature beyond the fear of uselessness and a lonely death. In each injured area, I was going to have to cultivate sensitivity despite pain. *Cultivating all good* would have to develop into specific skillful response to each condition. *Benefiting all beings* needed to spread the first two precepts first throughout my body and mind, then I must extend these insights to practice helping others.

To cultivate the ground for the arising of deep appropriate response, I took refuge in daily zazen practice with the community. I went to the zendo (meditation hall) at 5:00 every morning, even if I had been throwing up all night, even if I was too dizzy to walk, even if I had already meditated all night to help with disturbed sleep.

The very first day of return, I set my alarm an hour early to do some simple asanas for mobility. I chose simplified, nontrailing robes to reduce my risk of a fall. My walking stick was not sufficient to increase my confidence on the stairs. My assistant, Roger, patiently helped me down, one stair at a time. Once in the zendo, when I tried to sit in my seat, I could not lift my legs. Swinging forward and back increased my dizziness but allowed me to get up on my cushion. I internally recited Dogen Zenji's *Fukanzazengi* and the Three Refuges in Buddha, Dharma, and Sangha, recreating zazen posture moment after moment despite the increasing nausea and pain. Even my missing toenails hurt. Though in much pain, I did not feel less safe than I would have been at home. Beneath the pain was light, guiding me to wholeness.

That day and many other days, I realized more deeply than ever that sitting with others is a form of physical refuge in the awakeness of Buddha, the truth of Dharma, and the harmony of Sangha. I was back in my community. The light could manifest anywhere I needed to be sensitive and present, revealing both an inner sense of health and a sense of healing direction that could become as specific as it needed to be.

A great light began to grow in me, like the sun that calls forth transformation in a seed that has lain in the ground for eons. To grow the seed of health, I needed to manage my environmental conditions; to keep the ground fertile; to nourish, water, and weed. I needed to trust the abundance of nature, that helps seeds in the earth to soak in light and moisture, and to grow. I must sense changes in internal and external weather, and respond appropriately. The seed of health would be vulnerable to changes in internal and external weather. I would take the Three Pure Precepts as my gardening guide for fruition in my developing body, speech, and mind. These universal principles—when followed—cultivate an unshakably nourished wholeness at every level of the constructed self.

This way of working changed my life. For instance, I had been presented with the musculoskeletal issue of spinal damage. In my neck, this manifested as a change in how the weight of my head could be supported. I was told to refrain from many activities due to greatly increased risks. At first, *Refrain from all ill* meant finding out what those risks were, and stopping any activity that posed those risks. For instance, I wore a hard brace and refrained from bending forward or carrying anything. As sensitivity and skill developed, I learned to ask questions such as, "What stresses create spurs?" and "What are the specific risks to my strength? Endurance? Mobility? Coordination?" and "What duration and intensity of issues do I risk?" I learned that in my neck, training and appropriate risk go hand in hand. I learned to recognize ill when it arose, and to avoid inappropriately risking any health in my current baseline.

For my neck, *Cultivating all good* first meant to learn to distinguish good effects whenever and wherever in my cervical spine they arose. With experience came an understanding of how to use expert help to find specific tests and exercises that would comprise appropriate risk. I had to cultivate new habits such as raising my computer screen to keep my head and neck in a healthy relationship. I needed to learn to turn my head using support at the side of the temple. I asked a physiotherapist to teach me the five most important muscles that I might use to create a "tensegrity" rather than a "post and block" structure to support my head. Then I set dates and times to learn how to strengthen, move, and coordinate the developing functions.

As my neck began to heal in its new form, *Benefiting all beings* first meant learning how to use the increased function to promote increased wellness in other areas of my body. One time at the Ramamani Iyengar Memorial Yoga Institute in Pune, India, Sri B. K. S. Iyengar uncharacteristically decided to correct me in every pose, every day during my stay. His adjustments opened a new possibility of understanding how the functioning of the neck (the literal brain-body connection) influences every level and layer of embodied existence. Starting from the neck and other injuries, he shone a brighter light that extends *all beings* into my future, towards my students, and around my everyday and teaching interactions with everyone I meet.

A second example of organic refuge in the Three Pure Precepts is in healing my digestive system. *Refraining from all ill*, I sought medical help to analyze persistent nausea. After testing, I refrained from solid food for a year, completed two years of a medically restricted diet to help heal the system, and continue to observe various restrictions. *Cultivating all good* included phased medical interventions, a reintroduction protocol, the gradual replacement of medications with supplements, and further asana and *pranayama* practices specific to digestive function. *Benefiting all beings* developed from accepting restrictions as permanent, to cultivating a new set of skills that thoroughly nourish body and mind of self and others. As a result, some restrictions fall away, others remain as restrictions, and still others reveal themselves to be expansions.

And what about my ability to be with myself and the world, and to teach? After the first accident, my cognitive and executive damage meant that the language and practices of my recovery had to be simple. I understood and spoke so slowly that I was on a different timescale from people around me, and my words meant something different to them and to me. After the second accident, the damage to my balance centers, eyesight, and coordination meant that the physical disciplines of my recovery had to start from the ground. *Refrain from all ill*, in this situation, meant to stop comparing my abilities with others, to stop throwing myself at my activity to try to match their speed. I had to learn how to better sense truth in these situations, which deepened my understanding of what is. *Cultivating all good* took a long time to develop, as each section of brain and nerves needs its own "million-repetition" progressive approach for new circuits to be built. At first, I had to rely on my intuition about the direction of the inner light, much as a toddler relies on her mother in the game of Find the Thimble. "Warmer, warmer; colder, colder," I would say to myself. Learning came in layers of skill formulated as medicine for each issue.

Benefiting all beings was a conundrum. How could I teach when I felt less able than I had as a child? I had to find beauty in simplicity. I found that telling the truth about my process allowed others to understand and mature their own.

After a couple of years, my sense of connection with the light developed to the point where I could resume leading intensives and practice periods, both as a Zen teacher and as a yoga teacher. I grew past my old self. My students tell me I am a far better teacher than before, and here is why. When I learned to stop doing anything that further hurt me, my sense of the individuality and interconnection of specific parts of body and mind developed and matured. When

I did good at that place instead, I became able to discriminate the subtle wholesome feelings arising from a practice, which built refinement. Whether the situation calls for spreading a benefit within my own body or to others, I am now more able to discriminate small areas of progress and to find ways to spread the healing above and below, out to the sides, and from the depths to the surface.

Refrain from all ill. Cultivate all good. Benefit all beings. The Three Pure Precepts have never once failed to help me become more curious about what is, instead of more anguished about what no longer was. I am free from being a model patient. Despite some impairments, I am not a patient at all. When I can touch base with the light of my deepest intention steadily, day after day, I can do what my neurologist deemed impossible: to heal suffering, to diminish pain. The process of healing has become self-sustaining and unshakeable as it becomes more accurate. A great light of hope and faith has arisen in me, and spread to those around me. Looking back at the past eight years, I see definite stages of development nourished and sustained by each of the Three Pure Precepts. The seeds of practice germinated, grew, and are coming to fruition. And every morning as I wake, the Three Pure Precepts shine for me, leading me from my room, back into our life.

Nine bows to Buddha, Dharma, and Sangha
Beginner's Mind Temple, Fire Season, 2017

Myosho Ann Kyle-Brown is a Soto Zen priest and disciple of Gengo Akiba Roshi. Her early training was at Aichi Senmon Nisodo in Nagoya, Japan. She is founder and head teacher of Kumeido, the Mendocino Zen Center on the north coast of California. In addition, she works to support the development of Tenpyozan Monastery in Lake County, California. Myosho is also a poet, writer, wife, and mother.

The Four Noble Truths of Practice in Times of Challenge and Struggle
Myosho Ann Kyle-Brown

Is There Any Other Time to Practice?

The First Noble Truth is the recognition that suffering exists. Here's how it began for me.

Once upon a time, I was raising four children all on my own. You might think they'd arrived by virgin birth, as no one else seemed to be responsible or involved. I did not understand. Nor did the children. This was great suffering.

Then, after many years, I met a man who was also raising four children. Like packhorses climbing the same rocky mountain, we recognized each other. Who else could possibly understand? We married. Just like that, I doubled my yield. Stepchildren. A blended family. Apparently, I was the blender.

The first years of our marriage I was on call, without surcease, day and night.

Then, one dark, rainy, winter Sunday, making my rounds, room to room, I found everyone happily occupied. Not only was I not needed, I was actually in the way. They had taken over the dining room as a photo studio and the kitchen as a darkroom. My hard earned sense of self flopped over like a dusty stage set.

What do you do when there's nothing to do? Well, people take walks, I guess. So I did.

• • • • •

Our community newspaper had reported that a Zen temple was being built down the street from our home. Neighbors were complaining. What, I thought, too quiet? But I'd been following its progress. Carpenters from Japan, wearing Spiderman shoes, skittered all over the building. It arose like a mirage.

On this particular afternoon, it was quiet. I peered through a crack in the fence. Deserted.

I loved Zen. Never knew it first hand, but when I was twelve years old, my big brother had brought home a book by Alan Watts. He also listened to Watts on the radio . . . KPFA. Sitting outside his bedroom door, I listened. I learned the word *zazen*.

Now it was the last Sunday of the year 1993. I was forty-eight.

Perhaps I can learn to meditate here. On impulse, I rang the bell by the front gate, then stood, very straight and tall, and waited.

Nothing. Silence. I looked around. No one. I was disappointed. I climbed up onto a narrow toehold on the gate and peered over.

A Japanese home. A Japanese garden. A wide gravel path leading to the temple. A koi pond. It was a winter garden. Bare trees. Wet. Bleak. Spacious. Lovely.

Holding to the top of the gate, I took it all in. Took my fill. Took my time. Time passed. My knuckles turned white.

Suddenly it occurred to me that someone might be home! Maybe they were in the shower when I rang. Instantly, I hopped down. Heavens! Now I better apologize for loitering at their gate. Head down, slumped, chagrined, I rang the bell again.

Nothing. Silence. No one. Now, I was truly sad. In grief, actually. Who knew if I'd ever have the courage to return. I stepped back up onto the toehold and this time, because no one was home, I let my arms hang down over the top of the gate and dangled there like an Alaskan king crab. Looking, looking, looking. Time passed.

Finally, I thought, I better go home. Somebody probably needs something by now. Reluctantly, I stepped down. Then, just for the hell of it, I rang the bell a third time!

Instantly, a Japanese monk popped out of the house. He had a shaved head and was wearing long black robes. He looked at me. I looked back, scared. Slowly, he walked towards me. My god, I thought, what am I going to do now?

Just then, a shadow passed overhead. I looked up. A white

crane! In Oakland! It glided towards the pond, rose, and began a dive. Instantly, the monk whisked his long black sleeves up into the air. The muscular crane flapped its big white wings in the sky. Again, the monk shot his sleeves out, snapping them at the very heart of the crane. Back and forth they went, black and white. My hair blew in the wind they created. Instantly, all the buildings around the temple disappeared. Only mountains, valleys, gorges, rivers and streams remained, far as my eye could see. And silence. Where am I?

Then, just as suddenly as it had arrived; the magnificent crane flew off vanishing into the vast grey sky.

The monk looked back at me. Oh, my God! He came and opened the gate.

I didn't know if he spoke English. I only knew one word.

Zazen?

Welcome, he said.

• • • • •

I followed him. He showed me an unlocked side gate where I could enter day or night. He led me to the temple. Paint cans and a ladder still stood in a corner. But already it smelled of incense. A flyer on the wall announced an upcoming retreat, something called a *sesshin*. May I attend, I asked? Yes, he said. Do I need to wear special clothes, or read a book, or take a class? No, he laughed. You already Buddha. You sit, you remember.

Of course, I misunderstood. I thought he had recognized me as a special human being. Finally!

It was a long time before I realized that everyone is Buddha. If everyone sits, everyone will remember. Nonetheless, deluded by encouragement, I went on *sesshin*.

• • • • •

Starting at 5 a.m., we sat cross-legged in zazen without moving for fifty minutes at a time. Ten times each day. Then three times a day we stood barefoot on the cold floor and chanted in deep, monotone Japanese. Then we did many full prostrations—foreheads to the same cold floor. We ate our meals in silence. No eye contact.

Zen Teachings In Challenging Times

This was to go on for seven days.

On the fourth day, there was an interview with the monk. His wife was present to translate. I sat cross-legged in front of them and started talking right away. I was so excited. Who can remember what I had to say that day!

His wife interrupted. Where are you from?

Down the street, I answered.

No, no, she said. I mean, what Zen center?

No Zen center.

But where do you sit?

Here.

You mean this is the first time you have meditated?

Yes.

And you started with a *sesshin*?! You're crazy! She screeched something in Japanese to the monk and immediately leaned over and lifted up my skirt.

"Let us see your posture!"

They stared at my underpants and my bare, sore legs.

· · · · ·

Why? Why would I put myself through this—a middle-aged woman, with a completely whacked adrenal gland and the strong suspicion I would never know rest again? Why?

Because, I had come to the end of the known world. And, if you are a mother and you come to the end of the known world, your children are in danger.

· · · · ·

The Second Noble Truth is that there is a cause of suffering. What is the cause?

Each of our children is a whole story. As am I. As are you. They took turns teetering on the outer edges of reality.

The eldest struggled with mental illness. Another flirted with an eating disorder. One used drugs. Another had fragile nerves and was dyslexic. One was a surly member of the Punk movement. The youngest had a genetic condition that made him look different than other people. The others were garden variety neurotic and wonderful. What kind of people would have children like these? Our kind.

But if you came to our home for dinner, you would have thought they were quite lovely.

At that moment, I was beset with worry for the one on drugs. She was also in trouble with the law. And she had tried to kill herself. The nuns found her on the roof of the Catholic recovery center. She hadn't known the right way to cut her wrists. Not a small blessing.

I was terrified. I was also confused, ashamed, desperate, embarrassed, angry, righteous, judgmental, blaming, sanctimonious, apologetic, frustrated, guilty, and powerless. Nothing I did or said helped. Every conversation ended badly.

What do you do when you don't know what to do? My grandmother used to say, when in doubt, don't. So I didn't. I sat.

· · · · ·

It was hard keeping my back straight. Such was the weight of my sorrow. I tried to clear my mind, count to ten, follow my fractured breath. But all I could see was my daughter flailing at night in a stormy sea, waves crashing all about her, drowning. All I could hear were my useless platitudes and admonitions, as well as those of my mother and grandmother and on back in time. The only feeling available was dread.

Finally, I gave up. I slumped. I surrendered to the unknowable mess of it. In that instant, all moral judgments of her and of myself fell away. It was clear. She wasn't bad, rebellious or ignorant. She was sick. My daughter was sick!

I left the zendo and rushed home to call her.

It is mysterious how the heart opens, how minds heal, how people connect. What was different in that phone call to my daughter? Two things. I was compassionate and I listened. She felt it and opened up. Her healing began right there.

Zazen is the mystery. It is also the practice.

What is the cause of suffering? It is actually quite simple. We want what we want. When we don't get it, we get mad. Some of us turn that anger against ourselves. Some of us strive to get even. Some do both. That's the mess of it right there.

Zen Teachings In Challenging Times

• • • • •

You can't practice Zen without learning the wisdom of Eihei Dogen, who founded Soto Zen in Japan, in the thirteenth century. He wrote, "To study the Buddha way is to study the self. To study the self is to forget the self. To forget the self is to be one with all beings."

But how do you study what you do not know? Like, for instance, that you are Buddha?

You sit zazen.

• • • • •

My teacher did not give traditional dharma talks. It's not because he didn't speak English well enough. He didn't give dharma talks to Japanese people either. Here is one of his typical dharma talks.

Meditating on a spring afternoon . . . after days of Sesshin . . . after hours of silence . . . shoji screens open to a warm breeze . . . after a big lunch . . . feeling drowsy . . . he suddenly roared, "SHOYOKU!"

That woke me up.

Then he roared it again, only deeper. "Shoyoku!" Then he rolled the word around in his mouth like marbles. "Shoyoku!" Then, in a long rumbling growl, "Shoyoku!"

Then a pause.

I waited, wide-eyed, in acute suspense.

Then he roared, "GREED!"

I almost fell over.

He roared it again, "Greed!" He rolled it around like marbles. "Greed!" He growled it like an animal, "Greed!"

That was it. The entire dharma talk.

What did I begin to meditate on? Greed. My greed. Starting with lunch . . . descending down to my childhood . . . running up through all my relationships . . . great, ravaging, unquenchable greed. Greed for everything . . . people, love, attention, respect, money, things . . . bright shiny things . . . numberless things . . . stuff! Insatiable desires . . . deplorable manipulations to shore up my pride, deny my fear, assuage my insecurity! Shoyoku!

Thus, I finally saw myself and what I saw was a woman full of greed, anger, and delusions.

Still, if you came to my house for dinner, you would have thought I was quite lovely.

• • • • •

The Third Noble Truth is that there is an end to suffering.

How do you end greed? I turned to my teacher for instruction. But, as he didn't really teach with words, I was flummoxed.

I thought it was rude to stare. Still sometimes I would sneak a peek at him. If he caught my eye, I would quickly turn away.

Then one day I realized that whenever I did look at him, he suddenly started moving in slow motion. How does one suddenly move slowly? Well, if lifting a teacup, for instance, he would stop and look at the cup as if he had never seen one before in his entire life and had no idea how it had gotten into his hand. Watching him inspect the cup, I could feel his wonder, his curiosity, the heft of the cup, its heat, the texture of its glaze.

Then I looked down at my own cup, the one I'd been using for months already and realized that I had never really seen it before.

To look is not to see. To see requires letting go of, well, you're usually looking at—which is more than likely greed, often in the form of desire for something more or different.

After that, I didn't take my eyes off of him. He was teaching me!

• • • • •

Still, he traveled frequently to Japan. As a result, his wife became my new North Star. She can be ferocious. She is perfect and imperfect at the same time. Fair and unfair at the same time. Inspiring and daunting. Dedicated and generous. She overcomes tiredness like an athlete... pushing through. She is a dancer. Though we were almost the same age, I followed her around like a puppy.

In a specialty shop I saw some fine linen handkerchiefs, with beautifully embroidered linen envelops. One said Mother. One said Friend. One said Teacher. I gave her the one that said Teacher.

Zen Teachings In Challenging Times

What she teaches is tea ceremony. Many young Japanese women come to study tea. Japanese mothers send their daughters. Zen priests send their wives. Tea ceremony is one of the Zen arts. Often, an older Japanese woman named Yoko-san would be there. She and my teacher's wife were good friends. Yoko-san loved to laugh. Westerners came as well.

It takes years to be granted the right to make tea. You start as a Guest. After a very long time, you become the Second Guest. After an even longer time, you become the First Guest. Then, finally, after time immemorial, you become Otomae—which means that you are the one who gets to make the tea. By that time you are as graceful as a tendril.

The First Guest and the Second Guest speak to each other in set Japanese phrases. The First Guest bows and offers the Second Guest her tea and sweets, saying, "Osaki ni chodo itashimasu." Which means, "Please excuse me that I will be receiving this before you."

The Second Guest bows and says, "Dozo." Meaning, "Oh, no, please, you go ahead and enjoy it first." These phrases are repeated all the way down the line, Guest to Guest. It is difficult to learn to say them correctly.

Then, after you finish your tea, you lean over and carefully inspect the cup, tilting your head gracefully to the left and then to the right. You appreciate it. The first time I inspected the cup, I went too quickly. My teacher's wife stopped me.

"Sihothing," she said. I offered the cup to the next Guest, bowed and repeated. "Sihothing."

Yoko-san burst out laughing. You are a good monkey, she said. My teacher's wife had spoken English. "See whole thing."

If you want to see the whole thing, you can't take your greed, anger, and delusions with you. Thus I saw that there could be an end to suffering.

· · · · ·

The Fourth Noble Truth is that there is indeed a path to the end of suffering. Zazen is the path.

My family moved. Just like that. Last child still at home. Just two years before he'd go to college. I was happily planning for the rest of my life . . . at last. Oh, the places I'd go!

My husband got a job opportunity in a small town, hours north of our home, way out in the countryside. One day I'm preparing for my future, the next he's carting my grandmother's standup mirror out the front door. Where do you think you're going with that?! In thirty days flat we moved.

There are many, good, practical reasons for this, my husband said.

But for me, it was a disaster, a hurricane, a tornado, an earthquake, a firestorm. An act of God. As you may know, there is no insurance for acts of God.

I did not miss our friends, family, or neighbors. I did not miss the shops, cafés, or morning walks. I missed my teacher. I missed his wife. I missed the sangha.

There was no Zen temple in our new community. So, no new Zen teacher. There was a collective of Buddhist practitioners from many traditions - Thai, Tibetan, and American nondenominational. Two people were Zen. One very old and one a hermit. It was a democratic group. They had meetings to decide the way forward. Thus there were politics. But a group cannot vote to become enlightened. Only an individual can step onto that path. Without a teacher, it is tricky.

Unaware of what I was doing, I commenced the life of a peripatetic monk. Traveling farther and farther afield, I sought out every temple, monastery, and Zen center within a day's drive. Within two days. I would land on their doorsteps like a snowdrift. If they did not sweep me away, I would enter and practice with them. One hour. One day. Three days. Seven days. Ten days. A month. Thus I met many teachers. Thus I tasted many flavors of the Way.

One day I spoke with my teacher and his wife about becoming a monk. It was decided. I would go to Japan to train.

My husband was nonplussed. He had not married a monk. He put his foot down. Both of them.

There are many good practical reasons for this, I told him.

No! he said.

I looked right at him . . . . Do not say you love me, and then tell me I cannot go to Japan. He was silent for a time. Then, he said, I love you.

I shaved my head. I took new vows. I was ordained. I asked my teacher what I needed to do to prepare for Japan. Go to Japan, he said.

I was terrified.

• • • • •

Monks in a monastery are leaves in a forest. The wind blows them this way and that. You do everything together. You work together, eat together, study together, bathe together, sleep together. At night, if you roll over, you might find your nose inches from another's nose. You are never alone.

I did not speak Japanese. I didn't understand anything. I was profoundly uncomfortable. At first I thought, well, I'll get used to this in a week or two. But no . . . on and on it went.

I projected my fears and insecurities onto everyone. I imagined insults and slurs. I took umbrage at I know not what. I came up with clever rejoinders to emptiness. I rehearsed retorts to the unknown. I craved a free moment to translate these words using my English-to-Japanese dictionary. That moment never came. If I approached mastery of any task, they took it right away and gave me a new one. I was appalled. But slowly, very slowly, I moved from paranoia to realizing that this was not personal. It was training. They were helping me.

Then, two months or so into my stay, during afternoon tea, on a lovely summer day, a feeling of deep well-being and spaciousness came over me. It was startling. Words came spontaneously. Japanese words. *Kore wa nan desu ka?* What is this? I looked inward. Yes, indeed, I was still uncomfortable, but now I saw that I had grown comfortable being uncomfortable. I was free.

• • • • •

But what is freedom?

I met many people in Japan. One priest invited me to come to Bangladesh to help in an orphanage, a dangerous place of deep need. A Korean nun asked if I would come to Switzerland with her and speak at an international congress of women in Buddhism. Good Heavens! Other opportunities arose, all of the sudden, like a white crane in Oakland. I realized I could just raise my foot and step out into a new world.

I was at the airport in Tokyo waiting to go home. The loudspeaker announced the imminent departure of the plane to Seoul, Korea. My friend waved to me from the next gate. I waved back.

I was free. I raised my foot.

I thought of my eldest daughter who was going to have a baby, my husband who was so good to me. They were my first vow, my first sangha, my family.

I was free.

I was free to join the line of folks going back to San Francisco.

Kumeido—The Mendocino Zen Center
January 2018

Epilogue

In order to carve out time to write this story, I went on retreat to Genjoji—the Sonoma Mountain Zen Center in Santa Rosa. It was autumn. Lovely. I finished a rough first draft. The next day I would start the rewrite. But at 1:30 that morning there was a loud knocking on my cabin door. Myosho! Wake up! Fire!

We had to evacuate. We scattered like leaves.

The next day, some monks went back to try and save the temple. Others came to my house. To my husband's surprise, we kept the monastic schedule to steady ourselves and support their efforts.

The fire consumed thousands of acres, but Genjoji was spared.

As the deadline for this story lurked and loomed, I turned seventy-two. There were two trips to LA for pressing family matters. Then I had a planned minor surgery, after which, I sandwiched *Rohatsu* (the winter meditation retreat) between Thanksgiving and Christmas. Then my sister got very sick.

On it goes, right?

Is there any other time to practice?

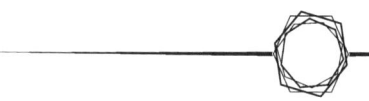

Melissa Myozen Blacker is the abbot of Boundless Way Zen, and resident teacher and priest at Boundless Way Temple in Worcester, Massachusetts. She is a dharma heir of James Myo'un Ford. She co-edited *The Book of Mu*, and her writing appears in Buddhist magazines and collections of Buddhist essays, including *The Hidden Lamp* and *Best Buddhist Writing 2012*. For twenty years, she was a teacher and trainer at the Center for Mindfulness, founded by Jon Kabat-Zinn at the University of Massachusetts Medical School. Websites: melissablacker.com, boundlesswayzen.org, worcesterzen.com.

Cutting the World in Two
Melissa Myozen Blacker

Nanchuan's Cat

>The priest Nanchuan found monks of the eastern and western halls arguing about a cat. He held up the cat and said, "Everyone! If you can say something, I will spare this cat. If you can't say anything, I will cut off its head."
>No one could say a word, so Nanchuan cut the cat into two.
>That evening, Zhaozhou returned from outside and Nanchuan told him about what happened. Zhaozhou removed a sandal from his foot, put it on his head, and walked out.
>Nanchuan said, "If you had been there, the cat would have been spared."
>
>—from the *Gateless Barrier*, case 14(1)

This koan is often quite disturbing to modern Zen students just starting out on the path. It seems so violent and cruel. Why is a Zen master threatening to kill a cat? And what is he trying to prove through carrying on with his threat after no one speaks up? Aside from the reality that this story arose in a very different time and culture (ninth-century China), the impact of cutting a cat in two may have been just as startling and disturbing to Nanchuan's students as to our contemporary sensibilities.

The koan appears repeatedly in our Boundless Way Zen training, as we encounter it in three different classical koan collections: *The Gateless Barrier*, case 14, *The Blue Cliff Record*, cases 9 and 10, and *The Book of Equanimity*, cases 63 and 64. At first, it certainly seems to be primarily about a cat being killed. But as we look more deeply into the story, as with all koans, we realize that it contains many layers. And these layers of meaning can illuminate some of the struggles we encounter every day in this burning world.

In koan practice, we learn to identify with all of the characters we encounter in the story, as a means of illuminating our own unquestioned habits and biases. Our teachers guide us directly into what is most perplexing, in order to free us from these blind patterns of behavior, thoughts, and emotional reactivity.

Some of us enter Zen practice with certain romantic notions and fantasies. We have dreams of peaceful monks and nuns chanting and walking slowly in beautiful gardens and temples, among singing birds and blossoming flowers. But Zen practice can be ruthless, and Zen teachers are determined to point us to a new view of reality, toward something beyond our usual world of good and bad, right and wrong. Zen shows us something bigger than the limitations of duality.

Both Nanchuan and Zhaozhou, who later became a great Zen master himself, do something unexpected in this story, something outside of what we might consider normal behavior. Nanchuan kills a cat. Zhaozhou puts a sandal on his head. It's important to know that these are not random or senseless acts. Zen is not about doing whatever you want, or acting crazy to get a rise out of people. The direct teaching of Zen is disturbing on purpose. And what it disturbs is our ordinary view of things. When the cat is killed, when Zhaozhou takes off his sandal and puts it on his head, we are forced to look at the world in a new way.

When we look at our own suffering, and the distress arising all around us, we can see that all the varieties of pain that we encounter have something in common. We suffer because we divide the world into pieces, into separate categories of "good" and "bad." This is a normal healthy human activity, and we depend on it for our survival. Without this capacity to categorize all of our experience, our ancestors would not have been able to distinguish dangerous situations from safety. Being able to differentiate in this way, we can tell whether the dark shape ahead on our night path is a stick or a snake. To improve our chances of survival, our brains appear to favor interpreting the unknown as a snake. However, seeing everything as a potential danger can get us in a lot of trouble.

It's clear that when things are going our way, when our presidential candidate wins the election, when what we decide is fair and just becomes the law of the land, we believe that all is well. We are happy and relaxed. When the opposite of these things happen, we go into a reactive mode, and suddenly, snakes appear everywhere. People who don't agree with our views are bad; people who see the wisdom of our beliefs are good.

Recently, I spotted a button on the backpack of a dear friend of mine who has been active all of her life in leftwing peace and justice movements. It said, simply, "Not my president." I was quite touched by the simplicity and directness of this message, and how much it reflected my own feelings at the moment. I told her that I admired it, and she gave me a small handful of buttons. I put one on my backpack too.

Like my friend, I was an active supporter of Hillary Clinton for president in 2016. On that cool November morning after the election, along with many of my family members and friends, I mourned the election of Donald Trump to the presidency. I wept when I watched Clinton's concession speech. In my heart, the words "Not my president" rang loud and clear as the absolute truth.

And then, as I looked at the button on my backpack, I remembered a sign in the yard of a neighbor after the election of Barack Obama in 2008. It said, "Impeach Obama." Every time I drove past that sign I felt sick and angry. How could someone not support the legally elected president of the United States? Suddenly I felt uncomfortable. I realized that any Trump supporter could see my new button and feel the same way. As much as I despised this current president's behaviors and views, he was, in fact, my president.

The monks of the eastern and western halls are arguing about a cat. Nanchuan asks them to speak a word of Zen to save the cat, and no one says a word. They are deeply caught in their binary world of right and wrong, and can't get away from this fixed view to see what is right in front of them. A cat is going to be killed. A war is going to be declared. Someone is going to pass legislation that will restrict the rights of citizens. What do you do?

Nanchuan shows us the consequences of doing nothing. As the author and historian Howard Zinn said, "You can't be neutral on a moving train."(2) Just standing by while a cat is being threatened, while the world spirals into destruction and despair, may contribute to the death of the cat, to the movement toward chaos. It's essential to speak out against injustice. The problem for us human beings is that most of our speaking out sounds like the arguing between the monks of the eastern and western hall.

Before the U.S. election of 2016, I had personally been lulled into a view of the modern world as moving toward healing, justice, and fairness. I had been a social activist as a young woman, participating in my share of protest marches and political work. The election acted as a disturbing factor, something like suddenly being told that sandals are meant to be worn on heads. The world had turned upside down. I was forced to look at my own role in the endless causes and conditions that had caused the election of a man who was the very opposite of how I believed a good leader should sound, look, and behave. I had been standing by while a cat was going to be cut in two, and I had said nothing. I was focusing on all the positive steps I was witnessing in social and political life: the election of a black president, the legalization of gay marriage, and the presidential candidacy of a strong, intelligent woman. Meanwhile, young black men were still being gunned down by police officers, global warming had reached the point of ecological crisis, there was rising unemployment and deaths from opioid addiction throughout the country, cities were in crisis, sexism, racism and gender bias continued to inform the views of many people, and wars, famine and violence filled the lives of people all over the world. Turning away from this suffering had become a habit.

One definition of suffering is that it is the product of our desire for things to be different from the way they are. I want a different president. I want all wars to end. I want sexism and racism to disappear from human hearts. I want resources put into turning the direction of global warming. I also want to be taller, and healthier, wiser, and more compassionate. Some of these things may come to pass—well, probably not the getting taller thing—but the path to those changes does not lie in investing all of my energy in fighting reality. When we fight reality, reality always wins. And all of the effort we put into being oppositional is exhausting. We get caught in an endless loop of anger, resentment and hopelessness. Turning away from suffering may seem like a logical response, a way to find relief, but it is simply our primary human way of fighting reality.

In Zen practice, we learn to turn toward suffering, to bear what might feel unbearable. This developing capacity to face what is actually happening, rather than turn away from it, also sharpens our ability to experience joy, happiness and contentment. We feel more alive in our lives. This great aliveness, which we sometimes call by its Sanskrit name, Dharma, is simply the way things are. Everything, including the events in the world outside us, and all of our behaviors, thoughts, and feelings, is an expression of the Dharma, with no exceptions. We are challenged, as Zen practitioners, to see the Dharma arising in all circumstances, even when it's not what we want. Even though we may hope that our practice will lead us to a fixed state of happiness and contentment, we come to recognize that everything comes and goes, including joy and suffering. Nothing is permanent, and everything is fully alive just the way it is.

The first step in meeting reality is to embrace whatever is happening, which may include our own grief and anger. If we meet reality as it appears, with interest and courage, and maybe a bit of warmth, we can learn more about it, and, crucially, we can clarify what it actually is. We can see it clearly as a manifestation of the Dharma, of the great aliveness that fills the universe.

And then we can choose to respond in a way that aligns with the energetic trajectory of what is happening, and perhaps find a way to actively, or subtly, influence its direction. This could take the form of doing something, saying something, or even doing or saying nothing.

In sitting with whatever is arising, we can find a way to act with integrity and clarity even in the most difficult circumstances. If we are caught up in our endless arguments about right and wrong, we will certainly become better at arguing. If our practice can show us the great pain of the divided heart, the cat cut in two, then we can see that there is something else that we must do. When we face into suffering directly, our hearts open in a compassionate response. The derivation of the word compassion, from the Latin, is literally "suffering with." This opening up to "suffering with" is what saves us.

We need to turn our views upside down and then take action, doing whatever we can to contribute to healing the great division that is the natural state of human beings. We can begin to base our lives on compassion rather than division, and in this way, gradually, if not always steadily, the cat comes back to life, and what we thought was impossible can be achieved.

Notes

1. Adapted from Wumen, *The Gateless Barrier, translated and with a commentary by Robert Aitken* (New York: Farrar, Straus and Giroux, 1991)
2. Howard Zinn, *You Can't Be Neutral on a Moving Train* (Boston: Beacon Press, 2002).

Mary Mocine, HoUn ZenKi (Dharma Cloud Total Joy), is the founder and abbess of the Vallejo Zen Center (Clear Water Zendo). After a career in law, Mary began practice in 1988 at the Berkeley Zen Center and Green Gulch Farm Zen Center, and she later spent four years at Tassajara Zen Mountain Center, followed by five years at San Francisco Zen Center. Mary was ordained by Sojun Mel Weitsman Roshi in 1994 and received dharma transmission from him in 2005. See also vallejozencenter.org or the Clear Water Zendo page on Facebook. There is a link to the series "Practicing in Interesting Times" on the website.

I Hate Donald Trump
Zenki Mary Mocine

In November 2016, we elected a very divisive president, Donald Trump. Many of us found ourselves profoundly upset and disappointed that he had won. It was quite a surprise. I gave a dharma talk with this title: "I Hate Donald Trump." It was partly to focus our attention, but also, it was the truth. The hate grew out of fear and disappointment that he had won instead of Hillary Clinton. It also grew out of the sense that he and his supporters hated me and people like me. I'm not proud of my reaction. It concerns me.

My strong reaction also grew out of feeling helpless before suffering. There is income inequality. There is unemployment in the Rust Belt. It is true that folks no longer think their children will do better than they have. There are real wounds left from slavery and racism in this country. Women and the LGBTQ community feel under threat. The anger and fear generated by these facts are real. What I find daunting is the reactivity triggered by these facts and what I see as the administration's exploitation of those fears. So, what's a bodhisattva to do?

Of course, the question (and the real topic of the talk), became "How Do I Practice with This?" Our sangha already had a podcast series, "Practice in Interesting Times," which ran during the election, but the fact of the result took the matter to another level. The usual advice is to sit still and check in and be aware of one's own shadow in operation. The usual advice is to take care of oneself, rest, exercise, eat right, sit zazen, and find one's center. The usual advice is to work to operate from that center. So, if you choose to be politically active, it comes from your zazen and not your reactivity. The usual advice is to remember the *Dhammapada* about hatred sowing only hatred and that love alone nurtures love.

For example, the following is the sort of thing I usually say about practicing with difficulty. I lead a dharma group for lawyers and I send some words to consider before each meeting. Recently, the Clear Water Zendo has been studying the ancient Chinese poem by our ancestor Xiquan Shitou, "Song of the Grass-Roofed Hermitage," so I sent the lawyers this:

> I've built a grass hut where there's nothing of value.
> After eating, I relax and enjoy a nap.
> When it was completed, fresh weeds appeared.
> Now it's been lived in—covered by weeds.

This is the opening stanza of the poem. In effect, it is practice instruction. One way to understand this is that the author, a monk, built a simple shelter for practice and to live in. It was built of nice grass. Soon, however, weeds appeared. After he actually lived there, it got to be covered with weeds. Oh well.

I think we want our practice, both law and dharma, to be clean and efficient. We want to feel that we know what we are doing and that we are in control. We don't want a bunch of distractions. We don't want our less attractive traits to show nor to trouble us. So, we reject the weeds. Oh well. Of course, it doesn't work to reject the weeds. What about making friends with them? Getting to know them? Many have traits that are helpful. Weeds can be medicinal, after all. Nettles are good for the blood. Tibetan teachers say that an enemy is a great jewel. This "enemy" can be a person but it can also be one of our weeds. An enemy is a great jewel because such an item has much to teach us if we can calm down and pay attention.

Please pay attention and notice your "weeds," and see what they may have to teach you. If you are resistant to this practice, notice that and see how well the resistance serves you . . . . Oh well.

This is good advice and relevant even regarding Donald Trump and his administration. But, it does not feel like enough in these difficult times. I want to say, "Yes . . . and . . . ." What about when it feels like the hut is threatened not simply by the weeds of garden-variety neuroses and difficult people or situations. What about if it feels threatened by a huge brick wall falling on it? Do I make friends with the bricks and my resulting broken leg? Are these jewels?

The answer is still yes. It is just harder. Sorry. But this is the practice of a bodhisattva. These are very difficult times for folks who think like I do. The environment is under siege. People of color, the LGBTQ community, religious minorities, immigrants, women, the First Amendment, basic civility and the office of the president, health care, and the poor and middle class are all under siege. There is fear of nuclear war. Science is seen as a threat somehow.

The answer is still yes. We must find a way to practice with this. Even when folks who think differently view me as dangerous or evil. Even with folks whose views I see as dangerous. Particularly in those situations, we must find a way.

It is useful to remind ourselves that things have been worse or at least as bad as now. We did, after all, have a Civil War and the aftermath of Reconstruction, which gave birth to the Ku Klux Klan and many of the Southern army statues that are at issue today. We had the Palmer Raids after World War I, in which the Justice Department, under A. G. Palmer, rounded up and arrested and deported hundreds of leftists without benefit of charges or trials, in response to what was known as the "Red Scare." We had the interning of the Japanese Americans during World War II. And, we had the McCarthy era. Many of us remember the divisions around Vietnam, particularly during the early 1970s. All of these events set people against one another, sometimes leading to bloodshed and sometimes tearing families apart.

What is a bodhisattva to do? Listen. Keep breathing and listen. Sounds easy but it is very difficult. This listening does not mean that one needs to give up one's views. It does require an openness and willingness in the face of others whose views we may find repugnant. It does require the courage to be quiet and calm before folks that may be expressing hatred toward you or toward views that you cherish. I find it useful to note my own feelings with care and to note that others who appear angry and hostile to my views are probably experiencing a similar level of fear and anxiety about me.

We can encourage one another. I listened to the *TED Radio Hour* yesterday. The topic was dialogue and exchange, and it was very encouraging. The first person featured was Meghan Phelps-Roper, who had been a lifelong member of the Westboro Baptist Church. That is the church whose members picket and protest at funerals of service members who have died. Ms. Phelps-Roper spoke of finally questioning and then leaving the church because folks online listened to her with kindness, not hate. They asked her questions in a respectful manner and eventually she came to see that she had been full of hate and not Christian love. She felt supported and encouraged by her online friends.

Two other pieces on that *TED Radio Hour* struck me. One was a social psychologist at Stanford, Professor Robb Willer. He spoke of "moral reframing." He pointed out that we all have a moral or ethical view of the world. We tend to speak from our own values and expect to convince those who think differently because our view is so very self-evident. He suggested we try to frame our argument instead in the moral terms of the other person. This does not mean being dishonest or manipulative. It does mean paying attention to those to whom you are listening and making the attempt to speak in terms that will resonate. I'm reminded of the descriptions of the Buddha teaching and being understood by people in the assembly who spoke different languages.

The last piece featured Celeste Headlee, a mixed-race journalist and author from Georgia. She has recently written a book, *We Need to Talk*, and is the host of *On Second Thought* on Georgia Public Radio. She was inspired by the story of Xernora Clayton, a civil rights leader, and Calvin Craig, a grand dragon of the Klan. They talked for years, and eventually Mr. Craig renounced the Klan. Ms. Clayton told Celeste Headlee that she never tried to persuade Mr. Craig. She just listened.

Just listen. What a daunting thought. I must start from the fact that I am frightened. I am angry. I feel helpless and hopeless. I do think that it is self-evident that we should be in the Paris Agreement. I do think it is self-evident that the Iran nuclear deal is a good idea in a difficult situation. I do believe science and the scientific method are useful. I do think that coal energy is harming the environment and that taking tops off mountains is a bad idea. I am frightened by the racism, gender issues and income inequality I see in our country. How do I meet those who disagree?

The folks featured on the *TED Hour* very much encourage me. If listening and asking respectful questions could turn someone from the Westboro Baptist Church, whose web address is godhatesfags.com, then anything seems possible. If listening could turn a grand dragon, anything seems possible.

Just listen. This is our practice, after all. Sit down, get quiet, and pay attention. Simply listen. Avalokiteshvara goes down to the hell realm to save beings. That is just what she does. It took a number of rounds before she got that that was it. Her head kept exploding when she emptied hell and looked back to admire it empty, only to find it full again. Eventually she saw that she must just do her job and take care of beings in hell, no thought of final success. We can take encouragement from this. Our job now is to engage with those who worry us. We can find the courage to just listen. Our zazen practice supports us to do this courageous listening.

We begin with listening to ourselves. What is going on inside? Fear? Hate? Anger? Impatience? Start with your body and your breath. Know your tendencies when you are upset. The more you know about such tendencies and the more you know how they manifest in your body and breath, the less likely you are to act or speak from them. The more you know about your own reactivity in the face of fear and anger, the more you can cut another person some slack—understanding that they also suffer. You know already that no one wants to suffer. When you can remember your common humanity in this way, the more likely you are to be able to hear what another is saying.

Just listen. We can listen to others without agreeing. The fact of respectful listening does not mean that one agrees or is validating views that one finds dangerous or repugnant. Let Xenora Clayton encourage you. Let Meghan Phelps-Roper encourage you. When you meet someone with a "Make America Great Again" hat on, holding a sign calling NFL players who take a knee sons of bitches or worse, consider listening. What would it be like to ask the person to go get a cup of coffee and find out what their concerns are. You might be surprised. You would almost certainly be challenged.

There is a technique I learned in a mediation course. It is called "looping." It is a form of "active listening." I teach it to the lawyers that I work with. They often have to listen to clients who are angry and upset and simply want to vent. In "looping" one listens then repeats what one heard and asks, "Did I get it all?" If not, the process continues until the speaker says that the listener did get it all. When the lawyers did this practice, they were moved by how great it felt to be really heard. Perhaps you have experienced this. It is indeed moving. Perhaps if you can listen that simply to your acquaintance with the MAGA hat, you may support that person to feel heard and maybe be able to calm down. Then, if a question arises organically and with respect, perhaps it will be heard. Then you can listen again to the response.

In her powerful book, *Strangers in Their Own Land*, Arlie Hochschild writes of getting to know Tea Party folks is southeastern Louisiana. She learned about their lives and their troubles. For them, white, middle-class and working-class, the modern world is full of threat. They feel they need the petrochemical industry, even with its pollution of their land. They worry that their way of life is under threat. They see themselves as church-going, monogamous, straight, and hard-working people. They see themselves as following the rules for living the American dream. And yet, to them, people of color and gay folks are somehow butting in line ahead of them and getting an unfair advantage. There is terrible pain in this worldview. It is important to be willing to feel that pain, I believe. That does not mean that one need agree with their view. But, can you listen? Arlie Hochschild did, and we can all be grateful that she did. And we can all be encouraged to listen too.

It is just what bodhisattvas do.

II

Yo Butsu u in, Yo Butsu u en

Related to all Buddhas
in Cause and Effect

Byakuren Judith Ragir is a senior dharma teacher at Clouds in Water Zen Center in St. Paul, Minnesota. She studied with Dainin Katagiri Roshi for seventeen years and received dharma transmission from Joen Snyder-O'Neal in the Katagiri lineage. She was the guiding teacher of Clouds in Water Zen Center from 2006 to 2015. She now works with senior students, writes about Buddhism, and makes Buddhist temple art. More information about her can be found at judithragir.org and cloudsinwater.org.

Emergency Spirituality
Byakuren Judith Ragir

I most appreciate my practice when I'm facing a personal difficulty, particularly when it concerns my health. Ill-health, which brings up my worst fears and anxiety, is the most serious and confrontational of teachers. My ego or frontal lobe never wants to be sick. How inconvenient it is! And how preposterous in its implication that I might die! Sickness inevitably brings up the fact that human beings die, an awareness that my ego and thought patterns particularly don't like. My ordinary mind thinks of death as an annihilation and therefore very scary. My Buddhist mind has been trained to go down another route. When I'm in a health difficulty, I especially appreciate this training.

There is one particular *gatha*/mantra that addresses these concerns. At my Zen Center, we often say this as part of our morning wake-up service. Called The Five Remembrances, it goes like this:

> I am of the nature to grow old. There is no escaping growing old.
>
> I am of the nature to get sick. There is no escaping getting sick.
>
> I am of the nature to die. There is no escaping death.
>
> All that is dear to me, and everyone I love are of the nature to change. There is no escaping being separated from them.
>
> My deeds are my closest companions. I am the beneficiary of my deeds. My deeds are the ground on which I stand.

How many times have I repeated those phrases? Especially in the last few years when Clouds in Water Zen Center has used them as a morning *gatha* for practice period. When a health crisis happens as it did a few years ago, I have this mantra as a back-up already planted in my brain. Even though my illness was not life-threatening, I was scared. At the Mayo Clinic, where I had gone for numerous tests in preparation for surgery, I called up this mantra. It was already emblazoned in the pathways of my neurons and brain through repetition, and because of practice, it did not take much reflection to bring the *gatha* up to meet the conditions of the moment. These recurring mantras help me face life and death directly.

There are a number of such strong reminders practiced at a Zen monastery. Every night we call out the evening message:

> I beg to urge you, everyone,
> Great is the matter of life and death.
> All things pass quickly away.
> Awaken, awaken, take heed!
> Make use of this precious life.

This urgent message sinks in, and in a practiced Zen person, it comes up automatically. A Zen teacher once told me, the land of practice needs to be cultivated *before* an emergency strikes. Then, in the face of extreme difficulties, you have something to rely on.

In 2015, for a stretch of months, I was sick. During the most intense of those days, I entered into what I called a "health *sesshin*"—a day so filled with pain and the inability to move normally that I had to use my practice and my concentration all day long. This intense concentration is similar to the feeling of single-minded focus practiced during one of our strict Zen retreats or *sesshins*. As Zen students well know, these *sesshins* often consist of ten or more meditation periods a day, with food served at your meditation seat. They require a type of concentration and attention to the breath that is uniquely demanding. The attention must be focused on each breath, relaxing on each exhale, to get through the ups and downs of the psychological suffering and physical pain that naturally arise when you sit down and face your life and your karma. I learn from these *sesshins* how to use my body and my mind to endure pain and difficult circumstances that my whole being registers as adversive. This "laboratory for life," as I call it, teaches me how to get through periods of my day that I hate and want to avoid but if I don't face them will cause even more suffering. This is the strengthening value of *sesshin*. It teaches us how to face pain without trying to run away. It provides us a spiritual stability that is unshakable or nearly so.

My six-month period of disability and illness had many days of difficulties. I couldn't leave the house. I couldn't do my work in the world. I barely could rise out of my chair, let alone help someone else. I had to stay at home and let my body heal. This circumstance was painful or scary enough that I thought I couldn't do it, but when that thought entered, "I can't do this," my mind switched back to "emergency spirituality."

It all started in February, 2015, skiing in Colorado, when I fractured my humerus and twisted my ankle and knee, in a downhill ski accident and had to be brought down the mountain on a toboggan. Now that I look back on it, certain moments make me smile—like the memory of chanting in the toboggan as we skidded and bounced through the snow. The ski patrol comes to get you, straps you in a covered toboggan, zips you in so you can't see anything but darkness, and snow-plows you down the mountain. The runs are too steep for a snowmobile. A very young, slight woman took me down the mountain; I was surprised and admiring of her skill and strength. How much I appreciated the caring of the first responders.

When I was waiting for the ski patrol to come, I watched my mind start to accelerate into worry and future-thinking, imagining all the bad things that were in store for me. One thought, "I'll never ski again," upset me as I had loved skiing since I was fifteen years old. Let alone the thought "I'll never walk again." So as I watched my mind spiral out of control, the Zen teacher in me kicked into gear. As I entered the toboggan, I decided to chant. I chanted the "gate gate, paragate parasamgate" mantra from the end of the *Heart Sutra* in an English translation by Tibetan Buddhist teacher Dan Brown, which is:

> Gate, gate—beyond thought
>
> Paragate—beyond personal identity
>
> Parasamgate—beyond constructions of Time

>   Bodhi—awakened awareness gone beyond individual consciousness
>
>   Svaha—ohh, ah, wow!(1)

I chanted this in English, finding a certain kind of rhythm that was reassuring. The mantra is often chanted in the classic Sanskrit, but I really appreciate understanding the concepts behind the chant. It helps me so much, in an emergency situation, to bring to mind the Buddhist ideas of; calming the mind, no centralized self, the illusion of the mental constructions of time, and my inter-connection with all beings. That repetition can truly revolutionize my mind!

Then I chanted the mantra for Kuanyin—*Namo Kuan Yin pusa*, and for Jizo bodhisattva—*Om ka ka kabi san ma e sowa ka*. The bodhisattvas, for me, represent the archetypal energy I want to bring forth in myself and in the situation. When I want to produce kindness, gentleness, and fearlessness, I can call on the bodhisattvas to help me strengthen my intention to bring my inherent kindness, gentleness and courage to the forefront as a response to any given situation. In the twenty minutes of being cocooned in the toboggan going from the top of the mountain to the emergency room at its base, I had calmed myself down and reoriented my thinking. My mind was surprisingly at ease. I had radically accepted that this was my new "now." I wanted to go to the emergency room as my best self and not as a crabby, complaining, angry, scared person. When this young lady who was my ski patrol guardian unzipped the toboggan zipper, she peered in and with a huge smile, said, "Wow, I heard you all the way down, it gave me so much strength." I recognized the blessing of practice. It was a great relief to enter the hospital with a calm mind and a radical acceptance of the situation I was actually in. It couldn't be taken back. This was the karma of the day and now, by my chanting, I had accepted it.

After I had somewhat recovered from my ski accident, I was diagnosed with a benign tumor on my parathyroid, which had to be surgically removed. I was operated on at the Mayo Clinic, and felt the blessing of practice in that circumstance too. All day long I was in testing rooms with scary names like the "Radioactive Medicine Waiting Room." I spent an hour and a half in the MRI machine and an hour with a sonogram technician. What a miracle western medicine can be, allowing them to take pictures of the inside of your body! However, as much as I appreciated the equipment, I was scared. The first photo in the MRI took ten long frightening minutes. I counted my breaths—sixty breaths in ten minutes. That concentration brought me back to myself and helped me calm down.

In the waiting room, I did *tonglen*, a meditation practice of taking in the black smoke of suffering and exhaling the white moonlight of love, peace, and acceptance. I did *tonglen* for all the people in the hospital and in the waiting room. One by one, I concentrated on each person in the chairs against the walls, and prayed for them through the practice of breathing, taking, and sending.

Through the years I have developed practices for spiritual emergencies. Here are some of the practices that work for me when I enter a personal crisis.

> 1. The first is *Guard your mind*. I have a visual image of setting up these ferocious guardian bodhisattvas at each end of the stream of my thoughts. As my thoughts enter and exit my mind, the guardian bodhisattvas decide if that particular thought is going to help me stay calm and stay in the present, or not. My guardians refuse any thoughts that bring fear of the future into my brain. They protect my concentration and do not allow unwholesome thought.
>
> 2. *Bring your concentration practice to the forefront.* You can't guard your mind if you are not concentrating. Usually I do a type of concentration practice for much of the day. That can range from following my breath, relaxing on the exhale, practicing *tonglen*, or a chanting practice that is coordinated with my breath.
>
> 3. *Practice tonglen.* This is my go-to practice in an emergency and I have used it many times in my life. It is best practiced before an emergency so you understand it and get the hang of it. Practice it in the cloistered situation of formal meditation. But *tonglen* in activity is one of the finest practices I know of when you are in a day of difficulty. The practice is to breathe in the dark smoke of suffering and ill-health and difficulties on your inhale. You allow the suffering to break open your heart and let the Buddha that resides in your heart come out through

the cracks of your brokenness. The Buddha light can penetrate your exhale in the image of moonlight. Your exhale is love, peace, emptiness: any quality or image that you think might help the situation. Do this type of breathing over and over.

4. *Practice using Divine Abode phrases.* Because I have worked with the phrases so much in my life, many of them are memorized and just come up as I face different situations. The Divine Abodes are loving-kindness, compassion, joy, and equanimity. There are phrases for each abode and I choose them according to what I need at any given time.

Loving-kindness: May I be happy and know the causes of happiness. May I feel safe. May I be healthy and strong.

Compassion: I care about this pain. May this suffering deepen into wisdom and compassion. May I be free from anger, fear, and anxiety.

Joy: May I know the joy of my own true nature. May I know gratitude. May I be grateful for _____. May I see the miracle of life in everything.

Equanimity: May I accept things as they are. We are the owners of our own karma. May I be at peace and let go of my expectations.(2)

5. *Chanting any number of repetitive phrases to yourself.* You can use a *mala* to help you concentrate. I have memorized various chants for Kuanyin, Jizo, the *Heart Sutra*, the medicine Buddha, Avalokiteshvara, and so on.

6. *Open up your prayer or extend the tonglen.* This is a very important practice for me. I start out doing all the above for myself but at a certain point, I extend my practice to include others. I do the practice for everyone, including myself, who are in the same circumstances. In a hospital, that is quite an obvious practice, for most everyone you meet is suffering and anxious. In the waiting room, you can do it for everyone there; or you can imagine all the people in their hospital beds. This practice really puts my own *dukkha* in perspective. It helps me join the human race. We are all suffering. This is what being a human feels like. When you extend the prayer to others, you can release a self-centered way of being. For example: I breathe in and out for myself and everyone else waiting for important

test results. I breathe in and out for myself and everyone else who is on the cold stretcher, in the busy corridor going into surgery and facing that huge overwhelming light above the surgery table. We can find endless circumstances to pray for ourselves and others in this way.

My root teacher, Katagiri Roshi, used to call our practice "attaining spiritual stability." This is the ability to hold all life circumstances with equanimity and strength—not an easy thing to do, especially in the face of your own or a loved one's ill-health. But if there is anything I'm deeply grateful for, it is my practice that helps me endure the low points of my life. The Buddha has two arms: one of compassion and one of wisdom. The compassionate arm allows me to be gentle and love myself and others under any circumstance.

> May the power of loving-kindness sustain me.
> May I connect with boundless love that flows endlessly.

The wisdom arm is where we get true perspective over our life and our karma. What is a life? Does it end? Where does it begin? Can I view my situation from the largest perspective I have and see how small my individual story is in the face of the whole world of humanity?

> May I realize the truth of impermanence.
> May I be open to the true nature of life.
> May I remember that my consciousness is much vaster than this body and this story.

These two approaches, wisdom and compassion, intertwined, are a true gift. That is spirituality at its finest. This practice is grounded and practical and also sublime. We can accept the worst of our circumstances and be calmed by the widest sky of understanding. We can find some peace with the facts of our life, which include old age, illness, and death. Buddhism at its best!

Notes

1. From my notes on a lecture given by Dan Brown on the *Mahamudra*, during a retreat at Mount Madonna Center, Watsonville, CA, February 2012.
2. Adapted from Sharon Salzberg and Joan Halifax, "Four Boundless Abodes," *Meditations*, https://www.upaya.org/dox/Meditations.pdf, 260/www.

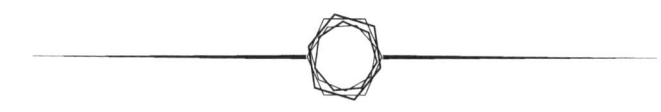

Shunzan Jill Kaplan received tokudo in 2001 and dharma transmission in 2013 from Misha Shungen Merrill, in the Suzuki Roshi lineage. She is a dharma teacher with Zen Heart Sangha in Woodside, California, and with Willow Zen in San Jose. Jill is also a psychotherapist offering sandplay therapy and Jungian depth work to children and adults in her private practice in San Jose. She has also trained in mindfulness-based stress reduction. Jill has written many articles for the Journal of Sandplay Therapy, often on Buddhist images and symbols and the spiritual aspect of psychotherapy. Website: kaplanmft.com.

Deep Connection to the Dharma
Shunzan Jill Kaplan

Siddhartha did not have a smartphone; Mahapajapati did not have Facebook; Ananda did not have Google search. Without Google search, Ananda had to rely on his memory to access all of the words of the Buddha. He couldn't look things up if he forgot. Without a smartphone, Siddhartha spent many years traveling around with no Google Maps, no calling home, no connection beyond where he was at the moment. He truly had to rely on himself out there in the dusty world. Without Facebook, Mahapajapati couldn't check up on what her wandering son was up to, she didn't post notes to her friends lamenting his disappearance.

The "tools" available to us today, via pocket computers, are meant to be time savers, organizers, and they carry troves of information. I did not imagine twenty years ago that I would be able to carry in my pocket more information than I could have found at my local library at that time, all of the news from countless sources around the world, connections to everyone I know (and countless ones who I don't) via phone or some form of message, a map of every place in the world, and endless sources of amusement and games if I wish to play them. While these are meant to assist us, they have actually become hindrances, as problematic as sloth and torpor or aversion or doubt, in our lives and to practice. In fact, they seem to support and exacerbate the classic Five Hindrances. Want to avoid how you're feeling? Play a game of Candy Crush. Want to avoid spending any time in your own mind? Check Facebook. As a comedian said, when explaining why he did not want his teenage daughters to have smartphones, "They keep you from ever having to feel sad." It turns out that among teens today there is a correlation between smartphone use and increased depression: people are not connecting in ways that we're used to, and it's hurting us.

These devices keep us from feeling a lot of things, actually, one of the hallmarks of addiction. They keep us from ever being bored, which also means it keeps us from being creative, because boredom is often the seed of creativity. They are meant to keep us connected, yet they actually serve to disconnect us, from others, and from our deepest selves.

The speed of access to information has another effect on us: we barely take in one disaster before the next one is upon us. We are delivered suffering on a global scale daily, hourly, on news sites, Twitter feeds, Facebook. Suffering may not have changed markedly since the days of our first ancestors – sickness, old age and death are ever with us – but the 24/7 news cycle means we are ceaselessly reminded of them. There is no palace where a Siddhartha of today could remain unexposed to war, famine, pestilence, violence for very long. In the past year, we have seen devastating hurricanes in the south of the United States and in the Caribbean, calamitous earthquakes in Mexico, uncontained fires burning in California, a mass shooting, and we hear threats of using nuclear weapons. No wonder we want to avoid how we're feeling by playing a game or reading the latest on Facebook.

The Five Hindrances—ill-will, desire, sloth and torpor, restlessness and anxiety, and doubt—are named in the *Sattipathana Sutta* as conditions that affect the mind's clarity and ability to observe the mind without judgment. These hindrances affect our awareness and concentration in meditation and are also states of mind that get in the way of relationships and our ability to function effectively at work and play.

There are of course many challenges of living a human life and at the same time tending to our spiritual nature; we are attracted by worlds of desire, thus the invention of monasticism. Zen, however, has a long and strong tradition of lay practice, of bringing monastic practice back into the marketplace, and probably has always struggled with the tension of spiritual needs in the midst of the material world. Harada Roshi, of Japan and Whidbey Island, described his desire to be enlightened, which he shared with his teacher after his first *Rohatsu* (winter meditation retreat) experience; for years, with the agreement of his teacher, he pursued this ambition, retreating to a mountain refuge. One day, students from a nearby town visited him, and remarked how fortunate he was to escape the world, while they struggled to maintain practice down below in the midst of their busy lives. Here a light shined, if not enlightenment itself: he realized that the real practice, true practice, was not to pursue enlightenment, but to be in the world and be of benefit to others. He came down from the mountain to teach and practice in the world.

The material world is so enticing and distracting. And the world that technology offers us is altering not just the material world, but also, I fear, our inner world. Our devices and the speed of communication and distraction they create increase the volume on the hindrances the Buddha named. Desire: we want the newest, we want to check our email, we want to play a game, we want something new and shiny and can order it with one click, desires multiply as fast as gigabytes can fly through cyberspace. Ill-will: misunderstandings created through email are notorious and all too frequent, access to the latest horror on the news is ever-present and unending, the divisiveness and polarization of online media often leaves us in a state of anger or despair, social media can be weaponized to cause great harm. Restlessness: distraction is seductive, ubiquitous, instantly available. We can soothe our anxiety with a bit of an Internet hit. But even worse, I worry that our use of media and smart devices is potentially retraining our mind in just the opposite direction of classical Buddhist mind training: to be distracted, inattentive, in a state of hyper-alertness much of the time.

In 1998, the Microsoft executive Linda Stone coined the term "continuous partial attention" to describe the effect computers might potentially have on our minds. Computers are designed in a way that almost dictates this state of never really fully concentrating on one thing: I can have as many "desktops" on my computer as I want—writing, emailing, the news, a spreadsheet, so much can be happening all at once. Right concentration, one of the eight limbs of our Zen practice, can be subverted by engagement with technology. Further, technology is actually teaching us not to pay attention, and rewarding us for distraction. It reinforces our restlessness, throwing new diversions in our path at every turn. Back in Psychology

101 I learned that the most effective technique for shaping behavior was intermittent reinforcement: this is our email inbox. We check it continuously, endlessly, banging away like a rat in an experimental psych lab, on the off chance there may be a reward in the form of a new message. Or when one pops up in the middle of my writing this, I go mindlessly to check it.

The answer, of course, is to turn it off.

The answer is to renew our determination to practice with the Eightfold Path, to renew our vows to follow the bodhisattva way. The opportunities that lay practice presents, as well as the challenges, hold the potential for healing self and others. In the midst of our cyberdriven life, demands of speed and instant replies and media overload can be mitigated by attention to right view: that all of this is a dream and we needn't be driven by it at all. The demands are mitigated by the essential connection between meditation practice and Buddhist ethics, arising out of right action, right speech, right livelihood. Basing our everyday life and everyday practice on the faith that we are Buddha changes us and changes others around us. The answer is to renew our determination to practice in this way, moment by moment.

While the Buddha and his followers did not have to contend with technology, the wisdom of the path they set out remains relevant, if not even more vital than it was 2,500 years ago in India, 1,500 years ago in Bodhidharma's China, 800 years ago in Dogen's time. If in their time, our ancestors needed to train the mind to pay attention, we similarly need the training that meditation and practice offer. Delusions have ever been inexhaustible, and the ones offered up to us today seem immeasurably deeper, more seductive, ubiquitous. Moreover, we look to meditation as a counterbalance to the speed and seduction of the many forms of media.

Abraham Heschel wrote that we need Sabbath to survive civilization: "Gallantly, ceaselessly, quietly, man must fight for inner liberty. Inner liberty depends upon being exempt from domination of things as well as from domination of people."[1] For Heschel, keeping the Sabbath holy meant taking time out from the material world; for us as Zen practitioners, meditation is or can be, like Heschel's description of the Sabbath, a path to inner liberty, to survive being enslaved by the material world. It is the medicine that Shakyamuni prescribed so long ago, to ease the bonds of dissatisfaction with conditioned phenomena.

The Buddha saw clearly the source of our dis-ease, clinging and aversion, never being satisfied. The smartphone, all our devices and apps and social media, are not liberating us or connecting us as much as they are sources of suffering, training us to want more and more, believing in connections that are virtual and not real and hence never satisfying.

What about technology that offers the dharma: websites, blogs, audio dharma, apps that offer teachings, ring meditation bells, send us inspiration. Aren't these a good thing, don't they help? Perhaps, but we have to be careful of marketing mindfulness and meditation, commodifying Buddhism in attractive packages, which may potentially reinforce our clinging and desire.

It's really all about balance and intention. Audio dharma and links to *Lion's Roar* may bring relief of suffering to many who might otherwise not encounter the dharma. It may make it possible to work with a teacher when we move far away, or to access teachings and research for dharma talks (*mea culpa*). Yet if we confuse the Internet or our apps for actual practice, if we neglect the silence of sitting, if we are not connected to Sangha in a meaningful way, then the websites and blogs and audio are merely diversions, one more product we want and buy and want more of. If our intention is to connect more and better and faster (which Stone identified as the intention of continuous partial attention), we are headed down the path of delusion, endless desire for more. If our intention is to end suffering, then we can't help but see the benefit of sitting still. Just sitting, since before Buddha's time a necessary simplicity, is even more today a necessary counterbalance to cyberspeed.

Mindfulness has become as popular as popcorn. It is taught in the workplace, in schools, in hospitals, in psychology courses, and trainings, and it has no doubt relieved many people and opened the door to deeper practice. The first three of the four foundations of mindfulness are well-taught: mindfulness of the body, of feelings, of the mind. However, the fourth foundation of mindfulness (mindfulness of the objects of mind) is seldom mentioned in secular mindfulness teachings and curricula, yet it represents the radical revolution of Shakyamuni. When he sat beneath the bodhi tree, he was drawing upon the meditation practices he had learned; most likely the first three foundations were nothing new in his day, as meditation was practiced by sadhus and seekers of his time. "All the dharmas," as the fourth foundation is called by Thich Nhat Hanh, specifies several pivotal teachings of Buddhism: the Four Noble Truths, the Five Hindrances, the Seven Factors of Awakening, the six senses and their objects. In this foundation, we see clearly the Buddha's intention to get to the bottom of suffering, as he offers the means to realize the truth of ending suffering. We can learn mindfulness, but the intention of understanding and ending suffering brings mindfulness to a deep level of healing for oneself and others, to the bodhisattva way. Mindfulness is one of the eight limbs, but it's not the whole path.

The Buddha saw how humans suffer through clinging and aversion, and that the way to end this suffering is to train the mind in a different direction, to see greed, hate, and delusion as clearly as we can. Our practice is to investigate over and over how we are motivated by these misunderstandings of the true self, reality as it truly is.

Buddhist teachers over the centuries developed specific antidotes to the hindrances, and there are perhaps specific antidotes to technology-dependent hindrances. We can see such antidotes in the Eightfold Path. The antidote to the negative mind training of devices is found in right concentration and right mindfulness; the antidote to the divisiveness or alienation we may feel as a result of the onslaught of news and tweets and emails is found through right understanding, the understanding of connection and no separation; our guides through email and Facebook and hateful trolling are right speech and right action; most important, the answer to the seemingly unending seductiveness and distraction of media and devices is right practice: being still, clarifying the mind, listening to silence.

Right practice with technology is to remember to turn it off. Spend a day without a device, turn screens off in the evenings, go to the library, read a book, sit quietly—most importantly, sit quietly. Otherwise we are feeding the poisons and cultivating the hindrances.

Sometimes I wonder, have things really changed in 2,500 years: would one awakening to suffering today have a different perspective or a different prescription from the Buddha? Would she need to add any truths to the ones he saw, any precepts, any additional step on the path? I don't think so. Though the Buddha, Mahapajapati, Ananda, and our early ancestors weren't faced with weapons of mass destruction or technological overload, their understanding of suffering and its remedies remain relevant. Hatred still does not end hatred, though sometimes it's hard to know if love and compassion are enough to save all beings. Delusions are still inexhaustible, and the capacity to create new ones seems unlimited. The good news is that dharma gates still remain boundless, and we can walk through them every moment. We can offer a hand, listen to those in distress, witness injustice and speak out, stand up for those who cannot stand. Just the simple act of allowing others who are in such a hurry to go first on the freeway or in the grocery line alters the flow toward kindness. The Buddha's way is unsurpassable, and the vow to become it remains a radical enactment of awakening in service to others.

The Buddha said, "I am awake," and this became how he was known. He was awake in a very crucial sense: he was awake with the intention to bear witness to others in order to end suffering. This intention is carried through the practice of the fourth foundation of mindfulness: understanding the Four Noble Truths, practicing with the hindrances, cultivating the factors of enlightenment, awareness of all the sense gates. Being awake is to experience true connection, to express vital connection, to cultivate human connection.

Note

1. Abraham Joshua Heschel, *The Sabbath* (New York: Farrar, Straus and Giroux, 2005), 77.

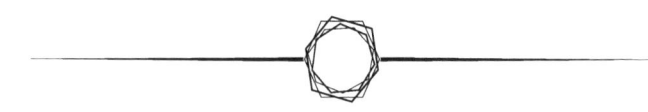

Sosan Theresa Flynn is the guiding teacher of Clouds in Water Zen Center, where she has been practicing since its incorporation in 1994. She was ordained as a Soto Zen Buddhist priest in 1997, practiced with several teachers including Byakuren Judith Ragir, and received dharma transmission from Joen Snyder O'Neal in 2012. Sosan has a master's degree in counseling psychology. She worked in both community mental health and staff training before coming to work at Clouds in Water in 1998, first in administration and later as a teacher.

Disillusionment

Sosan Theresa Flynn

I adored my first teacher. I felt that he had a deep understanding of the Dharma that I longed to know. I was willing to do just about anything to attain that understanding. I let go of so many things. I was shaving my head when I hated to shave my head. When I took up the razor once each week, I practiced letting go of the hatred. I also practiced letting go pretty much any time that I had a non-Zen social interaction with someone who wondered about my shaved head. I hated getting up at 4:20 every morning during our twice-yearly one-hundred-day practice periods. I'm a night owl . . . and so are my husband and son, so this was really difficult. And still I did it, even though it made me chronically sleep-deprived. I didn't like that he asked us to call him Sensei (an honorific term for "teacher," which I found pretentious at the time), but I did it anyway without complaint. I was really doing my best to let go of attachment to my way of doing things. In Zen practice, there are a million little details, and I had an opinion about almost every one. How to light or put out the candles. How to hold the incense. What translation to use for the chants. While there were occasions when I did share my opinion, mostly there was neither time nor space to do that. In those cases, even though I mostly thought that my way was "right," I did my best to let go and taste the bitter pill of just going along with someone else's idea. I thought the bitter pill would eventually lead to a great awakening. And perhaps it did, but not in the way that I expected.

It was a great shock when my teacher stumbled. I felt deeply betrayed. It seemed that he had abandoned the very principles that he had been trying to teach us. But, perhaps more than that, it was my own horror of seeing how completely human he was. What was his betrayal, you may wonder? This story is not about that. Simply imagine a child discovering that there is no Santa Claus, or Tooth Fairy, or Easter Bunny. This story is about me, and how I practiced waking up to the truth that my teacher was not a god.

I remember leaving our Zen Center on the day of my disillusionment. I was in my car, on the freeway, on my way to pick up my son from preschool. The sun was shining. The sky was a brilliant blue. "I have no idea what will happen to me," I thought. It felt as if an enormous weight had been lifted from my shoulders. The intensity of Zen practice and the way I had twisted that practice with a goal-seeking mind was suddenly exposed, and I had no idea what would happen next. It suddenly seemed clear to me that this man, who had ordained me, would never again be my teacher. "With no teacher," I thought, "how can I have a Zen practice? What will happen to the Center? Since I work at the Center, will I even have a job?" I drove along at sixty miles per hour. "This is the truth of my life. My life can be anything."

The next day, my alarm sounded at 4:20 a.m. I got up, put on my Zen clothes, left my husband and son sleeping in our bed just as I had the day before, and drove down to the Zen Center. Once there, I put on my priest robes and joined all the other students in morning meditation. I still didn't know what would happen next, but I remembered my vow, inspired by Dogen's Great Inspirational Vow: "I vow with all beings, from this life on throughout countless lives, to hear the true dharma; that upon hearing it, no doubt will arise, nor shall I lack in faith; that upon meeting it, I will renounce worldly affairs and maintain the buddha-dharma; in doing so, the great earth and all beings together attain the buddha way."[1]

After meditation, I did my personal morning service, including chanting Dogen's Great Inspirational Vow and dedicating the merit from this to my former teacher. There is a practice in Zen of doing something that would be wholesome for oneself, such as chanting a sutra, and then dedicating any merit that might be gained from this to others. I continued this daily practice for a long time. Thus, even in the midst of deep suffering, I planted the seed of remembering the good in my former teacher, and allowing gratitude to arise for all that he taught me.

After a month of very difficult communications with our board of directors, priests, and senior students, this teacher, the guiding teacher of our Center, decided to resign. A short time later, one of the other priests left and I was in the unenviable position of being the only ordained priest in the sangha. I was not ready to be a leader, nor was the community ready to have me lead. Yet there I was. As the only priest, I was the container into which many sangha members poured their projections, fears, anger, and spiritual longing. The board of directors decided to bestow upon me the title of "temple priest," and I continued to be on the payroll, shifting from my position as assistant executive director in charge of fundraising to that of a priest overseeing programs, classes, and dharma talks.

While many were projecting onto me this role of "our only priest," I was having a crisis of faith. "If someone with a deep practice could make such a big mistake," I wondered, "then what is the point?" For a couple of months, I didn't believe that practicing was necessarily a good idea. I wanted to say to new people coming in, "Don't learn how to meditate. Just go home. Try to be kind to your partners, children, parents, and friends. Take walks by a lake and breathe the air. Enjoy your life."

Fortunately for me and for our community, many other teachers were willing to help. But first, we had to ask. Our sangha had previously prided itself as being "the best," but we knew that if we were to survive, we could not go it alone. With deep humility and gratitude, we asked and received generous offers of support. In the first few months, we had guest teachers giving dharma talks every week. And then Joen Snyder O'Neal of Compassionate Ocean Dharma Center and Dokai Georgesen of Hokyoji Zen Practice Community agreed to serve as interim teachers, which was a huge gift to us.

About seven months after our former guiding teacher resigned, I received a card from him. A beautiful hand-calligraphed card that said, among other things, "I am sorry if I have caused any pain." While I didn't feel the apology went far enough, I felt some softening of my heart. However, when I discovered he had sent nearly identical cards to many of the other students at the center, my heart hardened again. Joen reminded me that even if he said the same thing to each of us, his apology was no less sincere.

Struggling with feelings that I somehow wanted more, I decided to let these difficult feelings be my teacher. I put the now-offensive card on my altar at home. There it stayed for one week, until I met with my therapist. I tried to explain to her the Buddhist practice of allowing the "enemy" to be one's teacher, of not turning away from difficulties. My therapist surprised me by saying, "You should put that card on top of your toilet!" Wow. She who never gave me any advice or direction was giving me a direct order. I decided to try it. The card sat on top of my toilet for another week. I never felt good about having it there. It didn't seem to be helping me any more than having it on the altar. Next I met with Joen again. "The toilet! That's no place for a card like that! Put it on your altar or put it away!" she cried. Back it went onto the altar. When I meditated at home, the apology card took its place along with the Buddha, *Mahaprajnaparamita*, and Jizo. I bowed to the card, along with the statues. During meditation, if difficult thoughts or emotions arose in connection with my former teacher, I invited myself to simply breathe and be with those thoughts and emotions.

I often did loving-kindness practice. However, instead of using the four classic phrases (May I be free from danger, May I have mental happiness, May I have physical happiness, May I have ease of well-being), I used the classic list of the eleven benefits of loving-kindness as a meditation:

May I sleep easily.

May I wake easily.

May I have pleasant dreams.

May people love me.

May angels and animals love me.

May angels protect me.

May external dangers not harm me.

May my face be radiant.

May my mind be serene.

May I die unconfused.

May I be reborn in happy realms.

I would silently say these to myself, one with each breath, saying each one three times before moving to the next. Then, I would start again and go through all eleven for someone near-and-dear, a benefactor, a neutral person, a difficult person, and then for all beings everywhere. My near-and-dear person was usually my husband or son. My benefactor was one of my parents, my current teacher, Joen, or my therapist. My neutral person varied, usually someone I had seen on the street or in the Black Dog Coffee Shop. But my difficult person was almost always my former teacher. So I wished that he would sleep easily, would wake easily, would have pleasant dreams, would be loved by people, angels, and animals, would be protected by angels and free from danger, and so on. This was often a difficult practice. Sometimes, I had to imagine him as a baby in order to do this. I didn't want to just say the words, I wanted to actually cultivate a loving attitude. Now, it is easier. I still have psychic scars, but I only wish the best for him.

The time without a guiding teacher was quite challenging for our community. We realized that we didn't know how to proceed and at the same time follow the Precepts—the ethical guidelines for behavior in our Zen tradition. Some people had strong opinions about what to do, and there were a lot of disagreements. Others didn't say anything because they were overwhelmed by the intensity of the conversations. Some of us knew that we had to talk about what had happened and what was happening, but it was hard to do that, given the Precepts. Some of us were breaking the Precepts by speaking about others' errors and faults, blaming others, and being angry . . . and others of us were shushing that discussion, or saying "Don't be angry," and "Have some compassion." We were really in a sticky situation, but we were determined to find a way through.

After about a year of stumbling along, we invited Wendy Egyoku Nakao Roshi of Zen Center of Los Angeles to come and help us. ZCLA has developed a form of council practice, or talking circles, based on the work of Jack Zimmerman and Virginia Coyle.(2) Egyoku spent a weekend with us and taught us this practice. We found it provided a way for our community to be together. It didn't magically make our anger and grief go away, or suddenly make us perfect people who did not speak of others' errors and faults and did not blame others, but it did provide a container that could hold these strong views. Within that container of listening from the heart and speaking from the heart, we were able to move forward. We used the council process extensively in our search for a new guiding teacher, and in helping us to manage the business of running a spiritual community.

I think that we were able to do all this and survive because council practice provided a structure that fostered our connections with each other. It provided a safe place for the shadows to be uncovered and addressed. It gave us a way to be with each other and to hold all of the strong ideas, opinions, and emotions. It allowed those who were mistrusting of authority to speak out and be heard. It enabled us to talk about "hot button" issues, such as budget cuts or staffing changes, in a way that was respectful and productive. It provided a nurturing place for those who tend to be introverted to speak out.

This practice saved us, mainly because we stopped trying to save Clouds in Water Zen Center and instead shifted the focus to practicing with and for each other. I remember a sangha member who said at the time, "How we practice through this is more important than what we accomplish. What good is it if we save Clouds in Water but, in the process, destroy our relationships and fail to practice well? We need to go forward in an upright way, being kind to each other, keeping the precepts, and practicing letting go of attachment to outcomes. Letting go of being the best."

Right around the time of our learning council practice, I had a powerful dream, which I titled, "Behind Enemy Lines":

> My husband Rob and I are crawling across a countryside. It's night. We are going behind enemy lines for some sort of rescue. We have done this before. In the past, we have occasionally, in times of great need, used magic colored sticks. We would throw these magic sticks to the ground and the situation would change in a way that allowed us to escape from the danger. I don't know who we are rescuing this time, or who we have rescued in the past, but it is terribly important work. There is no question that we should risk our lives

doing it.

As we move across the land, we see to our right, far in the distance but close enough to feel the heat, the smoldering remains of Chernobyl, the exploded nuclear power plant. Some explosions are still happening and light up the night sky. I want to look, but Rob reminds me to close my eyes and also to breathe as little as possible to avoid damage to my eyes and lungs.

We go as far as we can and find a place to sleep. Soon, I feel the heat on the back of my neck, sense light behind my closed eyes, and begin to feel warm all over, sweating in my sleep. I think there is some awful explosion or fire. When I can shut it out no longer I open my eyes to find that it is only the sun. It is morning and we are in a ditch on the side of the road. It is near a crossroads, and there are a lot of other people here. I don't know if these people are friends or enemies. Maybe they are some of each. We don't talk much to them or they to us. We are behind enemy lines and must be very careful. I learn from Rob that we have no magic sticks to use this time and must escape by our own wits. I am incredulous! How can we do this, and why didn't he tell me before? But I know that, in a way, it doesn't matter. It is as if we are rescuing our own son from death: there is no way that we would not do it.

When I woke from this dream, I thought, "Yes. There is no way that I would not do it. How could I relinquish my vow to save all beings?" The dream pointed out to me the heat of being in difficult situations, the fear of not knowing who or what I could trust, the hope that there would be a "magic" solution, and the strong vow to continue. More than anything, my vow is what sustained me. And I can thank my former teacher for helping me to cultivate that strong vow.

Part of the vow to save all beings was realizing what I needed to do in order to maintain this practice for the long term. After working for over a year in the challenging role of temple priest, I asked for and was granted a three-month leave of absence with pay. I didn't leave the sangha. I still attended regularly, but I didn't work there. I remain grateful to the community for this much-needed rest.

During my rest period, I continued doing the healing things

that I had started soon after my disillusionment: yoga and exercise, reaching out to many teachers who helped me, and reconnecting with a number of old friends whom I had neglected in my single-minded pursuit of Zen practice. I felt that I was opening up to my life in a new and more wholesome way.

Joen was one of the teachers with whom I deeply connected. She later agreed to be my main teacher, and, a few years ago, I received dharma transmission from her. I will be forever grateful to Joen for her many gifts. Byakuren Judith Ragir was another person who helped me, and she later became the next guiding teacher of our Zen Center. My gratitude to Byakuren is also immense.

I finished my leave of absence and came back to work at the Zen Center. Around that time, I had another memorable dream that I call "Angels Dive In."

> I am on the earth trying to help people. Angels dive in from heaven. They start on the clouds and dive into the water. They look like regular people. I end up helping by coordinating things for the angels, but they get to do all the fun things—helping and healing people with their magic—while I am just behind the scenes.

This dream, of course, is about Clouds in Water Zen Center. And about how my role as temple priest was more about coordinating things behind the scenes than doing what I really wanted to do, which was to directly teach. But still, it was okay. My practice was to do what was needed. And that ended up being a very deep practice for me.

On the first anniversary of my great disillusionment, I went to my altar and looked at the apology card that I had received. Then, I carefully removed the card from my altar and burned it. We have a practice in our tradition of burning things that we remove from the altar, not just throwing them away. After we finish with prayer cards or memorial cards that were placed on the altar, we do a simple ceremony and offer them to the fire. Sometimes they are burned in a bonfire, and sometimes people just take them home and burn them in fireplaces. This time, I met with a couple of my dharma sisters. We went to a regional park, made a little fire, said some prayers, and chanted the Dai Hi Shin Dharani for those who had died, and then said goodbye to many things and placed them in the fire. We included over a year's worth of prayer and memorial cards from sangha members. We also spent time in meditation and reflection about what we wanted to let go of, wrote these things down on slips of paper, and threw them on the fire. Letting go of clinging to betrayal. Letting go of indulging in anger. Letting go of idealizing someone. Letting go of blame. Letting go of self-pity. Piece after piece we placed into the fire. The flames now towering, we were sweating with the heat of the fire and the warm spring sunshine. Letting go, letting go, letting go. Wishing happiness and ease for ourselves and all beings, even the being who had harmed us so deeply.

In the fall of 2006, a wonderful thing happened. Byakuren Judith Ragir agreed to serve as our new guiding teacher and was elected by unanimous vote by the entire sangha. This freed me to take another break, a short one-week solo retreat.

One of the insights I had on this retreat was that the image I had built up around my teacher was like a straw man, one without solid substance. Now, instead, I could see him as "a true man of no rank."[3] I saw that the true man is vulnerable and imperfect. The true man is intelligent, loving, and a great teacher. The true man is not manipulative, but realizes his interconnection with the whole universe, and trusts in the whole universe to take care of him. I realize that under the thrall of the straw man and the promise of a big awakening, I lost touch with my own buddha nature. I discounted my own insights and my own sense of what is true and good. I realized that I needed to burn the straw man.

Burning is not annihilation. Burning is a respectful way to release things. Just as the prayer cards and memorials are removed and burned, in the same way I wanted to burn this straw man I had built up. So, I made a tiny doll out of straw, even fashioning a little priest robe out of an oak leaf. My hands trembled as I held it and I was surprised at how much power it seemed to have, even after all this time and even though it was only straw. I respectfully placed it in a large ashtray, chanted the Dai Hi Shin Dharani, and burned it.

When there was nothing but ashes, I decided that they needed to be placed outside, not just in a wastebasket. When I got outside, I also realized that the ashes needed to be placed well away from my hermitage. So I walked all the way down to a prairie area, with the ash tray in hand. I held the tray up to my face and, with a puff, blew the ashes away. They were gone in an instant. Walking back, I felt free.

Of course, there continue to be difficulties in my life, but there is much happiness. In 2014, Byakuren transitioned to senior dharma teacher at Clouds in Water and I stepped into the role of guiding teacher. The guiding teacher role is not the same as angels diving from the clouds into the water and doing magic and healing, but I am really enjoying the opportunity to serve the sangha in this way. The challenges that I have faced, and that our sangha has faced, have made us stronger, but also kinder and humbler. I am grateful for all the ingredients of my life and to everyone who has helped me, including my current and former teachers. All of them.

Notes

1. Dogen, *Eihei Koso Hotsuganmon*, trans. San Francisco Zen Center, https://terebess.hu/zen/szoto/SotoZenTexts.pdf, p. 39.
2. Jack Zimmerman and Virginia Coyle, *The Way of Council* (Colchester, UK: Bramble Books, 1996).
3. Lin-Chi, *The Zen Teachings of Master Lin-Chi: A Translation of the Lin-chi lu*, trans. Burton Watson (New York: Columbia University Press, 1992). See also Brad Warner, "Person of No Rank," Hardcore Zen, http://hardcorezen.info/person-of-no-rank/3514.

Ganman Cathy Toldi is a priest in the Soto Zen lineage of Suzuki Roshi. She is one of the teachers at Santa Cruz Zen Center (sczc.org), and guides a sitting group in Hollister, California. She is most interested in how the relational realm is a practice field for waking up together with all beings. She is a coauthor of the *Facilitator's Guide to Participatory Decision-Making* (Jossey Bass) and has published essays in *BuddhaDharma* magazine, and *In Times Like These: How We Pray* (Seabury Books).

Feeling Our Way to Embodied Wisdom
Ganman Cathy Toldi

"I'm being such a bad Buddhist," my friend announced as she came through the doorway. "I feel hatred in my heart." This was November 2016, just after the U.S. presidential election. "And I feel guilty, too. Others are already taking direct action, and I'm not."

She was not alone in struggling with strong emotions during this time. Another companion said, "I feel sick to my stomach. I feel like something terrible is going to happen. I don't want to go to work. I feel paralyzed."

And a third confessed, "I feel so far away from the wisdom teachings of our tradition. *The great way is not difficult for those who hold no preferences.* Ha! I don't know how or whether I want to try to reach out of my swamp of despair."

These post-election days were filled with people seeking counsel about how to practice in the midst of emotional turbulence. As a priest in a community-based Zen temple, it wasn't the first time I'd heard sangha members struggling to find their ground. People gravitate toward the temple, the church, the synagogue, the mosque, during challenging times. We'd come together before after a catastrophic earthquake, during military invasions in our name, after fires and floods, or incidents of violence in our community. We want guidance from our religions when the external world feels like it's reeling out of control.

What do we hope to get from Buddhism in challenging times?

Many come with visions of becoming like the mellow meditators we see in the magazines, or the wise ancestors we read about in the sacred texts. Yet this state seems far away from our actual experience: burning with anger, trembling with fear, sunk in despair. Often, we use the discrepancy between our aspiration and our reality to conclude—as did my friend—that the presence of nonmellow emotions must mean that we're somehow failing in our practice. We judge ourselves, and others, against an idealized state.

This is nothing new. In the seventeenth century, Satsujo, a student of Zen master Hakuin, was found by her neighbor weeping profusely after the death of her granddaughter. The neighbor challenged her. "I heard that you received a certificate of enlightenment from Hakuin, so why are you carrying on?"[1]

The neighbor believed, as many seem to do, that "enlightened people," or those on the Buddhist path, somehow shouldn't feel emotions, or at least not show that they do. However if you look for guidance from Buddhist teachings about practice and the emotional realm, you will find mixed and often contradictory views.

In the traditional Theravada approach, practicing with feelings means paying attention to whether a sensation is pleasant, unpleasant, or neutral. The implication is that what we call feelings—emotions such as anger, fear, hopelessness—are distractions to having a calm mind. We are encouraged to let them go, and just focus on our mental concentration. However, contemporary Vipassana teachers, while rooted in the Theravada tradition, teach mindfulness of emotion as an essential part of practice.

The Vajrayana tradition teaches that emotions are energy, and, as such, a primary vehicle for awakening. As described by Reggie Rey, "In the Vajrayana, practitioners invite the chaos of emotions and attend to them with meditative presence and openness."[2]

In Zen, it would seem that we don't talk at all about emotions or how to practice with them. Yet the teaching stories are laden with descriptions of practitioners expressing emotion —joy, gratitude, irritation, insecurity, appreciation, sadness, grief. For example, the esteemed thirteenth-century Zen teacher Eihei Dogen described how he felt the first time he saw monks doing the robe chant: "This was the first time I had seen the kashaya held up in this way, and I rejoiced, tears wetting the collar of my robe."[3]

Or consider the dharma brothers Yentou and Xuefeng, out on pilgrimage, taking refuge in a barn during a storm. First, Yentou chastised his friend for trying to gain awakening by sitting zazen all the time. Xuefeng confessed his longtime confusion and insecurity about his practice. Yentou burst out, "haven't you heard that what enters through the gate is not the family jewels? It must flow forth from your breast. In the future, your teaching and mine will cover heaven and earth!" These words provided the catalyst for Xuefeng to finally awaken to the way.(4)

And then our grieving grandmother, Satsujo, set her neighbor straight by replying to his criticism saying, "Idiot! My tears are a better memorial than a hundred priests chanting. My tears commemorate every child that has died. This is exactly how I feel at the moment." These ancestors teach us that far from being a hindrance, or a sign of poor practice, the ability to allow, own, and understand our emotions helps us live from the embodied wisdom of our actual—rather than idealized—life.

Xuefeng expended so much effort trying to "be a good Buddhist" and yet his awakening was prompted by the passionate in-the-moment urging from his friend that he turn to his very own heart as the source of that which he was seeking outside. Dogen searched throughout Japan and China, looking for the Zen expression that would most authentically touch and guide his life—and knew he'd found it when his body was flooded with tears of joy.

This intimate contact with our inner felt sense of what is true connects us with the aliveness of the present moment, with the fresh, direct experience of life. This is the wordless shared understanding that is reflected between student and teacher, between dharma friends.

While some prefer the Buddhist schools that encourage awakening through releasing attachment to the physical and emotional realms, and some may see Zen itself as emotionally detached, I speak from the experience of all the tears I've seen and felt when touched by shared moments of raw presence.

> "What is the business beneath the patched robe?" the student asks.
> "Intimacy," the master responds.
> The student has a great awakening. Tears of gratitude wet his robe.
> "Can you express it?" the master asks.
> "Intimacy, intimacy."(5)

Biologically, emotions are flows of energy, states of arousal and activation, that pervade all mental functions and literally create meaning in life. They are the vehicles that allow us to have a sense of the mental states of others—a profoundly important dimension for a social species such as ourselves. When people feel met, they are able to bring their true selves forward, contributing their intellectual and emotional energy to the collective enterprise, rather than covering up these resources with defensive behavior.

Emotions allow us to cultivate wholesome states of mind—the "immeasurables" (*brahma viharas*) defined by the Buddha. To express *metta*, loving-kindness, you need to be able to feel kindness and love. To express *karuna*, compassion, you need to be able to feel the pain of others as your own. To express *muditta*, taking joy in the happiness of others, you need to be able to feel joy. To express *upekka*, or equanimity, you stand, rooted and calm in the center of the storm, feeling the waves of human emotion swirling all around.

What we consider "difficult emotions" serve to deepen our experience and understanding. Sadness and grief open the heart. Guilt and remorse true us up as moral beings. Anger can motivate us to take action in the face of injustice.

But then what about the suffering created by the emotional realm? This is where study and practice come in. In the same way that obsessive thinking separates us from the actual experience at hand, trapping us in a repetitive, self-referential pattern, so too can emotional obsession aggravate our suffering. Our brains are wired to preferentially scan for, register, recall, and react to unpleasant experiences. Ruminating on the negative colors our memory with intensified anxiety and fear. "Pain today breeds more pain tomorrow," Rick Hansen writes in *Buddha's Brain*.[6]

Through practice, we can release the grip of our emotional habit patterns by shifting our focus from internal storytelling, to noticing where and how the emotional sensations show up in our bodies. This allows us to experience emotions as energy. We can then learn to breathe into and with this energy, rather than clinging to and hence reinforcing our stories of pain. At the same time, we need to understand the underlying causes and conditions that give rise to emotional distress, lest we use our practice as a way to bypass dealing with emotional problems.

The psychologist and Buddhist teacher Rob Preece describes how many of his clients with deep spiritual practices, who think they should just "let go" of difficult feelings, nonetheless find themselves experiencing repeated negative patterns in their lives. He writes, "If we don't uncover the problems [that underlie our spiritual search] we risk placing a veneer of spirituality over deeply buried emotional wounds from childhood that do not simply go away. Spirituality can then lead us to actually split off from our emotional problems, repress them, and even deepen them."(7)

Emotions are energy, and energy has to go somewhere. In your idealized vision of yourself as a good Buddhist, you might convince yourself, "Oh, I'm not angry"—but meanwhile your heart is pounding, your stomach is churning, your adrenal glands are flooding your body with stress hormones. You're "not angry"—but your blood pressure is rising, you're tossing and turning at night, nursing revenge scenarios in your head about those others you find to be so annoying.

Healthy emotional practice is neither repressing our feelings, nor acting them out upon others. When we just allow sensations to flow through our bodies, we feel them arise, and pass—like a wave. We rest in present-moment awareness: the act of awakening, of being a buddha.

While we typically imagine such practice happening within our own beings on the meditation cushion, for many of us, especially in the most challenging times, we appreciate the support of our spiritual friends to help in our effort to regain equanimity.

This was certainly the case for our three struggling post-election practitioners!

Let's see how they found their way out of the grip of their personal suffering, to participate in the flow of their lives.

Practitioner number 1 came for support, feeling hatred and guilt, and judging herself a bad Buddhist because she had these feelings. What we *didn't* do was engage in a conceptual discussion about what makes one a good or bad Buddhist. We got present in our bodies, in the here and now. We started with a hug. Not just a momentary pat on the back, but breathing together, heart to heart. As we stood in silence, I felt her body begin to relax. This is where practice begins: stopping, taking the inward step, letting awareness settle down into the felt sense of the energy in the body. Then, listening to the wisdom of one's inner truth.

"You know," she said, "if I really touch my deeper experience, there's something under what I've been calling hatred. What I really feel is more like revulsion." She paused, and kept sensing. "And if I keep going deeper, what's there is a profound sadness. I feel like what I need to do right now is stay home and cry. I'm not ready to go out in the world yet, like my friend. I need time to mourn."

She was doing what my root Zen teacher Katherine Thanas called "listening to the voice of the body." Some Buddhist traditions and teachers say the body is a burden from which to try to be free. Not Katherine. For twenty years, she taught us to pay attention to the body as the very vehicle through which real-life practice happens.

Once during a meditation retreat, a student asked her how to practice with his fear. "Go into it," she told him. "Take a little step toward it. Keep it in view. Go as slowly as you need to. You can only go at the pace that your stomach and heart can handle. It's only scary because you put it outside. It's just a manifestation of some energy. It has to come into the body, because it's the body that put it outside. It's the body that closed down and said, 'I'm not going to know that.'"

She went on, "Just inhale and exhale. Don't separate yourself from the sensation, don't go someplace else in your mind and wish it would go away. We have an aversion to painful sensations, intense sensations, but that aversion itself makes it more difficult, more solid. Please study intense sensations. Don't study them intellectually, study them with your breath, with your awareness, with your mind and your body. Outside of the idea of it, actually know it from the inside."(8)

As Practitioner number 1 let herself feel her emotions, rather than deny or obstruct them, or rather than talk *about* them, her energy kept transforming, opening up ever-deeper layers of truth. "I realize if I'm acting out of hatred," she said, "that's going to be wrong action. I need to wait until I find my ground again, so that my action will be wise."

This was Buddha's counsel to a group of fighting monks, who asked for his help with their difficulties. He encouraged them to work through their differences with kindness. "In this world, hatred is never allayed by further acts of hate. It is allayed by non-hatred. That is the fixed and ageless law."(9)

Practitioner number 2 also let herself feel down into the underlying truth of her emotions, though in a different way. She did this with a room-full of others. She felt terrified and didn't want to leave her house, but that that wasn't an option for her. She had a class of students waiting for her at the art institute where she teaches. So she got in her car and drove to work. All but one of the students in the room were people of color. Many of the students were international. The tension in the room was intense. Practitioner number 2 set aside her lecture notes, and invited her students to share their feelings.

"Why do they hate us so much?"

"Are we going to be able to stay in the United States?"

"I'm afraid for my physical safety on the street."

As they allowed and bore witness to the truth of their feelings, she described how a sense of relaxation arose, as they realized they were not alone. They were in this together. This opened up into a conversation about their purpose in the world. They were artists, committed to creative expression! Throughout time, artists have always been on the cutting edge of supporting political and social change. They could feel their fear transforming into motivation, passion and purpose, to get out and *do their art*. This was their deeper wisdom.

And what about the third practitioner, the one who felt so far away from the teachings, who didn't know how or if she even wanted to try to reach out of her swamp of despair?

Well, that was me.

After spending the week focusing on the needs of others, I found myself finally overcome with my own emotional eruption. I escaped to the mountains to get at my own inner truth. As I hiked and cried and talked aloud to the rocks and trees, I realized I felt really sad, and afraid, for our country, and our planet.

I found a place to spend the night. The next morning I was walking through the forest, trying to come up with the best word to describe the underbelly of what I was feeling. I realized that word was *defeat*. This was unusual for me. I'm a pretty upbeat person, and can usually spin the dharma to create meaning and motivation to continue to serve the world. But not this day. I didn't want to return home, but I had responsibilities I needed to attend to. I asked for counsel from my dear dharma brother and spiritual guide, got in my car, and drove back to town.

"Is there any way," he asked, "that you could find some spaciousness? Take your place there? Perceive and touch that one bright pearl?"

"Ohhh," I groaned, "I hear you, and some part of me believes, of course, that this is true. But right now, your words feel like a distant voice in another room. I am in *this* room, and I can't get out, I can't reach out, I don't even want to make the effort to do so."

He offered other suggestions, but we also just sat and looked at each other with openness and sadness in our eyes. And then it was time to go lead the evening service in our temple. We had a good-sized group, and our chanting felt particularly robust.

I went downtown, had tea, and shared notes with a friend. We acknowledged that it helped to not check the news every hour, which only made things worse. We recognized that part of our discomfort was feeling so nakedly exposed to the reality of uncertainty, and impermanence. We noted that the fact we were disturbed was also a commentary on the relative privilege of our lives: millions live with the discomfort of uncertainty and impermanence every moment of every day, every night.

The next morning, when asked, "How are you feeling?" I said, in all honesty, "You know, I feel like my energy is shifting."

Nothing had changed in the external world to make me feel safe or positive. But it was like the way the wind shifts and disperses the clouds, or how a storm rains itself out and the air becomes electric and clear. Even as I felt the poignancy of my personal despair, I also felt connected to my near companions, as well as all of those strategizing and taking action in the public arena. I felt all of these currents of life-as-it-is flowing through me, simultaneously: the human dimension, with our troubling events and agitating news, as well as the rocks, trees, ocean, and sky. The one bright pearl. The crows eating the last persimmon off the tree in our back yard.

Whether taking refuge through touching the core of our own pain, or offering compassion to another; whether receiving support from a circle of colleagues or opening to be nourished by the great beyond, ultimately, this is the invitation of the Buddha way: breathing fully into the particular and personal truth of our own body, heart and mind, and then breathing out and connecting with the vast universe of beings,

> in this place
> grounded in the real
> open to the ultimate
> right action flows,
> as the natural response
> to the request of the world

Notes

1. Grace Schireson, *Zen Women* (Somerville, MA: Wisdom, 2009), 178.
2. Reggie Rey, *Touching Enlightenment* (Boulder, CO: Sounds True, 2008), 199.
3. Eihei Dogen, *Shobogenzo*, trans. Kaz Tanahashi (Boston, MA: Shambhala, 2010), 134, v. 1
4. Andy Ferguson, trans., *Zen's Chinese Heritage* (Somerville, MA: Wisdom, 2000), 238–89.
5. Jokin Keizan, *Record of Transmitting the Light*, trans. Francis Cook (Los Angeles, CA: Center Publications, 1991), 190.
6. Rick Hansen, *Buddha's Brain* (Oakland, CA: New Harbinger s, 2009), 68
7. Rob Preece, *The Wisdom of Imperfection* (Ithaca, NY: Snow Lion, 2006), 31
8. Katherine Thanas, transcription of March 1996 *sesshin* lectures (author's collection).
9. Bhikkhu Nanamoli and Bhikkhu Bodhi, trans., *Upakkilesa Sutta, from the Middle Length Discourses of the Buddha* (Somerville, MA: Wisdom, 1995), 1009.

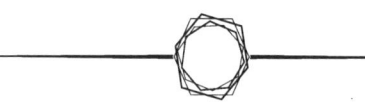

Myokaku Jane Schneider was ordained by Zentatsu Richard Baker at San Francisco Zen Center in 1972. She and her husband, Peter, were married in 1972 and lived in Japan from 1973 to 1995, where they studied with teachers, including Soto and Rinzai Zen, Shingon, and Tendai Buddhism. Jane also studied nihonga, traditional Japanese painting, and has had exhibitions in Japan and the United States. She received an M.A. in painting at California State University Northridge in 2004, the same year that Jane and Peter began Beginner's Mind Zen Center in Northridge (beginnersmindzencenter.org). Jane received transmission from Myoan Grace Schireson in 2009. She and Peter were installed as abbess and abbot of Beginner's Mind Zen Center in 2017. Jane contributed to two books featuring women teachers, *The Hidden Lamp* and *Seeds of Virtue, Seeds of Change*.

Breath Is Life

Myokaku Jane Schneider

In Beginner's Mind Zen Center we chant the Four Vows after evening meditation. The wording in other Zen Buddhist Centers may differ, but the heart is the same. In our version we say, "Beings are numberless, I vow to save them. Delusions are inexhaustible, I vow to end them. Dharmas are boundless, I vow to master them. Buddha's way is unsurpassable, I vow to become it." They seem like impossible tasks to carry out, but that is why the Four Vows matter so much. We take on the responsibility of actualizing them in daily life knowing that there is no end to it. They are the most precious jewels of our lives, but there will be no gain in following them, nothing to be achieved, no conclusion to the work, and no one's suffering will be ended for long by our struggle. The Four Vows are precious because good or bad results have no effect on our efforts. In dark times, they reveal a shining practice and clarify our way in confusion. We understand that no matter how much we do, there will always be someone who needs help. No matter how much we practice, delusions will still arise. No matter how much we learn, there will always be more to master. No matter how unattainable the Buddha way is, we will continue to practice. With no end in sight we work toward resolutions to problems.

The Four Vows are chanted as a ritual to follow the teachings of Buddha, but they are just a practical guide to live wholeheartedly in a world full of wonder, difficulty and change. In this beautiful world our news is filled with disasters, wars and corruption. One horrific event barely ends and another has already taken its place. We want to follow a compassionate way of life in this uncertain world, so we gather together in a community to find a way. We meditate together to create a harmonious center, a sangha that pulses with light and warmth. The harmonious center is like a radiant jewel that surrounds and supports us all. From that center we carry the tradition of warm hand to warm hand practice out into daily life. There we make a strong effort to live the Four Vows in every kind of activity according to our capabilities.

We are full of compassionate intentions, but before we can help others we have to find balance in ourselves. In meditation we regulate breath to calm our body and mind, let go of ideas and begin the first steps towards living the Four Vows. Through breath we unite inner life with outer life. We develop presence of mind enough to see that in a world where news is bad, yet friends are good; where peace seems impossible, yet we sit quietly in meditation; where fear of devastation is great, yet birds sing in the garden, we must remember to cherish what is already balanced here, in each moment. We can begin with that much. In a world of old age, sickness, and death, we find everything to live for. In the midst of loss and distress, we find warmth and kindness, help and hope. In the midst of catastrophic events, we find courage and compassion. We resist despair because if we look into the worst of conditions, we find the best in people at work.

Through our senses we can see, hear, smell, taste, and touch the world. Body, speech, and mind strengthen our experience of self-nature, but in our joy to explore all the particulars of self-nature we forget Buddha-nature. We avoid looking closely at the relationship between what we think and what our actual experiences are. We use memory to give history and credibility to our understanding of self-nature, but we ignore how often memory itself changes when we look at it. We spend a lot of time in thoughts dressing up our image of "I, me, and mine." Even though thoughts and emotions often cause us grief, their existence confirms our belief in a world that seems understandable, and therefore comforting. But self-preoccupation costs us dearly. With attachment to self-nature, or "I, me, and mine," we ignore the boundless, inclusive Buddha-nature that is our greater potential. When we become self-absorbed, we can overwhelm ourselves with dark imagination and hopelessness or too much anxiety, fear, and anger. Our ever-changing, unfathomable being, Buddha-nature, is forgotten, and we become like a beautiful butterfly pinned to a board.

But right in the midst of self-caused suffering, we can find freedom from self. In meditation we loosen attachment to our creation with breath and stillness, and step back from self-absorption. Without clinging to name or no name, taking each moment as it comes, we change things for the better, one breath at a time. For example, in anxious times we can stop, refocus our attention on the present, take one full, deep breath and look around with calmer eyes. As we listen to the natural sounds of ordinary life, or even stand in the midst of tense events, we can bring up composure, and with another deep breath, create some space between the events and us. For just a moment we can be still. Even one quiet moment can sort out a confused mind and heart. If instead, we look through the eyes of a self-absorbed person, we separate people into friend or foe and ignore the rest. We think as self, act as self, and are bound by gain and loss in a divided world. Even though intimate experiences of body, speech, and mind bring the world to life for us, we do not have to cling to an idea of a self in order to live. Without being entrapped in a rigid self-identity, we can wear it loosely in the midst of ordinary activity. With or without "I, me, or mine," we can express an abundance of life, in whatever way is needed. A person unattached to an idea of a self, who does anything, awakens everyone to a surface activity that reveals an awe-inspiring depth. It may be the sound of chanting, or seeing someone peacefully cut vegetables, or a child's laughter. On the other hand, a self-conscious activity, no matter how skillful, does not awaken anyone to a spacious present. It arouses surface interests, but nothing stirs underneath, nothing awakens us to "one-being/many beings/self, or being of all possibilities."

In a divided world we are often at odds with each other. But we can understand the sufferings and joys of others, because sometimes we reach beyond our self-imposed borders and touch Buddha-nature with all possibilities. At those times our self-identity comes to seem more like a paper doll, or a map of reality, rather than a transforming, evolving, creative presence. If we try to understand suffering and calamity through self-nature alone, then there is suffering and relief from suffering, help and apathy, success and failure. We struggle with guilt or shame and judge others and us unkindly. Either we try to fix the world or give up in despair. We are overwhelmed by our own suffering or defeated by the suffering of others. This is not the way of the Four Vows. To realize the Four Vows we may be called on to do a lot, or we may be called on to do nothing but listen. We may be called on just to be present. In the world of self-nature/Buddha-nature suffering is met with everyone's efforts working altogether, the obvious help and the imperceptible help. The world is full of those who are known and unknown, working together to help others. In a divided world of self-nature, we are alone among many others doing what we can against enormous odds. In an undivided world we are one of many working together. What we do as individuals may be inconsequential, but what is done altogether is enormous. We can trust ourselves to do what is needed, knowing that we move on the strength of both Buddha-nature and self-nature, and with self-discipline, the Four Vows are actualized everyday from simple, unknown acts to momentous ones.

The foundation of our practice is meditation, and it is our means to keep body and mind in balance. We face our dilemmas with calmness because of meditation. We develop self-discipline of body, speech, and mind with patience and perseverance. We learn through experience that a negative thought, an ill-considered word or a careless act impacts the world in a harmful way. In an undivided world of Buddha-nature/self-nature, experiences become deeper and richer. We find hope in despair, equanimity in stress, and joy in the midst of sorrow. In composure our world shines with exquisite possibilities, even when there are none to be seen. Without losing our ground of knowing that "we are here," we step into dark or light moments to help. Through compassionate action we understand that we help ourselves best by helping others. The Four Vows describe an endless round of suffering, delusions, learning, and practice. That might seem like a negative way to live, but, through practice, we know otherwise, and willingly step into the endless round. With meditation as the groundwork, we serve with an unwavering conviction that we can help.

We usually spend too much time in imagination about the world and people. Our thoughts combine facts and rumors with fears, and then our basic composure is shaken. We find no comfort in mind or emotions so we look for strength in meditation. We enter the zendo, the meditation room, and bring tragic events, raging storms and loss of life with us. We sit down with suffering and fill the moment with memories, too many thoughts, and an unhappy body. When we begin meditation, the day's affairs sit with us; the friendships, arguments, anxieties, bad news, anticipations, work problems, people problems, life problems, all come into the zendo and sit with us. We literally walk into the zendo with a crowd and sit on a cushion or chair. Too much space is taken up with the crowd, but we do not see it; we only feel the emotional and mental weight of it. The crowd was a problem when it came into our mind and heart little by little, and it will be a problem when we integrate it as we sit. Emotions, thoughts, images and body aches and pains will all have to be dealt with as each one pushes for attention. We have to be very patient and thorough. We begin to regulate our breath, but thoughts and emotions erupt through our patient efforts. It's overwhelming, but we continue anyway. We create a big space to rearrange all the furniture of emotions and thoughts in a better way. Before we were crowded in a very small space, our thinking mind. But then we sat down, regulated our breathing and included body and mind together in the search for balance. When we began to sit, mind and body relaxed and opened spaciousness. We continue to breathe calmly and let things go as fast as they come. We may be tempted to hold on to a pleasant experience, but even a sweet smelling flower will decay if it sits long enough. So our practice is to let everything go and meet each moment with original mind. We begin to sit with an anxious mind, but eventually, with patience, we calm our body and thoughts and then take a deep breath in and a long, slow breath out. Gradually the world disappears, other disappears and the clamor in our heads begins to fade. At last there is just a deep breath in and a long, slow breath out. For a short time, all of our sufferings, all the world's sufferings come together in one deep breath in and one long, slow breath out. For a moment there are no disasters, no birth and death and no one is suffering. Even in the midst of anxiety, there is just mind and body and breath in and breath out. There is no self and no other; there is just one breath in and one long breath out. Mind calms down and emotions settle without fuss. Body and mind let go of uneasiness as we wake up to the present and transform our whole world with the first long, true, deep breath.

We are united in an uncomplicated activity of breath and posture. Meditation will change us in ways we cannot imagine, because, like the hidden crowd that came into the zendo with us, the change is also unseen. It begins with breath and relaxation and moves through subtle loosening of mind and emotions. We sit down with anxiety, and as we relax, calmness appears. But anxiousness did not leave first, and then composure took its place. The same emotions and thoughts that produced the anxious state are still present, but through breath regulation and patience, composure arose out of an anxious mind. Through breathing practice the anxious mind is changed from an unworkable state of mind into a peaceful body and mind. Unpleasant emotions and thoughts are not discarded, nor interesting, new ones added. Instead, meditative awareness and patience creates spaciousness great enough to contain all of us, as-we-are. We have to be careful moment by moment because obstacles can change harmony into dissonance again, since the same unstable elements are present as before. Without discipline, words, actions and even thoughts can break our composure and we shift from reasonable to unreasonable and back again. Finally, we come to stand firmly on our own disciplined ground again. It's up to us to decide, through practice, whether we will command our presence or give in to pressures.

We entered the zendo with suffering and we leave it with a calm mind and body. We finish meditation and step out into the world again and reflect on how to reconcile our mind and heart with the daily world. How do we maintain equilibrium in such a difficult world? How do we take in the enormity of disasters, killings and suffering on such a large scale without becoming callous? How do we live the Four Vows without being overcome with suffering? A dualistic world is seductive because decisions seem easy; we are happy or unhappy, successful or unsuccessful, find loss or gain, feel depressed or joyful. We strive to have good experiences and fear bad ones. But in the undivided Buddha-nature/self-nature world, we are easily confused with the need to meet each moment unscripted, to let go of past experience and to stand firmly on one's own ground. Through practice we learn that suffering mind and compassionate mind are one. We can withstand sorrow because joy radiates through everything. Children play even in the midst of war. The natural world continues no matter the intensity of an event. In great loss, compassion springs up everywhere. And in the midst of this ephemeral life, if we want to actualize the Four Vows in our lives, we cannot hang on to anything, neither sorrow nor joy, neither accomplishment nor defeat. Whatever we grasp drags us down in the next moment and for that moment we die to our potential. But right in the midst of difficulty we remember that breath is life. Each moment is an awakening to new being, a deep breath in and a long breath out. We remember again to act, to experience it all, and to live one breath at a time. We are here now. That is enough.

III

Buppo so en, Jo raku ga jo

Our true nature is eternal,
joyous, selfless, pure

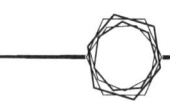

Josho Pat Phelan moved into the San Francisco Zen Center in 1971, and was ordained in 1977 by Zentatsu Richard Baker. In 1991 she moved from the San Francisco Zen Center to North Carolina to lead the Chapel Hill Zen Group, returning to Tassajara Zen Mountain Center in 1995 to receive dharma transmission from Sojun Mel Weitsman, abbot of the Berkeley Zen Center. In 2000, Josho was officially installed as abbess of the Chapel Hill Zen Center. In December, 2008, Josho traveled to Japan to participate in Zuise ceremonies at Eiheiji and Sojiji temples. She is married and has a daughter.

Friendliness to the Self

Josho Pat Phelan

Once, when I was a student at the San Francisco Zen Center, I asked my teacher, "How can I practice with the parts of myself that don't want to practice?" I meant the squirmy, restless part, the rebellious part that wants to skip practice and have fun, and the part that is tired or lazy and just wants to sit down and zone out, or watch a movie, and forget about everything else.

The path of Zen practice is sometimes referred to as a long iron road, and I expected my teacher to say something like "You must strengthen your resolve and persevere" or "Develop your self-discipline to get past resistance or past the part of yourself that is sabotaging your practice." I had heard him say things like this before. But instead he said, "There is no part of you that doesn't want to practice." This response stopped my mind because it had never occurred to me before that there was no part of me that didn't want to practice—I thought in order to practice, I had to struggle with the weaker parts and the parts that resisted practice and overcome them. When he said this, I was actually filled with joy because he was my teacher and I believed him. I didn't understand it, but I believed that somehow, in some way, it must be true. After that, when I wanted to sleep in and skip early morning zazen or meditation, I reminded myself that "there is no part of me that doesn't want to practice," and it became a kind of koan, or a way of examining, "What is practice?" If there is no part of me that doesn't want to practice, and if I'm feeling this way, then what is practice, anyway?

To practice fully, we need to wake up to and include all the parts of ourselves in our practice. We need to integrate the driven, achievement-oriented part, the irritable part that gets angry or constantly judges, with the part that is more open and accepting. Integration comes about first by becoming conscious of and bringing awareness to these different aspects of who we are, and getting to know all these parts intimately. It may not be easy to get a feeling for how to practice with the angry part or the part that's resisting practice and wants to escape. I've noticed that some people who have developed a regular zazen practice seem quite steady and disciplined. But sometimes self-discipline can be overdeveloped, so that slips into a way of controlling experience. People like this may feel like they need to step away from practice and do something like drink a beer in order to relax or enjoy themselves. If you find this happening, you might examine, "Can practice be fun?" or "How do you bring fun to practice?" or "How do you practice when you are having fun?" Is it possible?

Zen practice isn't the same thing as being serious. When I began practicing, the feeling in the zendo or meditation hall seemed pretty daunting and intense. And I internalized this intensity into a kind of rigid strictness. I only felt like I was practicing when I felt serious, which limited what I was able to bring my sense of practice to. The more we get to know and accept all the different aspects of ourselves, the bully and the part that is being bullied, the fun-loving parts, the angry or competitive parts, the threatened and defensive parts, and so on, the more we can practice with whatever we feel as just another state of mind. I have found working with self-acceptance has been one of the most important aspects in learning to just sit or to sit without moving, both physically and emotionally in zazen.

Part of my understanding of self-acceptance has been informed by Buddhist cosmology, which describes six realms of existence. These realms are taught both as the realms that beings are born or reborn into as well as states of mind that we enter and leave throughout the day. The six realms of existence are the hell realm, the realm of hungry ghosts, the animal realm, the human realm, the realm of the jealous and fighting gods, and the realm of the heavenly gods and goddesses. The states of hatred and anger are causes leading to the hell realm which is characterized by pain and anguish; and attachment, greed, grasping and desire lead to the realm of hungry ghosts where beings are characterized by physical hunger as well as never being satisfied with what they have or who they are; ignorance, doubt, and lack of clarity lead to the animal realm which is characterized by fear; the jealous gods are fiercely competitive, always trying to stay on top, to be the best, and states of mind leading to this are extreme pride; the heavenly realm of gods and goddesses is occupied by beings who have everything they want, all the time—all their desires are immediately satisfied so they have no motivation to practice, and self-absorption is one of the qualities leading to this state. I imagine we all can recognize aspects of ourselves in this description. The human realm is placed between the animal realm and the realm of jealous gods. These states or realms of existence are impermanent, just like our human lives.

In an article on these six realms, a Tibetan teacher said that the state of jealousy is the cause leading to the human realm which is characterized by "busyness."(1) So, being lost in our busyness, or driven by busyness, is characteristic of human beings, and its antidote is openness. Openness, like spaciousness, has been compared to the sky, which allows activity but isn't carried away, or pushed around, or pressured by the activity. The sky is big and expansive and can contain a lot. To be born as a human is considered quite rare and quite fortunate because the human realm is considered the only realm or the easiest realm in which the dharma can be heard and practiced. But when we are too busy or distracted, we miss the dharma right in front of us.

So, here we are in a human body, experiencing many different states or realms within this body and mind. But, if Buddhist practice is for human beings, if Buddhism is a human endeavor, then we have to be able to practice with all aspects of being human—not just our positive or uplifting qualities. We have to be able to practice with everything that makes up human character and experience. Wherever we are, whatever we're doing—that is what we have to practice with. It doesn't work to try to purify ourselves or perfect ourselves, to overcome our anger or desire or whatever so that then we will be able to practice. Whatever we feel as a human being is completely acceptable for practice. However, this does not mean that because whatever we feel is acceptable, that it is OK to express our feelings or to act on them. The activity of being aware of our thoughts, feelings and impulses, and accepting them is quite different from the activity of acting on them.

The Tibetan Buddhist teacher Trungpa Rinpoche taught that the way to work with negative emotions is not to repress them and not to express them. For a long time I wondered what he meant by this. If we don't repress our emotions and if we don't express them, what else is there—what other choice do we have? When we don't repress or express our emotional states, we have the opportunity to be present with them, to face them fully and directly in their "raw" form. It may sound strange at first, but acting on our emotions is a way of distracting ourselves from experiencing them fully. And if we aren't willing to experience them, we won't get to know them for what they are and we won't get to know what's propelling them.

Trungpa Rinpoche said that if we follow our emotions and escape them by acting on them, that is not experiencing them properly.(2) He said that the other way we try to escape from our emotions is by repressing them because we cannot bear to be in such a state. He talked about Milarepa, an important early Tibetan Buddhist teacher and yogin. Milarepa did a lot of solitary meditation in caves, and at one point in his training whenever he tried to meditate, he was confronted by a gang of demons, who interrupted his practice or who *he felt* interrupted his practice. He tried everything he could think of to get rid of them. He threatened them, he scolded them, he even tried preaching the dharma to them. But they would not leave until he finally stopped regarding them as "bad" and just saw them for what they were, just another form of distraction.

Once, someone who had been sitting zazen for about twenty-five years and who had a temper, told me that he had never been angry in zazen; while I, on the other hand, have experienced pretty strong states of anger while sitting, without even trying. When I experience anger in zazen, often it sneaks up, seemingly coming out of nowhere without warning so that I suddenly find myself angry. The experience of suddenly being enmeshed in anger comes from ignoring the physical sensations and psychological processes leading up to full-blown anger. Mindfulness is the antidote to our emotions taking us by surprise. But I think if we sit zazen long enough, sooner or later, we will experience in zazen just about every state of mind we have experienced anywhere else. One of the ways that zazen is misused is to block out feelings and emotions. It's easy to confuse letting go of thoughts with freezing or repressing our emotions in zazen, but we aren't trying to control our emotions. When we allow them to play themselves out with our awareness, but without our participation, we see them for what they are, an impermanent state of mind, not who we are, not our "self." Often when we feel physical or emotional pain, we react by tensing up trying to shield ourselves or to remove ourselves. This resistance strengthens pain, by making it try harder to get our attention. Instead, try leaning into the pain, relaxing and breathing into it.

In *The Power of Now*, Eckhart Tolle said, "When you deny emotional pain, everything you do or think as well as your relationships becomes contaminated with it . . . . Don't turn away from pain. Face it. Feel it"—he said, "don't think about it. Give all your attention to the feeling, not the person, event or situation that seems to have caused it . . . . Stay present . . . with every cell of your body." He said, "Full attention is full acceptance."(3)

My path to self-acceptance was and still is through loving-kindness. The traditional way loving-kindness or friendliness is practiced is by cultivating the warmth and open-heartedness that is evoked by such phrases as "May I be happy and joyous. May I be free from suffering, free from worry and anxiety. May I be healthy and enjoy a sense of well-being. May I be at peace." The practice is to radiate friendliness to yourself, to pervade yourself with loving-kindness. This is done so that you will have firsthand experience of loving kindness and know the benefits of loving-kindness personally, so that you will be able to take yourself as an example when you extend loving-kindness to others. For example, "As I want to be happy, as I am adverse to suffering and anxiety, as I want to be well and live in peace, may my benefactor or dear friend be happy, be free from suffering, be well, may my good friend live in peace." After cultivating loving-kindness for yourself and a benefactor or dear friend, continue extending this aspiration or wish of goodwill to a neutral person, then to a difficult person, ending with radiating loving kindness to all beings, "As I want to be happy and free from suffering, may all beings be happy and free from suffering." The ideal is to feel friendliness for all beings at all times. But the instructions from early Buddhism emphasize the importance of, first of all, directing loving-kindness toward oneself, again, and again, and again.

Buddha is quoted in the *Visuddhimagga*, or *The Path of Purification*, a classic compendium of all the practices in early Buddhism in the chapter on the Four *Brahma Viharas*. The *brahma viharas* are the practices of friendliness, compassion, sympathetic joy, and equanimity. Buddha is quoted saying, "I visited all quarters with my mind," which refers to Buddha's clairvoyance, meaning that he visited the four quarters of the universe. So, "I visited all quarters with my mind. Nor found I any dearer than myself. Self is likewise to every other dear. Who loves oneself, will never harm another." Reading this verse, I realized that Buddhist practice includes self-love, which is very close to self acceptance. Each time I read this last line, "Who loves oneself, will never harm another," I wondered, what kind of love is this that once you have it for yourself, you will never harm another? Can you imagine caring for yourself in such a way that you will never harm another?

Before I knew about this group of practices, I stumbled onto my own version of friendliness toward the self. At the time, I had been sitting zazen several times a day for seven years, and I was living in residence at a practice center for five and a half years where my boyfriend also lived. After a while I noticed that he had a growing interest in a friend of mine who also lived in the same building. Before long, I began to feel threatened and rejected and jealous. At that time I thought one of the goals of Zen was detachment, and so I reasoned that if I were feeling jealous then I must be attached; and if I was attached, then I must be a failure at Zen practice. Not only was I feeling pain and jealousy from the relationship, I also felt guilty and embarrassed for feeling jealous in the first place. My response to this was to reject myself out of disgust for my own jealous feelings. Sharon Salzberg said that "When we feel anger, fear, or jealousy, if we feel open to the pain of these states rather than [feeling] disgraced by their arising, then we will have compassion for ourselves."[4]

When I was going through this period of feeling jealous and rejected, I was really miserable, and this continued every day for several months. Then one day in zazen I spontaneously began a visualization process in which I visualized each part of my body starting with my toes and moving upward to my head. I would visualize my toes, then my feet, my ankles, my lower legs, my knees, and so on up to my head. And as I visualized my toes, some of which had ingrown toe nails that I didn't like, I directed these phrases to my toes, "I love you. I care about you. I completely accept you." I continued directing these phrases to each part of my body while visualizing it. One thing I found was how many parts I didn't like or thought were imperfect or inadequate. One of the benefits of doing exercise was that I became conscious of my attitudes toward by body, my physical being; and it gave me a way to consciously try to accept all the parts of myself just as I was.

The verse by Buddha is, "Who loves oneself will never harm another." It doesn't say, "Whoever is enlightened, or whoever is a perfected being and loves oneself, will never harm another." It just says, "Whoever loves oneself will never harm another."

This is not so easy for me to talk about, but this is the way I found to work with self-acceptance. Each of us will have our own way of accessing the open, supportive aspects of our being, which may be quite different from this. But the point is to find a path that connects your critical, self-rejecting voice to your open, understanding heart—the place of refuge in you that has the capacity for unconditional acceptance.

I would encourage you to find whatever way you can to welcome and cultivate the attitude of embracing the parts of yourself that aren't so uplifting, the parts that you are ashamed of or disgusted with or are a kind of taboo. So, for example, when I feel myself becoming jealous, I try to welcome it with the attitude, "It's my old friend jealousy" and I try to open myself to it with a friendly attitude and then try to feel what it is, what it feels like in my body and mind. To do this, you need to be willing or devoted to not moving away from what is difficult. This reminds me of being with my extended family when I was a child at Thanksgiving. Some cousins were really good friends, but one used to twist my arm behind my back and I hated it. I had my favorite aunt and there was an uncle who was pretty annoying, but they were all part of the family. Similarly, all of our mental and emotional states are a part of ourselves and are something to practice with. We may not enjoy all states of mind, but nevertheless, we can practice with them. Having the ability to work with emotional states in zazen makes it easier to work with emotions in daily life.

Zen emphasizes nonduality through a total acceptance of our experience right now, in this moment, as a manifestation of reality. This kind of total acceptance, especially as it is experienced in zazen, implies a kind and compassionate mind, although loving-kindness is not articulated directly or suggested as a practice in Japanese Zen. But because it was so supportive for my practice, and because we are part of such a judgmental society, I recommend it.

One of the traditional ways to help call up the actual feeling of loving-kindness is to visualize your own face in a happy, radiant mood. Then, when you are doing loving-kindness meditation, put yourself in that mood—recall the warmth and radiance you feel when you are happy. The traditional phrases for extending loving-kindness are a way of expressing these states of mind, and the actual practice is to connect with the boundless nature of our own heart and mind. If you have a hard time directing this feeling to others, especially to a difficult person, instead you can practice with the difficult parts of yourself. But again, it is important to spend the time it takes to really develop loving-kindness toward yourself.

One day after I had done the body visualization, directing loving-kindness to each part of my body, something else happened. It was as if my emotional terrain or emotional geography appeared. I called up my jealousy by recreating inwardly how I felt when I was in a jealous state, and I directed the same phrases toward my jealously, "I love you, I care about you, I completely accept you." Before this I had always hated my jealousy and hated myself for feeling jealous, so the idea of accepting my jealousy or accepting myself as a human being who is sometimes jealous was completely new to me, and it seemed like a pretty weird thing to do. One way to work with difficult emotions is, when you are alone and feeling safe and grounded, try to call up or replicate the difficult or painful state and stay with it, breathing into it the way you might relax and breathe into physical pain.

After I had called up jealousy, then I called up my comparative thinking or judgmental faculty, and instead of trying to stop it as I had previously, I directed this same attitude of acceptance toward it. I tried to accept myself as a human being who sometimes judges and criticizes. Not long after that, I noticed that sometimes when I was sitting zazen, I would have an uneasy or crummy feeling in my gut. I had been pushing this uneasiness aside for so long that I was barely aware that it was even there. When I brought my attention to it, trying to be present with it, I found that it accompanied a low level of comparative thinking, in which I was comparing myself to someone else or comparing my practice to an external standard; and when I compared myself in this way, I had the unpleasant sensation that accompanies feeling inadequate. So I tried to accept this—that judging or comparing is an aspect of being human; and it is completely acceptable for practice, completely acceptable as something to practice with—only when I judge, I feel uneasy. But it's OK to feel uneasy sometimes. I used to think that feelings like jealousy were the most shameful and difficult states to admit to and practice with. But I've come to find that the judging, self-critical, self-rejecting faculty is the most painful, and it needs the most forgiveness and acceptance. This was tricky for me because the process of judging feels superior or more adult-like than feelings like jealousy or anger, which tend to bring up associations with childishness and helplessness. I think we developed our ways of judging when we were children by internalizing what we were told and by how we were treated by adults. It has been much harder for me to try to find the vulnerability of "the judge" because my critical attitude is conveyed through an adult-sounding attitude. It has also been harder to try to be kind to the part of myself that is "doing" the judging and rejecting.

But I've found that when I do treat the parts of myself that I don't like, first with attention—an unwavering attention—and then with friendliness and acceptance, they become much less powerful, and lose their strength to push me around. Similarly, all of our mental and emotional states are part of ourselves and are something to practice with. We may not enjoy all states of mind, but nevertheless, we can practice with them. Sometimes I wonder if the aspects of our selves that seem the most irritating or painful are just trying to get our attention, that because of our neglect they can't be resolved. Having the ability to work with emotional states in zazen makes it easier to work with emotions in daily life. Through awareness and acceptance of whatever states arise, when we no longer try to avoid or ignore what we consider painful, we can practice with all the parts of ourselves. And when all these parts join in and support our practice, it becomes a much fuller practice, allowing us to just sit without moving, no matter who shows up on our cushion.

Suzuki Roshi said, "To find complete composure when you don't know who you are or where you are is to accept *things as it is*. Even though you don't know who you are, you accept yourself. That is 'you' in its true sense."[5] The way I understand "who we are," is who we *really* are, beyond our thinking, beyond concepts and definitions. So, even though we can't define it or pin it down, when we can accept the vastness of who we are, that's "you" in its true sense.

Notes

Some of the material in this essay was published previously in the journal *Mindfulness* 3 (2012): 165–67.

1. Geshe Tenzin Wangyal Rinpoche, "Everyday Life Is the Practice," *Shambala Sun*, November 2005, 41.
2. Trungpa Rimpoche, *Cutting through Spiritual Materialism* (Berkeley, CA: Shambhala Press, 1973), 239.
3. Ekhart Tolle, *The Power of Now: A Guide to Spiritual Enlightenment* (Novato, CA: Namaste Publishing, 1999), 185.
4. Sharon Salzberg, *Lovingkindness: The Revolutionary Art of Happiness* (Boston, MA: Shambhala Press, 1995), 81.
5. Shunryu Suzuki, *Not Always So: Practicing the True Spirit of Zen* (New York: HarperCollins, 2002), 130.

Isshin Havens, a native American and naturalized Brazilian, is an International Missionary (*kokusai fukyoshi*) representing Soto Zen in South America and leads the practice center Jisui Zendo—Sanga Águas da Compaixão in the Porto Alegre, Rio Grande do Sul, Brazil, as well as affiliated groups. She has honorary doctorates in Zen Buddhism and certificates in alternative therapies and conflict mediation, as well as postgraduate certification in humanistic psychoanalysis. At this time of writing, she is completing her clinical training as a humanistic psychoanalyst. She has published two books and coauthored several others, keeping a presence on internet through blogs and Youtube as she works to develop educational resources for Brazilians who wish to learn about Buddhism and Zen—all in Portuguese. This is her first work for publication in English.

A Bumpy Ride with Dukkha
Isshin Havens

Dukkha, what is it? Some forty days after his enlightenment, Buddha encountered the five colleagues with whom he had practiced asceticism. He had practiced asceticism with them for several years, but, having perceived that such extreme practice was not bringing him any closer to the answer for his search for freedom, he had left them, eaten a rice porridge given by the maiden Sujata, and sat under the bodhi tree until reaching his goal of enlightenment. When they first saw him from a distance, these former colleagues thought of him as a weakling, unworthy of respect, but, coming closer, they perceived a special quality about him and decided to listen to him.

So, it was then that Buddha gave his first teaching, which is transmitted to us in the *Dhammacakkappavattana Sutta*, SN 56.11 (with the title translated as *Setting the Wheel of Dhamma in Motion* in Thanissaro Bikkhu's translation). In this sermon, he presents the Four Noble Truths, the first of which tells us that life is *dukkha*.

Quite often, we find this word, *dukkha*, translated as "suffering," and Buddha's First Noble Truth is frequently taught as "Life is suffering." But this translation can be confusing for many people. After all, there are countless pleasures in living, so how on earth can we possibly make such a black-and-white statement as "Life is suffering"?

Let's look at this Sanskrit word, *dukkha*. According to some scholars, this word is based on two components: *du*, which means "bad" and *kha*, which means "sky," "ether," or "space" in later Sanskrit, but for which the original, Aryan meaning was "hole," a reference to the axle hole in the wooden wheels of the ancient vehicles. As a result, the term *dukkha*, at that time, meant "having a bad axle hole." So, when this word came into Buddhism, it brought up the image of the bad, off-center axle holes in the wheels of the early carts and wagons. When an axle hole is bad or off-center, the ride in the cart can get very bumpy. There can be instants of the sensation of smooth rolling along, but then the ride gets broken up by a sudden jerk—and that is a good analogy for our lives.

When we ourselves are not truly centered in our essence, living out our lives can indeed take us for a very bumpy ride, just like being a passenger in one of those ancient carts with its off-center wheels. Death, illness, accidents, loss of employment, debt, the end of a relationship—all of these represent challenging bumps in our ride that can overwhelm us and drive us into questioning and crisis.

Then we also have those social, commonly-shared challenges that we face as groups: violence and crime, prejudice (racial, ethnic, gender, religious, and so on), economic and political crises.

And, finally, there are those huge potholes in the road, when whole groups of us are hit by a major disaster and many of us seem to be getting completely thrown out of our carts, tossed about by the forces of nature (tornados, hurricanes, earthquakes, flooding, drought, wildfires, and so on), wars, and threats of nuclear war—the list seems endless.

I especially recall the tsunami that swept away entire towns in Japan in 2011, when 20,000 people were lost, as well as the 2004 tsunami that claimed 200,000 lives and erased entire villages from the maps. Not only had these people lost their families and friends, as well as their homes with all of their belongings and workplaces, but they also lost their official records with the disappearance of municipal offices and schools. So, in a way, they had also virtually lost their personal histories and identities as well and literally had nothing left except the clothes on their backs.

One of the nastiest sides of *dukkha* had shown itself—that aspect that justifies that word so often being translated as suffering! Tsunamis like that one, as well as the one in the Indian Ocean some years before, cause levels of suffering that are beyond words.

But even less extreme events can leave us feeling completely overwhelmed and throw us into deep crisis.

The Japanese word for crisis, *kiki*, is written with two ideograms, as follows 危機. The first one, 危, means danger or fear, and the second, 機, signifies opportunity. And when *dukkha's* pain hits us, we find ourselves facing a crisis, with its mixture of danger and opportunity.

What do we do then? How can we bear our suffering? How can we possibly find opportunity when our lives are falling apart? What happens to our practice? Is there some way that we can truly prepare ourselves for the possibility of having to deal with future disasters, either in our own lives or in those of people around us?

Naturally, the most obvious answer would be zazen (a sitting meditation focusing on the breath or, ideally, just sitting, exclusively sitting). And we definitely should try to sit zazen, if possible—even if it's a two-minutes-here and five-minutes-there kind of zazen practice. But if we are in the middle of an earthquake, we almost certainly will not have time or place to do sitting meditation.

So, despite that fact that the sitting practice of zazen is the heart of our practice, there can be moments when it is time to remember that the Buddha was a highly pragmatic teacher and taught about forty different kinds of meditation. Sometimes, Zen practitioners can seem to forget these two facts and get too hung up on an idea of a "pure practice," losing their creativity and pragmatism. Let's look at practical actions we can take while we are going through a crisis, even if we are not able to do much actual sitting practice.

1. Whenever possible, stop and take one or two conscious breaths, turning your attention to the physical sensation of the expansion and contraction of the body—especially in the trunk of the body—during this breath. This helps counter the tendency to breathe superficially in the upper thorax during a crisis by pulling the breath down to the energetic and gravitational center of the body. This act, in some subtle way, also pulls "us" back into our bodies and helps us to center ourselves in the middle of turmoil.

2. Repeat a mantra, with or without using a *juzu* (*mala*, or bracelet of prayer beads) to keep count of the repetitions (or to occupy our nervous hands). This could be reciting—even if just in thought—the Three Refuges, which could even be simplified to "I

take refuge in Buddha, Dharma, and Sangha" instead of the full, one-at-a-time traditional recitation. Mantras can help us to remember our faith as we also invoke the associated potentialities in ourselves. Remembering the iconography of Buddhism with all its symbolism,(1) during the recitation of mantras, especially with the use of a *juzu*, can also help calm feelings of anxiety. Upon occasion, this kind of practice has proven to be useful in helping students learn to deflect the start of anxiety attacks. Here are some other mantras (an Internet search can help you find recordings or videos demonstrating the pronunciation):

a. Kannon Bosatsu: *On arorikya sowaka*. Kannon, or Avalokiteshvara, symbolizes compassion both for oneself and for others. A special characteristic of Kannon's compassion is that it is not only the kind, gentle compassion that we usually imagine when we think of this word, but she also represents a tough love kind of compassion that can give strong, unconditional limits and protection.

b. Jizo Bosatsu: *On ka ka kabi san ma ei sowaka*. Jizo is thought of as a protector of children (especially those unborn), animals, and the earth itself.

c. Fudo-Myo: *No maku sanmanda bazaradan senda makaroshada sowataya untarata kanman* (long version) or *No maku sanmanda bazarada kan* (short version). Fudo-Myo, whose name means "unmovable protector," represents steadfastness.

d. Daikoku-ten: *On maka kyaraya sowaka*. A deva from the Hindu tradition, Daikoku-ten is one of the Seven Gods of Fortune whose images can be found in the kitchens of monasteries and private homes; his task is to provide food.

e. Idaten: *On ken daya sowaka*. Originally seen as the son of Shiva and a warrior god, Idaten is considered to be a protector of the Dharma as well as a caretaker of the kitchen. A fast runner, he is able to go to wherever there is trouble quickly.

f. *Om-mani-padme-hum*: Originated in India and made popular by Tibetan Buddhism, this mantra, according to the Dalai Lama, reminds us that the practice of the Buddhist path leads to the transformation of our body, speech, and mind into the purity of the body, speech and mind of the Buddha.

3. Feel your emotions, without acting from them. A surprising number of practitioners have a fantasy of the attainment of a Buddhist equanimity in which they will never again experience painful emotions. What a disappointment some of them feel when they discover that equanimity simply does not work that way—fortunately. Our practice is not for the purpose of turning us into robots! Quite the contrary, we will be able to live fully, vibrantly, right now, right here, centered in the present moment.

Sometimes, this does mean we will experience unpleasant emotions. But we do not have to suffer because of these emotions if we can simply permit ourselves to experience the feeling fully, without trying to repress and deny it or else telling ourselves stories that will be like wounding ourselves with the second arrow (or third or fourth, or however many extra arrows we create in order to feed our suffering) that Buddha described in his teachings. Some research findings tell us that a fully experienced emotion may take no longer than ninety seconds to pass, as the body processes the hormones related to that emotion.

So, instead of trying to act like the "perfect Buddhist," when you feel anger, let yourself actually feel it. Experience the imaginary steam coming out your ears, feel the tension in your hands—feel it all in your body, but don't get involved with stories and don't take any action until the anger has cooled and you are no longer "seeing red."

Obviously, there are emergencies, such as a fire, where we must focus on dealing with the immediate situation and should not give in to our feelings of, for example, fear. Once the immediate emergency has passed, however, according to researcher-therapists such as Peter Levine, it would be good to give ourselves a chance to let the body tremble and shake off its natural response to the fear of our example, instead of keeping it locked up in the muscles.

Emotions, such as the sadness over the loss of a loved one, often come in "waves." Some stimulus sets off the emotion and there we are, feeling crushed in the pain of our loss. But if we can just stay with the emotion itself, without getting involved with it or trying to pretend it doesn't exist, the emotion will pass surprisingly quickly for the time being, until another stimulus causes another "wave." With time, the waves start to become spaced further apart, as well as starting to pass more quickly, until gradually, we are past the greater part of our mourning.

4. While we're talking about feelings that come up with the loss of a loved one, this brings up another important aspect of maintaining our practice during difficult moments: self-acceptance and compassion for oneself. When we suddenly lose a loved one, perhaps through an accident, in the middle of that confusion of emotions such as shock, desperation, grief, and a wish to deny what has happened, we may suddenly find ourselves feeling angry, with thoughts of "how could you leave me like this?!" directed toward the person who died and anger at the universe. While this is a perfectly natural feeling that is part of the grief process, we run the risk of getting into overly critical judgments of ourselves as the human beings that we are for having such "ignoble" thoughts and feelings—which only add to our difficulty. This is a moment when it is very important for us to exercise self-acceptance and self-compassion.

Many people confuse self-acceptance with passivity and believe that if they develop self-compassion they will become lazy and worthless—or some variation of these attitudes. This is not at all true. In reality, as we learn to accept ourselves as we are at this exact moment, we then become freer to make the changes we may be needing to make in our lives. Shunryu Suzuki Roshi describes this in delightful fashion by telling us that the best way to have a contented cow is to give it a large pasture—and contented cows do usually produce more milk!

Let us cultivate self-acceptance and self-compassion until we are so filled with these qualities that they virtually overflow, transmitting peace and tranquility to all beings.

5. Finally, we should always remember that Buddhism is very realistic and pragmatic. Therefore, if things are truly becoming too much to bear, we should not hesitate to use non-Buddhist resources. Music for relaxation, guided meditations, counseling, psychotherapy—even tranquilizers, appropriately used, may offer us important support during difficult times.

As our practice matures, we will discover that we have more and more resilience for dealing with difficult moments. It is as if we connect with and then anchor ourselves to a deep current of the ocean of life that will carry us through the rough waves created by the storms of violent painful events. And this is when we begin to truly live out the fearlessness that Buddha discovered and taught through this wonderful practice that has been transmitted to us down through the centuries.

> May all beings be safe. May all beings be well. May all beings be happy. May all beings be free from suffering.
>
> May the merits of our practice extend universally to all, so that together with all beings, we realize the Buddha way.
>
> Gassho.

Notes

1. You can find a wealth of information about Japanese Buddhist iconography in the *A-to-Z Photo Dictionary of Japanese Religious Sculpture & Art* at http://www.onmarkproductions.com/html/buddhism.shtml.

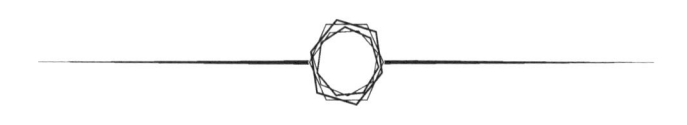

Hobu (Dharma Warrior) Beata Chapman was ordained by Sobun Katherine Thanas Roshi and received dharma transmission from Meiji Tony Patchell after studying intensively with Surei Darlene Cohen. She leads Open Zen Community, which is virtually without walls (hence, open)—sitting zazen and chanting online each day and meeting twice each month for body-to-body practice. Beata works full-time as a career coach in San Francisco and, in the teaching tradition of Darlene Cohen, offers meditation groups for people living with chronic pain and illness. Because of her own life experiences, Hobu has a great interest in trauma and its effects, which continue to lead to the marginalization of African Americans in the United States.

Taking Refuge in Sangha: How Wide Can This Buddha Field Be?
Hobu Beata Chapman

> I take refuge in Buddha
> before all beings
> immersing body and mind deeply in the way.
> I take refuge in Dharma
> before all beings
> entering deeply the merciful ocean of Buddha's way.
> I take refuge in Sangha
> before all beings
> bringing harmony to everyone
> free from hindrance.

Refuge: sanctuary, protection, shelter, safety. Refuge means all of these and it would come to prove itself as my life began to transform in following the Buddha's way. Transformation is a mystery; PTSD is a mystery. Neurological, yes. Psychodynamic, yes. Relational, yes. Spiritual, definitely—about one's place in the universe, one's worthiness to be alive, one's right to have needs, to take up space, to belong. Love escapes. Powerful grief. Rage. Hate. Things very unacceptable in this world, maybe even more so in Zen. From the beginning of practice I've been very struck by the tenth grave precept, "Do not be angry." Frankly, it made me mad. It seemed to run counter to what therapists were telling me, to let myself be angry. How could religion tell me how to feel? I feel what I feel; I can't just not be angry. This conundrum would take many years to reconcile.

Although I'd love to be able to offer deep wisdom full of helpful guidance for practice in difficult times, I can only tell my own story.

In so doing, I try to paint a picture of how Buddha, Dharma, and Sangha transformed this heart-mind through excruciatingly difficult times and gave me the ability to feel loved, to stay with my own life, and to experience real joy. Through years of practice, the realization that staying with my own life brings the experience of real joy has become an essential touchstone. Years and years of being seen and known in Sangha brought the ability to feel undeniable love—after all, I can't say they don't know me because they do, intimately. Nothing is hidden in Sangha. My hope is that others may be able to glean something useful from my story of practice-transformation.

The suffering and pain of PTSD, in all its forms, is excruciating and convoluted to live with. Its symptoms can be scary to those around the sufferer because there is often confusion about boundaries and relationships, fear, and anger/self-defense as the first-line response to events and interactions. My deepest wish is that by revealing my experiences of living in Sangha all these years and making myself vulnerable to misunderstanding and criticism, other teachers will be more able to stay open to students who show up in the state I was in, in the early days of my practice. I will never be able to express my gratitude to those who opened themselves to me, even if they felt some sense of risk.

Years ago, I attended a four-day workshop my teacher was co-leading. I had only known her for a few weeks at this point; she was not yet my teacher. There were twenty-five or so students there, all pulling on the energy and attention of the three teachers. Since something that had happened gave me reason to doubt whether I wanted to be there at all, I decided that lunch would be an opportune time to slip out unnoticed and call a colleague to check out my read on the situation. I drove off the property and made my call; I was gone for about an hour and a half or so.

When I returned to the retreat center, several students came to my car, concerned. They said the teacher had been walking around in the heat looking for me. She was upset, they said. Immediately I sought her out. When I found her she looked at me with her piercing eyes and said, "Let's meet." We walked slowly across the way, student lagging just behind teacher, until we were sitting face to face. "Why did you leave?" the teacher said.

I explained that I thought she would not miss me at all. There were many others looking to talk with her and sit with her, so what difference did it make that I slipped out for a little bit to make a phone call. I really didn't think she'd notice, I stated.

The teacher looked directly at me and expressed warmth and total awareness of my leaving. It had never before occurred to me that what I did or said, my presence or lack thereof, made any difference whatsoever to anyone. I had felt more-or-less invisible and at the same time big and overwhelming. I expected rejection, not love, punishment, not talk, and certainly not forgiveness. The teacher chose love, talk, and forgiveness. We moved on, growing more and more intimate in our Dharma exchanges.

Several years later, I brought this story up to her. I told her how much I learned from her response, her ability to show love in such a difficult situation, and to meet me right where I was while also pulling the rug right out from under me. Very skillful, I concluded. She said, "Many selves arose that day and I chose that one to show you." For the nth time in my practice life, here was the vast one, the wise one, the one I longed to be like.

From the very beginning of my exposure to Zen practice, specifically service, I was in trouble. Extreme PTSD, hard earned through eighteen years of extreme sexual, physical, emotional, and spiritual neglect and abuse, had left my bodymind hardwired for unwelcome defensiveness and self-protective reactions. In truth, by the time I was seventeen years old, I had been tortured, held captive, publically humiliated, starved, beaten, kicked, and entirely abandoned. I had been sexually abused as a small child for years on end by a man I can only describe as a sadist. To escape from him, I moved to Northern Idaho and entered what it would take years to learn was a religious cult. I was lucky I made it through that time, although each and every day I wished I would die. To tell the complete truth, I believed I was stupid for surviving because the personal and relational costs of living with the effects of my early life were a hell realm of their own, seemingly eternal. Victor Sogen Hori's comment on Tozan's *Song of the Jewel Mirror Samadhi*, "Unaware it was a jewel, he thought it just rubble," describes well my view of myself, Beata Chapman, at that time, such self-loathing being a deep core issue in persons with developmental, chronic PTSD.[1]

Don't get me wrong. I am a privileged white woman who grew

up until age twelve in a working-class family in Tempe, Arizona. We looked like those around us, the kids in Catholic school, my parents' friends. Surrounded by family, I lived for a time with my father on his father's ranch called the Big Sandy. There we raised bees, hauled water from the well, built huge fires in grandpa's oversized fireplace, and ate pork and beans out of cans in great-grandpa's old abandoned house down the road. The bats that lived in the house fascinated me, as did Steve, our pet cricket. It was a wonderful life, riding horses and wandering in the orchard; the Big Sandy would give me great relief as things unfolded. The truth is, what was going on in my day-to-day existence did not resemble what happened at the Big Sandy.

The secrets I held about the truth I was living were changing my body and mind, having their way with my neurology, and building foundational tracks that would be with me for the rest of my life. Or, as Uchiyama Roshi might say, for this period in the life of the Self. Thirty-five years of therapy would eventually convince me that I had done all I could and the scars left in me were well earned. I came to know that there will always be the residue of PTSD in this body-mind. And yes, that meant I would sometimes suffer and those around me would sometimes suffer. And so it is with all of us in our total interdependence; the fact that we cause suffering for one another seemingly without wanting to do so is part of the mundane anguish of all our lives.

When I came to Yokoji Zen Mountain Center in 1991 and first experienced Zen practice, I was completely taken aback by my reaction to what I experienced. The priests and monks came into the Buddha Hall for zazen and service all dressed in black robes and everyone was so serious, looking down and not talking. Wow! That threw me right back to the religious cult, and I bolted out of the zendo and down at a table outside. Roshi, a young priest at the time, followed me. She patiently listened to me cry and say that they were all from the devil and that obviously I had misunderstood. "Who are you bowing to?" I wailed, and she smiled calmly. The woman was unflappable. There was a pause while I tried to recover a little dignity. Roshi sat forward and I thought she was going to say something like, "Can I help you pack up?" But what she said was, "What would it take for you to be here with us?"

My heart blew open. So vast was she; I wanted to be like that. She could include even me! Without a doubt, it was the most shockingly wonderful and terrifying thing anyone had ever said to me. She didn't even pause, as if no other thought crossed her mind except to include even me. That's how vast she was.

Apparently to be like her I would have to learn to sit still and do zazen. There was nothing merciful in that zazen, I knew for sure, but it was a small price to pay to be that vast, that open, that able to include whatever comes. Roshi's vastness blew my mind in every sense of the word, and changed my life forever. Zen practice became an indelible and undeniable part of my life through thick and thin, from then on.

The Yokoji Sangha made wide space for me and met me right where I was in my high anxiety, panic, and fear. When I ran out of the room sweating because my body could not remain, Roshi followed slowly and patiently. Maybe I was her assignment; I'll never know because they were so big-hearted, so genuine, and so present that it all seemed quite ordinary to them. As time went on I asked another priest to be my teacher, and she agreed. That, too, took me by surprise. How fortunate was I?

She made the field wider and wider as I showed up in various ways. Undaunted, she made ways for me to be a respected part of the sangha and also to practice zazen and study no matter what was presented. One time I was very restless, and she suggested I get an all-white cushion to paint during our upcoming sesshin. That cushion saved my life! I painted the outside rim like a rocket taking off—with fire and smoke. It allowed my bodymind to know that I could always rocket out of there, and in so doing, it allowed me to feel more confident and to stay longer. Perhaps it gave me permission to leave. In some way internally, it overcame parts of the deep injuries of having been held captive and tortured as an adolescent. Little by little, with just a teaspoon, moving the mountain of snow—incomprehensible, wrenching confusion and pain. Teacher and sangha right alongside me. Refuge in Buddha, Refuge in Dharma, Refuge in Sangha right there living and breathing.

While in the cult in Northern Idaho, my mother died; I was sixteen. At her wish, she was buried in the cult's cemetery on their property called the City of Mary.

In the mid-1990s, therapy and practice led me to make a pilgrimage to my mother's grave in Northern Idaho, at the risk of entering the property of the religious cult for the first time since I escaped. Although I had been out of the cult for more than twenty years, the prospect of being there and running into people I knew was nearly paralyzing. I shaved my head and prepared to go with my teacher's blessing. The trip was a watershed, and when I returned we held a posthumous jukai (lay ordination) ceremony for my mother. I received my mother's rakusu (Buddha's robe) and name. The ceremony was powerful and gave me a tremendous sense of continuity with my mother's own lifelong religious practice. It was a way to include my mother and to wrap her into my practice, to accept her fallibility and desire for salvation as simply part of the human condition, conditions I also experience (though most of the time now salvation doesn't seem nearly as interesting as the mess of the moment).

Teachers over my twenty-five years of Zen practice have been intrepid pillars of patience. Seisen Saunders, Nicolee McMahon, Katherine Thanas, Darlene Cohen, Tony Patchell—each and every one has met this bodymind with great, vast witnessing, presence, and gentle (or sometimes not) guidance. They are my spiritual friends, my great companions ahead of me on the path, who with their lives showed me Zen, and immersed me in the way of practice. They held me and my life with Right View—it exists, it suffers, it is impermanent, and it is entirely interdependent with all being. I have been given the great gift of wide open space to slowly absorb these liberating, transformative teachings. I did not transform myself; I just kept showing up. Embodied Buddha, Dharma, and Sangha transformed me. And this "me" is always conditional, as is transformation.

Back then, I went to my teachers naked and vulnerable, and they met me over and over again. As I moved from Orange County to Santa Cruz, even though they were very different people, unflinchingly each teacher met me at my place. It felt like they had no expectation of change, no requirement that I be different, no pressure to improve or to stop being so reactive. My relationships with my teachers were not always easy, but in each case both teacher and student remained devoted to the other and we both kept showing up. When it was joyous and when it was sorrowful, there we were, face to face. I cannot measure this kind of love, nor can it be put into words. For me, the relationship with my teacher was the salubrious aspect of practice that allowed me to keep going back to the hard work of facing myself on the cushion. The teacher never asked me to leave.

I moved to Santa Cruz after a back injury took me out of work and out of my life-as-it-was for about two years. The injury and subsequent related events left me with a permanently damaged sciatic nerve on the left side. Nerve pain flashes down my leg and more-or-less hangs in that leg all the time. My back feels extremely fragile. I put on weight as movement became more and more difficult. Aging did not help the situation, bringing arthritis and less strength. Chronic pain became a bigger and bigger issue over time. The zazen I learned from my teachers, treasured by them and all the ancient sages, practiced by folks for over 2,500 years, was not possible for me because it was excruciating to hold my body in the cross-legged position, and the kneeling position, *seiza*, caused hot shooting pain down my leg. It was simply intolerable, and zazen became an experiment with every possible bodily configuration.

As I tried every conceivable way to sit on the floor I gathered an amazing collection, a veritable museum, if you will, of sitting implements and devices. Above all, I was not going to lie down, period. My teacher at that time said it was fine to lie down and taught me the corpse pose. Okay, that sealed it. No way was I going to do that pose. Zen really was trying to kill me, as I had suspected! I struggled, left, recovered, returned, left. Always disappointed in myself at having to leave before the end of sesshins or even before entering the zendo, it was years later that I learned the sangha understood my coming and going as my practice. That's how generous they were—when I showed up on the porch and looked in the zendo, then turned and left, the sangha was allowing and witnessing and knowing—and it, too, never left and never asked me to change or to leave. Looking back, I believe this embodied Zen way of looking upon my behavior as a practice, a necessary cycle, and simply bearing witness, was wisdom beyond wisdom. Nothing could have been more beneficial for this one.

About sixteen years into practice, I was asked to be *shuso* or head monk for the spring practice period at Warm Jewel Temple, Santa Cruz Zen Center. As I was preparing to be *shuso*, it was suggested that I attend a workshop called "A Day of Practice for People Who Don't Think They Can Practice Because of Pain." At that workshop, I not only met my next teacher for the first time, but also wept at learning how to lie down for zazen in a real posture that included all the elements of upright posture. There was no compromise. I was so happy to be able to embody the ritual enactment of zazen in a way that worked for my body, that all I wanted to do was sit zazen (lying down).

As *shuso*, I was assigned a seat with two *zabutons* (floor cushions) side by side on the *tan* (sitting platform), right where the *shuso* usually sits. This was extremely meaningful to me. The sangha made space even for me. The sangha cared about me just as I am, further rewiring my lifelong painful love and attachment pathways. The effort of showing up and leaving, staying when I could, over and over and over, and being met, my "leaving practice," was indeed practice. Up until I was *shuso*, zazen had been extremely difficult. During this time, becoming more comfortable with lying down in the zendo and abandoning a bit of ego, zazen was filled with joy. The zendo made space for this bodymind, and my practice shifted again.

Those teachers who have met me in this way have all had a huge impact on my transformation, including allowing it to be transformation without requiring some definition of perfection to be met. Zen Buddhism, ultimately, is not two, not one. There are many ways to describe this, but that fundamental teaching, and its embodiment by the sanghas I've had the great good fortune to practice with, saved my life, transformed my life, and still to this day make my daily life possible.

These teachers and sanghas have done this without talking to me about therapy (although that might be because I was nearly always in therapy back then) and without any deep knowledge of PTSD or childhood trauma. They met me in their vastness and called me there unflinchingly. What they did was not, and is not, easy or simple. They gave me their very lives, opening to searching within themselves when difficulties arose between us. They never weaponized the Dharma or made me bad or wrong. Amazingly, they were willing and I was willing, and that willingness was the most important thing—tremendous willingness, guts, and firm resolve.

Nowadays, when I arrive, it is still difficult. I often cry, want to leave, and profess that the new situation is just not livable. Through my teacher's support, along with years of driving to strange new places for residential practice, arriving over and over again, changed me in some deep way. Under my tears and protestations, I now know it will be okay. I stay much more often now than I used to. I feel I belong in sangha and with other people in general. I know for a fact that everyone suffers, everyone struggles, everyone is growing older and knowing impermanence day to day. Everyone brings themselves to practice just as I do. That's what we do. And we don't get to leave certain parts of ourselves at the zendo door, or the interview room door. We bring this one everywhere, just as it is. Teachers and students both as we are—this is what we have to offer to Buddha, Dharma, and Sangha.

Unlike my mother before me, I am surrounded by bounty and actually feel bountiful. I can feel loved. I can arrive, albeit roughly, and even stay. Zen has taught me to hold lightly and allow, to include and wrap into myself whatever arises, as we are not two. Anger, yes, that too. Hate, yes. Joy, yes. Love, yes. Compassion, empathy, caring, yes, those too. I often practice with the question, "What am I excluding from me right now?" And I open, open, open. This capacity gives me great joy; the farther I push myself the greater the joy. The beautiful flowers I encounter on the way to an appointment. All me. And I offer that joy overflowing, that vastness, to my mother who, although she was surrounded by love and laughter and other bounty, never felt bountiful.

For the most part, my contribution to this transformation was simply coming back again and again, and leaving again and again, until the fundamental teaching nested within me. It took over eighteen years. We are all, each and every one of us, not separate from our experience in any way. We are entirely interdependent and reliant on the common good. At the same time, the words of Sawaki Roshi, the homeless monk, cannot be better stated, "You cannot share even so much as a fart with another person." We are not one. Each must find their own way. As my late teacher, Darlene Cohen, said, "Moment after moment we have to find our own way. Each one of us must make our own way and when we do, that way will express the universal way."

In some sense, this practicing with the residue of PTSD will go on endlessly as long as this one practices the Buddha way. As Bhikkhu Bodhi said, "We have to see that our lives are not fully satisfactory, that life is impermanent, that it is subject to suffering, and we have to understand that suffering is something that we have to penetrate."[2] To penetrate suffering is to penetrate human life, to find complete refuge in life as-it-is.

Notes
1. Victor Sogun Hori, *Zen Sand: The Book of Capping Phrases for Koan Practice* (Honolulu: University of Hawai'i Press, 2003), 359.
2. Bhikkhu Bodhi, "Right View," sec. 1 of *The Noble Eightfold Path*, http://www.beyondthenet.net/dhamma/nobleEight.htm.

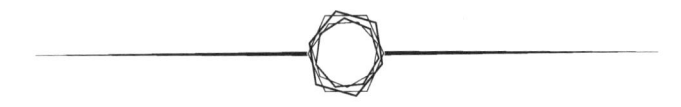

Joan Hogetsu Hoeberichts is abbot of the Heart Circle Sangha in Ridgewood, New Jersey. A successor of Nicolee Jikyo McMahon, she is a member of the White Plum Asanga. She is also a psychotherapist in private practice in New York City and Montclair, New Jersey. She and her sangha are involved in social action. In 2008 and 2009 she was recognized for her social action by the Buddhist Council of the Midwest and the United Nations International Women's Day Association for the Promotion of the Status of Women for her work in Sri Lanka after the 2004 tsunami. More information is available at heartcirclesangha.org and dharmateam.com.

Love and Fear
Joan Hogetsu Hoeberichts

A baby grew inside me. My breasts swelled and painfully tingled. I needed to rub them to stop the tingling. Was that gas or the baby moving? I felt so protective of this little being that filled my body. Was it me? My body was not my own. Whose was it? Ours? I felt this was what I was made for. This was my destiny. It felt primal, preordained. It felt like a biological imperative. I could only surrender to the process. The baby began to kick and move, punching me painlessly from the inside. Sometimes I pushed back. It was intimate. I could play with him in this way at work, at concerts, at all my activities. I was constantly aware of his presence in me. I loved him already. Were we one or two?

Lying on my back in the delivery room, I peered into the mirror overhead so I could watch his arrival into this world. I glimpsed his head, just the crown, and then he slipped back. Then he crowned again and slipped back again. "Push down, push down!" I was ordered. I pushed with all my might and suddenly there was a baby. I saw the doctor twist him slightly and ease him out. He began to cry. I was overcome with awe. I had participated in a miracle! I was struck by the sense of being part of a great flowing stream of generations of humanity. Sperm flowing in, meeting the egg, babies flowing out, over and over, throughout time. This was a live, crying, frightened baby human being who needed to be taken care of, who needed to be loved.

When he cried, my breasts would leak milk. This was an experience entirely of the body. It felt good when he suckled. I relaxed and nourished him, feeling nourished myself. His soft little hands would wander over my bare skin, touching me while he nursed. Caring for and loving this infant felt natural. I knew what all his cries meant: a hungry cry, a mad cry, a wet cry. Only when my grandchildren were born did I realize this was a special knowing. I had to ask their mother what their cries meant.

Fathers too, open to their new infant with vulnerability and wonder. They, too, are affected by the miracle of a newborn. Did I make this child? Many fathers are intimidated by the tininess and fragility of an infant, but they connect through loving it and are thrilled when the child begins to respond to them and to know them. My husband said the birth of our son gave him a profound sense of completion.

I had never imagined that family love could be a spiritual experience, but love is at the core of spirituality. Loving, I became more open, vulnerable, and accessible. I saw the world through a lens of love. It flowed into my feelings toward others. Compassion, empathy, deep caring, kindness, and tenderness just arose. I had become something beyond "me." Through loving I had lost my I-ness, my solidity as an autonomous, separate being. I felt whole, at peace and connected to the world.

I remember a warm summer evening about thirty-five years ago when our family was staying at a resort north of Toronto for a few days. Our fourteen-year-old son, bursting with excitement, came running to tell us of something happening outside. He insisted we all come down to the lake where we could see the stars clearly in the dark summer night. Meteor showers were lighting up the night sky. Following his lead, we all lay down on our backs on the warm wooden dock and looked up. It was as if I was expanding to hold that night sky. Meteor after meteor lit up the night; I was surrounded by people I loved. The beauty above was wondrous. My mind emptied out. I was open. I became the silent night sky.

Although longing to hold on to that experience, I knew that if I hung on, I would deaden it. Holding it as a lovely memory would be enough. Reflecting in quiet moments I could summon the warm, special loveliness that accompanied the experience. Remaining in that state of deep interconnectedness was not possible.

Weeklong *sesshins* (Zen meditation retreats) provide an experience of opening. I sit for the first few days with a busy mind, feeling very much as though I am there with my ordinary mind full of thoughts and plans and problems to be solved. Then gradually the thoughts slow down, sometimes even stop, and I fall in love with everyone around me. No matter the weather, it always seems quite perfect. No matter how exhausted I feel, I don't mind. Sometimes I am interrupted by crises in my life at home that require a response. They don't really bother me that much. I just respond as needed. I love *sesshin*. It always serves to remind me that this delightful mind space is always available. However, again, I cannot hold onto it. A day or two back at home and at work, and it is a memory.

So why can't I stay in that interconnected, loving state of mind?

It is mostly fear or anxiety that causes me to drop away from the sense of oneness. In the return to my daily affairs I become, like most of us, subject to the anxieties of my ordinary life. It was my own anxiety that brought me to meditation and a spiritual path to begin with. My anxiety comes from a false sense of self that arises over and over again, disconnecting me, leaving me alone, on my own, struggling to keep it together in a tough world. Will I have enough money to retire someday? Am I doing the best I can with a difficult patient? Is my grandson OK? With such concerns, I momentarily lose sight of the interconnected flow of the universe, and feel I am on my own with my problems. Meditation and spiritual practice do bring us relief from anxiety.

Recently we had a guest speaker in the zendo and only five students showed up to sit, I was painfully embarrassed. The pain stayed with me throughout morning zazen and through his excellent talk. I had no sense of interconnectedness. I was not full of loving feelings. I was shriveled with embarrassment. Toward the end of his talk he spoke of how we want our life to go the way we think it should go and how we suffer when it doesn't. Pulled back from my embarrassment, I realized I wanted to be sitting in a full zendo with all my students raptly listening to the guest speaker and asking intelligent and probing questions. My own expectations were the source of my suffering. A lesson I have been taught over and over again.

Indeed, it was my anxiety that brought me to practice some fifty years ago. I was also afraid of being free of anxiety, imagining anxiety kept me safe and on my intended path. I worried that if I started to meditate I would become some kind of hippie hermit that lived in a cabin on a mountainside like the Chinese hermits of old. That hermit life has more appeal to me now. But then, in my twenties, I feared becoming a nobody, laid back and penniless. I was ambitious and drawn to the competitive life that the world offered. Ambition and anxiety are closely linked. Letting go of ambition would have required giving up my dreams of achievement in the world. That very thought made me anxious. My parents expected me to succeed in a material world, not a spiritual one, and they would have been sorely disappointed in me. It took a few years more before I was brave and independent enough to learn to meditate. Eventually I took the leap. As a meditator, I became less anxious, more accepting of my ambitious part, and more comfortable with myself.

Meditation has provided the grounding I have needed throughout life's crises. When my husband was in the hospital, recovering from having a stent put into one of his arteries, someone had given me a book of poems about death. Reading it, anxiety reemerged in spades. As I read, I noticed the fear in my body. I was panting. I was having a mini panic attack. Taking some long deep breaths, I began to talk to myself as if I were a frightened child: "This was a very minor surgery and he is expected to have a full recovery. It has gone well and there are no complications. What the hell are you doing reading a book about death." I put the book down and drew more deep breaths. My anxiety abated.

Recently, I was stressed by a work situation. I was bothered by tension in my body that I could not release. Busy trying to resolve the actual problem, I neglected my morning meditation routine. Noticing I was having heart palpitations at night, I made an appointment with my cardiologist who diagnosed me with atrial fibrillation. My blood pressure was spiking. I knew I could lower my blood pressure by meditating but I didn't know if I could stop the palpitations. I gave it a try. Sitting zazen, I could feel my heart beating rapidly, but as I continued to sit, it seemed to slow down. By the end of thirty minutes, the palpitations had stopped completely; I felt as though my blood pressure had returned to normal. I resolved not to let anything interrupt my daily meditation routine again. I recalled Thich Nhat Hanh's clear directive that we not be too busy, that we make time to love and care for ourselves and others.

I am now seventy-four and my husband is eighty-three. We are in the end phase of our lives and these days we appreciate each moment. We know that life will become more difficult. The Buddha said that old age, sickness, and death were where the rewards of practice really pay off. Facing old age with equanimity takes courage, even though it comes whether we face it with equanimity or not. Although I am in "good" health for seventy-four, doctor's appointments dot my calendar, and there is no question that my body is in decline. My husband, too, is in "good" health, but his body is further along in its decline than mine. Already at eighty-three, he has lived longer than any of his male relatives. In the next twenty years, I will face his sickness and death. Then looming ahead, I will suffer without him, my own sickness and death. Old age is already here. I sit with this, facing it, living with it and allowing it to guide my choices. Now, my meditation practice has a greater urgency. Everything in my life is colored by this awareness. The Buddha describes this prospect as,

> Just as mountains of solid rock,
> Massive, reaching to the sky,
> Might draw together from all sides,
> Crushing all in the four quarters—
> So aging and death come
> Rolling over living beings—
> There is no escape.

I am grateful for my fifty-plus years of practice to remind me that birth and death are a flow, an endless cycle of energy, and that I have been only temporarily trapped in this body from the beginning. It seems that all my practice has simply been to bring me to this point in life.

Am I afraid? Yes and no. I was asked recently to visit a woman in a local nursing home who was a Buddhist, and one of the administrators thought that some Buddhist chanting would be helpful to her. Visiting her, I brought some recorded chants and a printed copy of the *Heart Sutra* we could chant together. However, when I found her, her advanced dementia had left her unable to speak or communicate.

She was sitting in a wheelchair at a lunch table in the common room with an attendant who was feeding her. When she was finished, I asked if she would like to chant with me. Perhaps she nodded an assent. I chanted the sutra, but she couldn't stay with it. I played the chants I had recorded on my phone and again she seemed to listen for a few moments and then drifted away. A few weeks later, I brought over a CD of chants to leave with her. This time I found her in her bed, which was an adult crib. She was awake and rocking back and forth, making unintelligible sounds, alone in her room. She looked up at my arrival, but did not greet me or appear to recognize me. I played the chants on a CD player with the same results as before. I left the chants in her room hoping the staff might play them for her.

Such a prospect is, indeed, frightening.

When my mother was dying ten years ago, I remember her lying in bed with her eyes closed. Moaning, she murmured, "It hurts," and I knew she was afraid. I offered to chant the *Heart Sutra*, which I found very comforting. Though not a Buddhist, she had seemed to relax when I chanted it before. She nodded. As I chanted, "It completely clears all pain. This is the truth, not a lie," her eyes popped open and she said in surprise, "It's true!" She passed away peacefully the next morning.

Last year I lost a senior student, a dharma holder, to complications from cancer treatment. He had made a point of preparing for death. His preparation involved reading everything he could find about Buddhist preparation for death. We would meet regularly to meditate on death and to talk. It was an intimate time. Eight months after his diagnosis, while still appearing to be healthy, he died unexpectedly from heart failure, in his sleep, after shoveling snow. He was only sixty-two. His death was a huge loss for me. We had practiced together for twenty years. I knew it was a foreshadowing of what it will be like to lose my husband of fifty years. That is a far more intimidating prospect than my own death.

Nothing to do but return to my cushion, my breath and this moment, full of love, joy, fear, life, and death. This is my life.

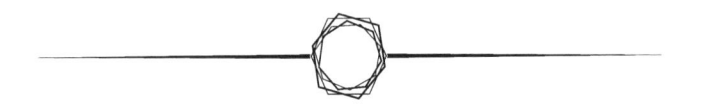

Carolyn Joshin Atkinson, a dharma heir and lineage holder of the late Kobun Chino Otogawa Roshi, is head teacher at Everyday Dharma Zen Center in Santa Cruz, California. She has been practicing Zen Buddhist meditation since 1973, and has also studied extensively in the Theravadin tradition. She is the author of two books, *Quiet Mind Open Heart* and *A Light in the Mind*. After training in San Francisco and China, she practiced traditional Chinese medicine for twenty years. She is the mother of two grown sons. For further information, visit everydaydharma.org.

Accepting Our Lives in Difficult Times
Carolyn Joshin Atkinson

Several months ago at our Zen Center, a new group of members stepped forward to undertake the *jukai* process. In English we call this "receiving the precepts." These precepts are part of a basic statement of our intentions for practice within the world of Soto Zen Buddhism. We see it as a period of training where we examine our lives: what we have inherited, who we imagine ourselves to be, how we can take refuge in our Buddhist teachings, and how we can bring more awareness to our relationships in the world, to our behavior, and to our choices. It's a big challenge to really pay attention directly to how we are living in and with the world, especially in difficult or painful times. And it's an important *choice* that we make: to turn in the direction of peacefulness when life can be difficult, to cultivate the Buddhist practices of mindfulness, of equanimity and of ethical behavior, when it might be easier to turn toward resistance to life as it is.

We try to bring our best awareness to all of these issues. And usually we notice that we feel fine about the places in our lives that are comfortable, but we tend to feel stuck in the places we don't like. This is not really a surprise, of course. But it is a challenge. I find that if I want even to approach choosing peacefulness in my life, I have to be willing to look at the question of acceptance. And of course, the only place where acceptance is an issue for me is where I do not want things to be the way they are. I can accept that the sun is shining and that I'm physically able to come to our Zen Center for meetings. I have no trouble accepting that I have people, so many people in my life that I love. Accepting any of these things is no problem. But the places where my mind is disturbed or resisting and where my heart is closed down—these feelings are, of course, exactly what I don't want to accept. I would rather not acknowledge such responses. This is where I do not want to be open to life, as it is.

I know that, for many of us, there are circumstances in our lives that bring up huge feelings of grief, of guilt perhaps, of shame, of injury, of anger or despair. One person said to me recently: "I can't seem to resolve my feelings of guilt about my life and what I've done. I know I need to accept that this is the way it is, but I'm finding it almost impossible to do." Another person asked this: "What do I do with all of my negative feelings, toward myself and others? I recognize my situation but I feel so much anguish about what others did to me. I can't seem to let go of the injury, and of wanting things to be different than they are." Haven't we all felt like this, at times in our lives? We're talking here about deep acceptance. And acceptance is a difficult task, a demanding undertaking. Sometimes, the challenge of acceptance feels impossible.

I'd like to tell you a story that looks at this issue very directly. And it touches close to my heart, because it's the true story (with changes for anonymity, of course) of a good childhood friend of mine. This friend was a classmate. I will call him "Andy." I lived just one block away from him when I first moved from our farm into town with my family, so he goes all the way back in memory for me to when I was four years old.

Andy was a rather shy person. He liked to play the drums in the kindergarten band. Otherwise, he was pretty unnoticeable. But we walked home on the same streets for years, and so I began to get to know him slowly. Now, Andy had a younger brother—three years younger—whose name was David. "Davey," we called him. And Andy and Davey were really close, unusually so, I would say. I didn't understand this exactly, but it was clear that Andy would always protect Davey. If something happened at school, Andy was right there on the playground, attacking anybody who even looked a little strangely at his brother. Andy got into trouble for this a number of times, as one might imagine.

I found out many years later that their parents, whom I almost never saw, were both alcoholics. So Andy and Davey were essentially on their own, having to raise themselves. Andy told me one time after I'd known him for a number of years that the fighting between his parents was so frequent and so bad that he usually slept with his ears folded over, to block out the sound. And his ears did indeed stick way out—which perhaps might happen in folding them over every night. I didn't know, but it seemed like a good reason.

So Andy went to college—he was smart—and he graduated in 1967. The Vietnam War was a huge shadow over the whole country at that time. Andy had gotten involved with draft resistance at college, and by the time he finished undergraduate work, the world for us young people was chaotic and polarized. We were either against the war or not, we were either finding some way to protest or not, but this was a defining identity issue for most of us during those years.

More and more people—our brothers, our friends, our lovers, those of us who were young then—were being killed. And the Vietnamese were being slaughtered. This war was about reasons that didn't even make sense: the domino theory, and so on. We learned later, of course, how much of it was actually about politics in Washington; it had very little to do with this remote area of the world that we seemed intent upon destroying.

For my generation, the Vietnam War was the formative experience of our age: we felt impotent and helpless, and there was great despair all around. Break-ins at draft centers, demonstrations and marches: we were trying everything. Then in 1970, protesting students were shot dead by National Guard members on the campus at Kent State in Ohio. The whole country watched it happen. And rage—horrifying rage—took up residence in many of our hearts.

Andy was one of those filled with rage; he had already been politically active for several years. He joined Students for a Democratic Society. He poured animal blood on draft cards. He went to sit-ins. He got arrested repeatedly. But remember, he graduated in 1967. There were still certain ways in which young men could avoid being drafted by slipping through the maze of deferments (joining the Peace Corps or Vista, going to graduate school, teaching, having children, and so on). Andy used as many loopholes as he could manage—until finally, he aged out when he was twenty-six, and then, he was no longer on the active draft list.

However, Davey was three years younger. So by the time he was

Zen Teachings In Challenging Times

eligible, the draft was a lottery and Kent State was a vivid experience for most of us. Davey's draft number turned out to be quite low. He was a very shy young boy, not political at all, not thinking about options like escaping to Canada. And, as expected, after an interval of a few months, he was called up for the draft. He was given a brief training and put on a plane to Vietnam. Andy was frantic with fear and anger for his brother; Davey was his only deep and close connection in the world. Six months later, news arrived that Davey had been killed somewhere in a swamp in Vietnam. He might have been stoned on drugs at the time. He must certainly have been terrified beyond belief.

These stories were common during those chaotic times. And after Davey was killed, Andy just basically went crazy. He entered a world of rage and despair that was to consume his life for years. He got heavily into drugs, finally he was living on the street or in parks, wherever he could find a place to lie down. We only heard news of him sporadically, because he basically dropped out of sight and out of contact with everyone who knew him. That was years ago.

Recently, when I returned to my hometown, I ran into Andy quite by chance as I was walking down the street. When we recognized each other even after all these years, we were so happy to meet again, and we took time for a long talk together. I asked him how he understood these experiences in his life. How does he make sense out of everything that happened? He said that for a long time he blamed himself. He had a kind of animal-like turning around and around, trying to figure out what he could have done differently. Wasn't there something that he or someone else should have or could have done—and then it would have all changed somehow, Davey would still be alive? He felt that way for years, but he said finally, he has found a kind of peace within his life. Now, he no longer believes that he should have found that perfect something else, and then things would have been different.

We talked directly about the question of peacefulness in Andy's life. And what was clear to both of us was that peacefulness depended upon his willingness to turn toward acceptance in his life. As long as he could not accept what happened, he could not find a peaceful mind. He talked about really accepting his life, beginning with his childhood, and his parents. He said he had to absolutely accept that all of his life was precisely what happened. It hasn't been easy. He mentioned that he is often lonely. He struggles with despair sometimes. But he has made a kind of peace with exactly what his life has been. When he shared this with me, I thought to myself, Andy didn't go to war in Vietnam, but he has been at war with life for so many years. Now, he has made his peace. Good job, Andy.

As we've been looking at the *jukai* process at our Zen Center, we've come back repeatedly to this issue of acceptance—how it is necessary to accept what's happened, in order to choose peacefulness in our lives. One woman phrased it in a different way recently when she said, "The question for me is not so much what I need to accept, but what do I need to give up, in order to approach a quiet mind?" These are good questions, both of them: what do we need to accept, and also, what do we need to give up, if we want to choose peacefulness in our lives?

Andy was asking the same questions of himself in his life. What do I need to accept? And what do I need to give up? Reflecting back on our conversation, I've come to a tentative list of possible things we might need to accept, if we really want to choose peacefulness in our lives. Here is a list, partial I'm sure, of what we might need to come to terms with.

> 1. We might need to accept that people we have truly loved have caused pain for us. This doesn't go into the reasons for these events. But yes: it does happen, and accepting this can be very difficult. How could they do this, we ask. And we can ask this for years, for a lifetime. So, I think we are challenged to consider: can we accept that this injury happened, sometimes from the people who especially should have loved us in much more skillful ways?
>
> 2. We might need to accept that what we think we know to be true may not be so for someone else. We can feel very certain, but others may genuinely disagree. In other words, we might need to accept that what we think is the way things are or the way things have been or should be is not what others experience. We're not necessarily right all the time about "the way the world is."

3. And this too: we might need to accept that often we don't know a lot. We don't know what's going to happen, or what is happening, or what did happen. Simply put, often we don't know what's really going on.

4. We might need to accept that being the injured party in a situation does not actually confer any special privileges upon us. Being injured doesn't automatically make us good. Absolutely, we can fight for what we think we deserve, but it's not guaranteed that we are therefore virtuous. I would suggest that what we can most beneficially learn is something the Buddha taught: that things are what they are, arising out of everything that has gone before. In the practice of cultivating *upekkha* or equanimity in the Theravada tradition, a phrase used frequently says: "May I accept this life, just as it is." This is very challenging; there's no question about it.

5. We might need to accept that we cannot do everything we think we should, or be everything we want, in our lives. We might need to accept that actually we are ordinary—so very ordinary—all of us. What we have is each of us, coming into this world, living and going out of it: just ordinary me and just ordinary you. We might need to really accept this, in order to have a more peaceful mind. Imagine what it might feel like to accept being not so special, but being instead, oh so very human.

6. And, as long as we're really looking at the nature of life, there's this very big challenge: we might need to accept several other demanding teachings from the Buddha. We learn that no matter how much we love or want or fear, we cannot hold on to anything. Everything and everyone we treasure will eventually leave us. The Buddha reminded us: all birth ends in death. There are no exceptions for anything that is alive. This means that everything we gather together, our best efforts to preserve what we value—all this will eventually drift apart, no matter what we may want. Just think how this would change our minds and lives—if we were really to accept all this.

One man in our sangha who lives with metastatic melanoma said recently: "I'm learning to live each day as if it were my last one." His face was calm and he had a smile of acceptance. This man didn't have a choice about his medical diagnosis. But he has a choice about how he will respond. Good for him, I say, making this choice to live the life he has as completely as possible.

I tell you the story about Andy, and about our sangha member, because I wanted to reflect a bit further on this question of choice. Here's the way it looks to me: Andy didn't have a choice about what family he was born into, and what problems they may have had. He didn't have a choice about his social inheritance. And he didn't have a choice about coming of age right as the Vietnam War was escalating. Obviously, he didn't get what he wanted for Davey's draft number. So, we can see, he didn't have a choice about what was going on in the world around him in these early years of his life.

And Andy told me that when Davey was killed, the despair was so complete that he didn't feel like he had a choice about blotting out his consciousness with drugs and alcohol in order to simply not feel the pain so much. He didn't have a choice about how he felt, and it seemed that he didn't have a choice about his response. But finally, he said, he realized that he *did* have a choice about how he would continue to respond. I would say that Andy's digging out of his own particular hellish hole was an act of great ethical integrity. It was difficult. It took him a long time. And he has done it. He has found a place of peace within himself that allows him to continue making ethical choices, day by day. Andy is able now to own his life—the one that he has—and to remain conscious within it.

When times are difficult—which means for many of us, much of the time—the question arises: how do we respond? What are we to do with our experiences, living in these difficult days and weeks and years? Why can't things be better? Do we have to give up, as someone suggested, all hope of a better past? This is important: how do we relate to the painful events in our lives? We actually don't get to choose what has happened in the past, or what is happening in the world beyond our own minds, and we don't get to choose what feelings may arise within us, in living our lives. However, we do get to choose how we will respond to these feelings and to life itself. And this can sometimes be quite difficult. As Andy said to me: "My life has been what it is, not what I wanted it to be. I'm making my peace with that. And it hasn't been easy." Good for you, Andy. I say, good for you.

Now just briefly, I'd like to share one more thought about

choosing acceptance. For a moment, let's look at the question of what acceptance is not. I want to be clear that acceptance is not condoning injury or cruelty or thoughtlessness. This is not a free pass for people to abuse others. And also, it's not a dismissive response of "Oh well, whatever, anyway. It doesn't matter." And I would say this as well: acceptance is not trusting that the perpetrator will not do it again. It doesn't mean believing that we're always going to be safe, and that everything will be fine. I like the Sufi expression "Trust in God, but tie up your camel." Acceptance doesn't mean that your camel may not wander away in the desert, or be taken by someone else. Really—it's smart to tie up your camel.

Also, acceptance is not the same as self-pity. Or self-justification. It is not a state of indifference or passivity or resignation. Nor is it quietism. Finally, I'd suggest that acceptance doesn't mean that we always have to like everything that happens. Rather, it is a state where we say: "This too. This too, I will acknowledge that this is happening. If I want peace of mind, I will accept this also." Our sangha member says, "I'm practicing living every day as if it is my last one." He's choosing to be present, to accept this very life that he has, maybe not the one he wanted or expected, but the one that he got. Good job.

The question I'm posing is this: what do we each need to accept if we want to have a quiet mind and an open heart? Or maybe it's the question—what do we need to give up wanting to have, in order to find peacefulness? What price are we asked to pay? I would suggest that nothing is free in this life. Acceptance and equanimity come at a price. Peacefulness demands a great deal from us. Nothing is free. So again, what price are we willing to pay for a quiet mind and an open heart? How are we going to cultivate quietness and peace of mind?

Sometimes I find myself remembering a fragment of writing from a man named Raymond Carver. He was someone who experienced a difficult life, partly due to a number of circumstances beyond his control, as well as to his own choices. And with all these issues, he was finally able to come to a place of stability in his own mind and heart. In the months before he died, he wrote this line: "And did you get what you wanted from this life, even so?" [1] I think of his question, and I notice that my mind stops on the words "even so." It seems to me that this speaks directly to all of us, whatever our circumstances. Are we getting what we want from this life, even so? When I ask this question of myself, I realize that what I want to get from this life is to embrace peacefulness, to choose peacefulness, even in times of difficulty, even in times of war. Even so.

I would just say that I feel like I have to painfully choose acceptance every single day. In fact, I have to do this consciously and repeatedly many times within every day. And of course, exactly what I need to choose is what I would absolutely rather not have to choose. Sometimes it helps me to ask myself the question: would I rather be right or would I rather be peaceful? Can I bear to bring myself to acceptance of this very life ... just as it is? With our Buddhist practices, with training our hearts and minds in the directions of mindfulness and kindness and equanimity, we do have choices in our lives. We may not get the choices we want, but it is clear to me that choosing the life we have is always possible. Andy has made that choice. Our sangha member is doing this. I found a sentence recently where Suzuki Roshi said, "Actually, good and bad is not the point. Whether or not you make yourself peaceful is the point, and whether or not you stick to it."[2] It seems to me, these words ask us if we can bring ourselves to turn toward acceptance? Can we bear to choose peacefulness? It's a demanding task, and I would suggest, an absolutely rewarding choice.

Notes

1. Raymond Carver, "Late Fragment," in *A New Path to the Waterfall* (New York: Atlantic Monthly Press, 1989), 122.
2. Shunryu Suzuki, *Zen Mind, Beginner's Mind* (New York: Weatherhill, 1970), 128.

IV

Cho nen Kanzeon, Bo nen Kanzeon

Morning Mind is Kanzeon;
Evening Mind is Kanzeon

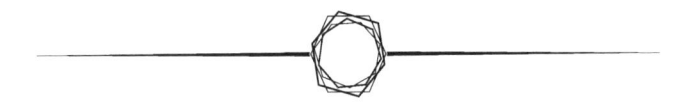

Enkyo Pat O'Hara studied with Daido Loori and Maezumi Roshi and received transmission from Bernie Glassman. In 1986 she founded the still-vibrant Village Zendo, a nonresidential Zen center in Manhattan. She holds a Ph.D. and taught for many years at New York University's Tisch School of the Arts, centering on new media technologies and social justice. Her writing has appeared in various Buddhist journals, Temple Ground Books, and her 2014 book, *Most Intimate: A Zen Approach to Life's Challenges*, was published by Shambhala.

Showing Up in Troubled Times
Enkyo Pat O'Hara

A beloved Buddhist image is that of a bodhisattva who steers a raft filled with suffering beings across a sea of troubled waters to a shore of peace and clarity. In thirteenth-century Japan, in the midst of fearfully challenging times, Zen Master Dogen wrote,

> What can I accomplish?
> Although not yet a Buddha,
> Let my priest's body
> Be the raft to carry
> Sentient beings to the yonder shore.[1]

It is a humble, poignant wish, to let one's own body serve to awaken others, awaken them to the reality of our interpenetrated universe, where nothing is separate, nothing exists without all the rest in that moment. That a devout, brilliant philosopher-monk might take on the profound responsibility of carrying suffering beings across the sea of despair seems to me to challenge each of us to investigate how we can make of ourselves a raft and thus survive and help others to cope with these troubling times.

And indeed, these days are deeply distressing and challenging for the many of us who, until recently, felt as if our world were slowly changing into a more compassionate and rational one. Perhaps naively, we thought that the threat to the health of our planet was beginning to be met, that hunger and disease, partisanship and violence, racism and elitism, were all on the wane. And we are shocked and awakened to the reality that the countervailing forces of greed, anger, and ignorance have gained strength and now are exerting control in different parts of the planet. Difficult as it is to take in to our consciousness, we are witnessing a harsh rebalancing of worldview and of power.

What raft can we construct that will serve to strengthen us, create resilience, so that we can act to serve skillfully? As in so many times in the past, I turn again to Dogen, and his opening words in an early writing, the "Genjokoan." It is a text beloved by many, and truly is a balm for these times.

Dogen initially wrote "Genjokoan" for a layman and dharma student, Koshu Yo, who lived in Kyushu province. At that time, that area faced threats from China and the Korean peninsula, both frighteningly close to this extremity of the Japanese archipelago. Moreover, at the time when Dogen began writing "Genjokoan," there had been weird weather—snow in summer—and crops had been ruined, and so there was a famine. It is said that corpses lay on the streets of Kyoto. And, within the political realm there was great change, with the samurai class taking over the rule of Japan from the emperor and his court. Buddhist groups fought one another; theft in the monasteries was rampant.(2)

It was a grievous time, and like today, called for wisdom and discerning Bodhisattva activity. Today, like layman Koshu Yo, most of us are living multidimensional lives, with the needs of our personal relations, work relations, sangha relations, our own inner struggles to understand our lives, the world around us—and our response as citizens in a world that needs us.

How do we show up for this? The first words of "Genjokoan" show me a way, helping me to balance my life, to live in buddha dharma and to act in everyday life. These are the opening lines:

> As all things are buddha dharma, there are delusion, realization, practice, birth [life] and death, buddhas and sentient beings.
>
> As myriad things are without an abiding self, there is no delusion, no realization, no buddha, no sentient being, no birth and death.
>
> The buddha way, in essence, is leaping clear of abundance and lack; thus there are birth and death, delusion and realization, sentient beings and buddhas.

Yet in attachment blossoms fall, and in aversion weeds spread.(3)

Here is the heart of the teaching: Dogen escorts us through the mystery of how we inhabit and receive the world, how we presence ourselves within the myriad things, and then within our own hearts. He begins, "As all things are buddha dharma, there are delusion, realization, practice, birth [life] and death, buddhas and sentient beings." What I hear in this line is the very *ordinariness* of awakened truth, or buddha dharma: in this awakened truth, we cannot deny that there is delusion, that there is awakening,—think of the many times a day when you experience delusion, and then, when you also "wake up" and realize that!—That's the power of practice, it helps us to stop and *wake up*.

And in the world around us, in this pathetic polis of a country pulling apart each day, there are wise ones and fools, there are the good and the bad and the confused, and the ones who are swallowed up by the classic Buddhist three poisons: greed, anger, and ignorance.

This, then, is *one* way to see our current situation in the buddha dharma: there is falling down and getting up, there are buddhas and sentient beings. Each of us, many times a day, inhabit these states, and when we stop and truly realize this, and accept it as the way things are, that this is a reality we humans live in and experience, we can roll up our sleeves and function in this reality. In order to serve the world, we must realize the way things are: this is a radical acceptance of *now*—we are not saying "This is OK," we are saying, "This is what is—now."

Immediately, in the very next line, Dogen reverses energy and reminds us that the ordinary ways we have of structuring reality are simply convenient, temporary tags, illusory ways of thinking. He says. "As myriad things are without an abiding self, there is no delusion, no realization, no buddha, no sentient being, no birth and death."

We stop again and imagine no edges to our being, no "self" that persists all day, but rather, just the moment, or not even the moment, but this vast empty moment.

There is such release, such succor, such bottomless truth in this realization: all that we think and hold dear, our own selves and our stories, and others and the world: it is all, on one level, merely a structure, a way of organizing the impulses to our senses. Dropping that, there is no "me" or "you" or even "Trump" or "cruelty" or kindness.

There is just this mind-moment: nen, nen, nen.

That this empty reality is *also* present in our lives offers us a glimpse of a deeper truth, a resonance we fail to notice in our "to-ing" and "fro-ing" through our lives.

Just this: the silence that has no name. Even the soft breeze, the warm sun, the night air, just just just—and no name or label. It is a showing up of everything all at once—with no walls or borders.

But wait! Dogen's next line brings us to yet another view: "The buddha way, in essence, is leaping clear of abundance and lack; thus there are birth and death, delusion and realization, sentient beings and buddhas."

The heart of the teaching: the Buddha way, the way of awakening, "leaps clear" or jumps over, is not stopped by, our views of reality as either just our everyday life or as emptiness. Instead, this line teaches that the Buddha way leaps over *both* getting caught in the everydayness of life, *and* getting caught in the empty vastness of undifferentiated reality.

This is to wake up! It is to neither grasp what is here, nor to ignore what is here. It is to *show up*.

Indeed, these times are very scary, and I must act to insure the well-being of those in need of food and medical care and housing and basic human rights. The demand is great, and all my efforts are required to meet this moment, the needs that are in front of me. *And*, I must also realize that even while in the heat of action, there is a reality also present at each moment that disentangles difference, disentangles you versus me, and unknots the knot of difference and inequality.

Allowing this "leaping clear" prevents us from becoming ideological warriors, or martyrs, and opens our hearts to the deepest truth: the interconnected quality of all of life throughout space and time. Thus we can express skillful, non-harming action towards everyone. We respond and act in accordance with these two truths.

To underline this, Dogen gives us this brilliant last line to this section, "Yet in attachment blossoms fall, and in aversion weeds spread."

Even in this moment when we recognize that things are as they are, and also are *not* what we think we see, and even when we leap clear of these dichotomies, and rest in a kind of wisdom, *still*, nevertheless, we lose what we love, and what we do not like increases.

"Yet in attachment blossoms fall, and in aversion weeds spread."

A poignant reminder of the sad and beautiful mystery of life, the preciousness of each moment, the necessity that we live in the multiple realities, the two spheres and doing that, we live a fully human life.

Can we show up for all of it, even the tender reminder that everything in us and around us is flowing in a stream of impermanence, and no matter how we *feel*, things move on.

In the final section of the "Genjokoan," Dogen slyly and humorously encourages to show up and serve the world and life we encounter:

> Mayu, Zen Master Baoche, was fanning himself. A monk approached and said, "Master, the nature of wind is permanent and there is no place it does not reach. Why then do you fan yourself?"
>
> "Although you understand that the nature of the wind is permanent," Mayu replied, "you do not understand the meaning of its reaching everywhere."
>
> "What is the meaning of its reaching everywhere?" asked the monk again.
>
> Mayu just kept fanning himself.
>
> The monk bowed deeply.(4)

This begins with an echo to the first lines of "Genjokoan," the ordinary world, and old Master Mayu, probably on a very hot and humid day, is fanning himself, rather as in: "As all things are buddhadharma, there are delusion, realization, practice, birth [life] and death, buddhas and sentient beings."

So, there is warm weather, there is a fan, there is cooling oneself: things just as we see them in our everyday life. Then, a monk approaches and says that the nature of wind is permanent, reflecting the view, "As myriad things are without an abiding self, there is no delusion, no realization, no buddha, no sentient being, no birth and death."

The monk has fallen into the thrall of emptiness, or oneness, where there is no separation and therefore the wind is everywhere! No need to act. The old teacher replies that the monk may understand that all is one, but he doesn't realize what it means that it reaches everywhere: "The buddha way, in essence, is leaping clear of abundance and lack; thus there are birth and death, delusion and realization, sentient beings and buddhas."

And, when the monk asks what that means, old Mayu shows him: he plies the fan, or, as we in the West might say, he puts "his shoulder to the wheel"—he acts! And we can almost feel the fan's gentle breeze.

In these challenging, difficult times, when the way seems really rough, Dogen's counsel can help us to understand and function with compassion and vigorous action. These lines of the "Genjokoan" can inspire us to let our bodies be rafts to serve sentient beings. And how might we do this?

It is a time in which we are called to practice strongly, to sit zazen, and to hold the multiple truths that Dogen generously shares with us: we are ordinary beings, and life is filled with what we see, and also on another level, not-this and not-that; and yet, as we witness blossoms fall, as we witness the harming of people of difference, of color and gender and religion and wealth, the ravaging of the earth itself, the ascendance of hatred and violence, we must leap clear of our ideas, and act. Old Mayu is fanning, what is it we must do?

There have been many helpful English translations of the title "Genjokoan" (The Koan of Everyday Life, Actualizing the Fundamental Point, The Issue at Hand, the Realization Koan). In this historically difficult time, I'd like to add my own title: "Showing Up."

Dogen was willing to "Let [his] priest's body/ Be the raft to carry/ Sentient beings to the yonder shore." I wonder, if we can let our bodies and minds serve the many who are in desperate need in this challenging time? Are we "Showing Up"?

Notes

1. Steven Heine, *The Zen Poetry of Dogen* (Cambridge, MA: Tuttle, 1997), 106.
2. Steve Bein, *Watsuji Tetsuro's Purifying Zen* (Honolulu: University of Hawai'i Press, 2011), 47.
3. Kazuaki Tanahashi, *Treasury of the True Dharma Eye: Zen Master Dogen's Shobo Genzo* (Boston, MA: Shambhala Publications, 2010), 1:61.
4. Tanahashi, *Treasury of the True Dharma Eye*, 1:65.

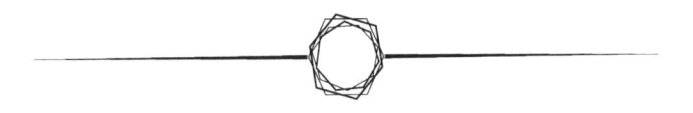

Konin Cardenas's current practice is to be the Guiding Teacher of Ekan Zen Study Center. She took up Zen in 1987, and was ordained into the Soto Zen tradition by Sekkei Harada Roshi in 2007. Konin trained at Hosshinji in Japan, at Tassajara Zen Mountain Center, and at San Francisco Zen Center's City Center, where she received dharma transmission in the Shunryu Suzuki lineage. Konin also teaches the dharma in Spanish and is trained as an interfaith chaplain to offer spiritual care in both hospital and hospice settings. She enjoys mothering her daughter.

Grappling with the Green-Eyed Monster
Konin Cardenas

A long, long time ago there was an illiterate Zen student who had been working in the kitchen and then, was promoted to abbot of a prestigious monastery overnight. The retiring abbot felt sure that this would cause a stir. So he sent the new abbot on a journey, on a long walk, and told him not to come back for several years. No doubt he thought that this would allow time for people to absorb the news. As expected, many of the other monks from the monastery were upset. They were so upset that hundreds of them actually set out in pursuit of the new abbot, to track him down, and retrieve the robe and bowl he'd been given as evidence of his new role.

This is the legend of Zen's Sixth Ancestor, Huineng, and the dharma transmission that he received from the Fifth Ancestor, Hongren. It is said to have occurred at East Mountain Temple in Huangmei county in China, during the Tang dynasty, in the late seventh century CE. The moments leading up to the transmission, and the dialogue that ensued when Huiming, the leader of the pursuing group, caught up to Huineng are recorded in the *Platform Sutra*. This ancient text has been studied for centuries, and you may find it just as relevant to Zen practice today.

Have you ever felt like one of the monks who went after the new abbot? Have you ever thought, "Who is this fool that landed that job?" Perhaps you have had the feeling that someone didn't deserve some special recognition they had received, or that they weren't qualified for some role for which they had been chosen. Maybe you have felt envy that someone you knew received a special gift or found that special life partner but you haven't. There is a lot of envy in the public discourse in contemporary Western society, people expressing dismay or upset or anger at the recognition given to others, or the gifts that are given to others. This is sometimes expressed as "critique," and it is sometimes expressed as "indignation" or "dismay." Yet, often, it is a form of envy.

Envy is defined by the *Merriam-Webster* dictionary as "the painful or resentful awareness of an advantage enjoyed by another, joined with a desire to possess the same advantage." Notice that the smart folks who compile the dictionary mention that pain is involved. Notice that they also acknowledge that envy has to do with the advantages and recognition we want for ourselves, regardless of whether we are actually able to obtain it. For this reason, envy has also been called "the green-eyed monster." When we are caught by envy, it can create deep suffering and states of mind that lead to other harmful thoughts, speech, and actions. Again, this process is clearly displayed in the public discourse, and is occasionally even celebrated. And it becomes truly sardonic when the critics cannot possibly obtain that which they envy.

So how can one practice skillfully with envy? A teaching from Shantideva, the eighth-century Indian Buddhist scholar, seems appropriate here. He taught:

> If you can solve your problem, then what is the use of despair?
>
> If you cannot solve it, then what is the use of despair?

That is, a skillful practitioner recognizes that envy is a personal judgment that rejects, or simply ignores, the present state of things. A practitioner may recognize that envy is based in a story about how things should be, according to one's own point of view. However, Shantideva's teaching suggests a different approach. Instead of being caught by the story, how would it be if you were to acknowledge the state of the present moment and seek an appropriate response to that? Can you do something about it? If so, then there is no need for envy, because you can set about doing that thing, or helping to put the conditions in place so that thing can be done in the future. Is there nothing you can do about it? If there is nothing that you can do, then there is even less reason to be caught by the story of what you think should be happening. You might simply see it as an idea, something that you can hold lightly. And because it is just an idea, you can choose whether to take that thought seriously or not. Thus, a skillful approach to practicing with envy begins by seeing that it is a feeling that arises because of inattention to, or a lack of acceptance of, present moment reality.

· · · · ·

But what happened to the new abbot and his pursuers? Were they able eventually to accept this new situation?

This part of Huineng's story is also recounted in the collection of koans titled No Barrier.(1) The word "koan" means "a public case or proclamation" and it is an abbreviation of the phrase "kofu no antoku," which referred to publicly declared legal decisions in ancient China. Therefore, the word has the connotation of something that applies to everyone. Today we might think of koans as precedents. They are cases from the past that are not exactly the same as our own case, but can nonetheless tell us something about how to practice with our own case. That is, they are pointers to a principle that is universally applicable because it is revealed in everyday life.

Here is Thomas Cleary's translation of the koan story that relates to Huineng and Huiming:

> When the Ancestor [Huineng] saw Huiming coming, he set down the robe and the bowl [that he had been given by the former abbot as proof of his succession to the abbacy of the monastery]. He said to Huiming, "This robe symbolizes faith; could it be right to fight over it? You can take it away."

This act is itself a profound teaching. It is a demonstration of Huineng's generosity with, and clarity about the Dharma. The robe symbolizes faith because it was said to be the very robe that the Buddha gave to Mahakasyapa as part of the first transmission of Dharma. Whether or not that story is historically accurate is not as important as the fact that, for many people inside and outside the monastery, the robe was very dear. One way to think about any Buddhist robe, monastic or lay, is that it represents deep trust—the trust between the teacher who gave it and the student who received it, the trust between the teacher and their teacher, and so on, stretching back for millennia. Clearly the new abbot's fellow practitioners lacked trust in the transmission that had occurred between him and their mutual teacher, Hongren. Thus, Huineng reminds his dharma brother of the trust that is implicit in the robe.

However, the pivotal teaching that Huineng demonstrates with this act is that it is neither the robe nor the bowl that make him the abbot. It is his unique, insightful expression of Dharma and the understanding of his own life as a complete teaching, that make him qualified to be the abbot. Thus, he can truthfully say that it is fine if Huiming or someone else were to take the robe. The robe doesn't make the person, in this case or ever. To put it another way, one cannot judge a person or their practice by their clothes. No matter how fancy the attire, or how modest, each person is a unique, momentary expression of the laws of interdependence. Regardless of personal history, one who truly understands that the clothes don't make the person, and can live that way, is unusual. This is one example of the teaching that the true nature of all things is formlessness. We would do well to remember this when encountering Buddhist teachers and people in every walk of life.

Huineng had a deep, experiential understanding of this, perhaps due to having lived such a humble life. His father had been a government official, but was later stripped of his position for reasons that are not now known. He and his family went from having the elevated social status accorded to those in positions of political authority, to being what Huineng would later call "commoners," people of no special rank. Then, as recounted in the *Platform Sutra*, when Huineng was three years old, his father died.(2) This meant that he and his mother experienced great hardships and poverty. They were so poor that Huineng sold firewood in the marketplace of Guangzhou City, rather than study, like other children his age. He was, therefore, illiterate. This also caused him difficulty because language arts and literary skill were highly valued in ancient China. Even when he entered the monastery, he was treated with very little respect and given heavy labor in the kitchen. Huineng had never had fancy clothes or a high status before his succession and, therefore, he knew that it wasn't necessary to have those things in order to realize the Way. He also knew that possessing things that indicate status does not necessarily mean that a person is aware of the Dharma they possess. He could see that very dilemma in his Dharma brothers who were higher in rank. For this reason, the contemporary Zen master Sekkei Harada teaches, "To be truly what you are without being jealous of someone else is what we call Buddha."(3)

Returning to the story:

> Huiming tried to pick up the robe but it was immovable, like a mountain. In fear, he said, "I have come for the teaching, not the robe. Please instruct me."

The pursuer has a sudden change of heart! He recognizes that he is feeling fear. And he allows the fear to be information, to be a signal that he should stop to consider what is happening. In retrospect, it seems natural that Huiming would be afraid at the moment of encountering his dharma brother. Seeing the robe and bowl may have reminded him that these items had been given to Huineng by their teacher, and that the succession has already happened. In fact, it may be at this point that Huiming realizes that he is doubting his own teacher's judgment by questioning the succession that has taken place. He also might be feeling fearful because, if he were to take the robe and bowl, he would be breaking his ethical vows. He was not named the successor. So even though Huineng has offered him the robe and bowls, they do not rightfully belong to him. To take them would be to take what is not given, a violation of the second of the grave precepts of the Zen school. Perhaps it is this very recognition of his own fear that turns Huiming toward the teaching, and away from breaking the precept vow. That would be a very skillful response, one that would reflect his years of practice.

At this moment, it seems that Huiming realizes that he cannot steal these venerated objects from Huineng. He cannot steal the role of abbot or the Dharma from Huineng. He cannot steal wisdom. Therefore, he wisely requests the Dharma, even though he is feeling fearful. Now, face to face with the reality of the situation and with his fear, he chooses a more skillful path.

> The Abbot [Huineng] said, "Not thinking good, not thinking evil, right at this very moment, what is your original face?"

This is the kernel of the koan. "Not thinking good, not thinking evil" is a pointer. It indicates that the response that brings forth the fullness of the Dharma is one that is free of dualistic judgments, one that sets aside the mental habit of dividing people or decisions into right and wrong. It points to the mind that recognizes the inherent harmony of all things. This harmony is always present because all things are interdependent. They must, by definition, fit together. It is not the harmony of good feelings he points to, but the harmony of the complete integration of conditions in each moment.

"Right at this very moment" is a pointer to the immediacy of the response. The manifestation of Dharma is not something that requires long years of study, is not repeating something that was learned in the past. Though it may be informed by study, it emerges spontaneously in the present. Simply put, we live in the moment now. We practice in the moment now. The complete Dharma resides in the moment now. The moment now is fully imbued with that which we are seeking. It is not something that emerges from dusty texts, awaits far off in the future, sits on a distant mountain, or hides in the folds of a particular robe.

The last part of the question is a pointer to the kind of Dharma expression that Huineng is trying to elicit. He asks to see Huiming's "original face." That is, Huineng is asking Huiming to demonstrate his buddha nature, the Dharma of great activity that harmoniously resolves all conditions in every instant. It is a function that is completely neutral, beyond any concept of good and evil, though not obstructing either good or evil. He asks Huiming to demonstrate a Dharma that is free of the constraints of personal identity, sometimes also known as "your face before your parents were born."

Continuing with the koan:

> In tears, Huiming bowed and asked, "Is there any meaning beyond the esoteric intent of the esoteric words you have just spoken?" The Abbot [Huineng] replied, "What I have just told you is not esoteric. If you turn your attention around to your own state, the secret is after all in you."

From Huiming's reply, it is clear that he has not fully penetrated Huineng's question, even though he is deeply moved by it. Here the word "esoteric" means "secret" or "private." Huiming's question implies that he has just received some special teaching from his Dharma brother, albeit one whose meaning is not yet fully clear to him. Huiming apparently believes he has now become an "insider," that he has been granted a secret word. He has gone from seeking a special robe to seeking a special teaching. It seems that he is still hoping to receive the Dharma from the outside, now a word rather than a garment, but still something that will give him more status than what he has. This is merely another version of the same mistaken view.

Immediately correcting this misunderstanding, Huineng replies by saying that the Dharma he has just shared is not a secret. It is not esoteric. It is a universal reality that is already equally present within Huiming, and everyone else for that matter. Huineng tells his dharma brother that he himself is the "secret teaching" that he seeks. This is true for all of us.

The special gift, the special recognition that you seek is already yours. Practice is to give it to yourself. It is simply a matter of turning your attention to align with your inherent integration with the true nature of all things. It is a matter of turning toward the activity of impermanence and emptiness that manifests as "you." Then there is no longer any need to feel envious of someone else's things or their position. You yourself have the most precious thing, the highest, most perfect Dharma. You yourself are a harmonious expression of the highest teaching. You have access to that if you are willing to make the effort to clarify the mind, and to stop looking for someone to hand the Dharma to you, or someone from whom to steal it. If you will turn your attention toward your own state of body and mind, it will show you that the special quality that you seek is integral to your everyday life.

Though there are certainly secret ceremonies and teachings you have not yet heard, those things will not enlighten you. There is no secret handshake or password or mantra that will make you a buddha. You are already of the nature of buddha, the crystal-clear awareness of reality and its principles. In fact, the verse that accompanies this koan says, "It is your true self; it has nowhere to hide." It is right in front of you, right within you, throughout you. Yet when you look for it to come from somewhere else, you won't find it. If you try to steal it from someone, you rob yourself of the chance to express it.

Does this mean that there aren't people who are unqualified for their jobs? No, sometimes a person is not qualified. However, even in that situation, you cannot take anything that is truly valuable from someone else. The most valuable thing in the world is the Dharma, and only you can find your own Dharma, with the support and trust of those who devote their lives to pointing it out to you. Having found the Dharma and living from that place, you can find a skillful response to a world that is subjectively imperfect, where people are not always suited to their role. Or perhaps, like Huiming, you will find that they are, but in ways that are not immediately apparent. Abiding in the Dharma, you can find a way to bring forth the generosity and clarity that meets the situation without thinking that you can, or need to, take something from someone else to become special.

Concluding the koan, Huiming told Huineng, "I am like a person who drinks water and knows for themselves whether it is hot or cold."

Now Huiming speaks as though he can appreciate his own experience and his Dharma brother's teaching. Having asked for the Dharma, he acknowledges having encountered it by saying he can know for himself the conditions that he encounters.

Zen is not an explanation, but a demonstration. Zen shows us a path of directly encountering that which is—in our mind or in our mouth, such as hot or cold water. It exhorts us to find the Dharma right where we are, in this very life. Zen demonstrates that our world, full of judgments and envy, cannot be made right by fighting or stealing, but by engaging with that which is already complete and harmonious. Thus, practice is a path of discovery, because taking what someone else has doesn't take the place of knowing your original face.

Notes

1. Thomas Cleary, *No Barrier: Unlocking the Zen Koan* (London: Aquarian Press; New York: Bantam, 1993), 110.
2. Andy Ferguson, *Zen's Chinese Heritage* (Somerville, MA: Wisdom Publications, 2000), 38.
3. Sekkei Harada, *The Essence of Zen* (Somerville, MA: Wisdom Publications, 2008), 59.

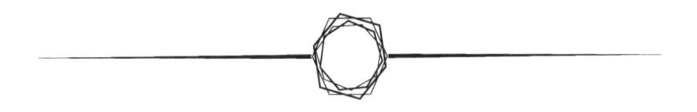

Diane Shoshin Fitzgerald, Sensei is a member of the Soto Zen Buddhist Association and the American Zen Teachers Association. Diane is a guiding teacher of the Boundless Way Zen school (boundlesswayzen.org) and the resident teacher of Zen DownEast in Pembroke, Maine (zendowneast.org), where the deep, cold Bay of Fundy, the towering spruce and pine, and a committed group of EcoSattvas create her home.

Finding Peace
Diane Shoshin Fitzgerald

As of this writing, war continues in Syria, Afghanistan, and Iraq. There are armed conflicts in Africa and Asia too numerous to list. The threat of a nuclear attack by North Korea or a preemptive strike by the United States fills us with dread. Russian aggression in Eastern Europe claims news headlines. Terrorist and "lone wolf" attacks throughout the world have become horrifyingly common. Species large and small are threatened with extinction in unprecedented numbers by habitat loss, climate change, pollution, and more. We find ourselves in an increasingly connected world that is at war with itself. I fear that even these atrocities may be eclipsed by something as yet unimaginable by the time you read this essay.

Throughout history, humans have battled each other and laid waste to massive areas of our incomparable planet. At the same time, most have longed for peace, and many in our Buddhist tradition have retreated to the natural world of mountains and waters to revive their broken spirits and open their hearts. Where can peace be found? Many Buddhist teachings, and those of Zen in particular, have responded to my own longing for peace, not in the way I expected but in a way that has come to sustain me. I have learned, however, that I also require the sustenance of the mountains and waters of which Zen Master Eihei Dogen so poetically wrote in the thirteenth century. To them I must retreat from time to time to remind me of who I am. With this essay, I hope to share with you some Buddhist teachings on cultivating peace that have changed my life and to encourage you to also find your sustenance in the natural, living world that surrounds and supports us all.

War in the world at large grows from the seeds of war within ourselves. The human tendency to divide self from other is deeply ingrained in most cultures, leading to endless categories of those with us and those against. Here in the United States, we find ourselves on either side of a seemingly unbridgeable political divide. President Trump's endless incendiary rhetoric stokes the passions of his supporters and detractors alike. Conflict pervades our daily life.

The war within pits not only self against other but also self against self. Feelings of alienation and loneliness are not new to human beings, yet their current manifestations—the opioid crisis and the spike in teen suicide to name just two—are heartbreaking. As adolescents spend more time alone in their rooms online, their unhappiness increases and life seems ever more unbearable. The longing for peace is acutely felt as the complete absence of even a moment of inner peace.

This longing for peace is what brings many people to Zen. The archetype for this longing might be case 41 from the *Gateless Gate* collection in which Huike, Zen's second ancestor in China, chops off his arm to demonstrate to his teacher, Bodhidharma, the depths of his longing for the master to pacify his mind.[1] Our longing can be just as sincere when we first encounter Zen. We envision a technique we might master to deliver us from our inner turmoil and outer conflict, imagining ourselves as that serene, robe-clad figure sitting silently in the light of the full moon as pictured in a Zen center's flyer.

I must confess to creating just such a flyer, which my students eventually come to realize is one of Zen's frequent bait-and-switch techniques that we who teach euphemistically call "skillful means." The flyer might be a technique for enticing future Zen students but there is no technique for finding peace. Instead of a technique, Zen offers a radical view of what peace might feel and look like and a radical view of how to cultivate it, none of which conforms to our conceptions of peace. It takes a bit of sincere practice to uncover that which can be learned but not taught, and a lifetime of practice to nourish and manifest it. While it is true that meditation practice, what we Zen Buddhists call zazen, can in fact make us feel calmer, more connected, more alive, and more resilient to life's many stressors, in Zen this is only the beginning of practice and not its purpose.

Zen invites us to discover much more and claims it is our birthright to do so.

When zazen is undertaken to achieve inner peace and reduce outer conflict, no matter how laudable these goals, the activity is inherently "dualistic" because it relies on a notion of a self that needs improvement (to become more peaceful) being judged by another self (that knows what that improvement looks like). This dualism creates the conditions for an internal war between the self that needs to be more peaceful and the imagined perfectly peaceful self. There might even be a third self engaged in this battle: the trainer self that imposes the regimen for attaining inner peace, like a marathon training coach. The hapless self, the perfect self, and the trainer self all engaged in struggle. A strategy such as this, born in conflict and separation, cannot possibly liberate us from our inner turmoil or guide us through an outer world of strife.

So, then, what does Zen offer as an alternative? Zen practice invites us to entertain the possibility that peace may not look the way we imagine it. Instead of trying to create a self that feels and acts more peaceful, Zen asks us to abandon our conception of a self at peace and consider the much more radical possibility that there may be no self that needs to find peace. Anything we imagine as "inner peace" may be nothing more than what the *Diamond Sutra* calls "a star in space, an illusion, a dewdrop, a bubble, a dream, a cloud, a flash of lightning."[2]

If we unhook ourselves from our idea of inner peace, we may find ourselves abandoning our strategies for achieving this constructed idea of peace. When we desist from conceptualizing what inner peace might look like, we can find ourselves in a place of profound not knowing. This state of not knowing can be very generative. Shunryu Suzuki Roshi famously called this state of profound not knowing "beginner's mind."[3] "In the beginner's mind there are endless possibilities," he said, "but in the expert's mind there are few."[4]

Having abandoned our idea of peace and our strategies for achieving it, we may find ourselves present to the ever-changing, groundless nature of being alive. What could this be like? We don't have a frame of reference for it. It's not about achieving some transcendent experience. Rather, it is about being alive to our life exactly as it is. Experiencing our life not as an observer but as part of it, as the whole of it. Is this "no self," or is it "everything is self"? It can't be pinned down by words.

Even our human frailty is part of it. Master Dogen wrote, "Therefore flowers fall even though we love them; weeds grow even though we dislike them."(5) Our regret, yearning, and wanting things to be otherwise are poignantly included, just like the flowers and weeds that cover the Earth. If we try to exclude violence and tragedy, we find ourselves back in the mode of trying to construct a reality from the safe distance of the observer even when we know it is the distance that brings us so much pain. When we risk vulnerability to life just as it is, truth can be realized in a moment of life springing forth unbidden. Then there's only the continuous dynamic functioning of life in which self and other are not two. The surprising thing is that this real, powerful and connected life is not different from the life we already have. This is the meaning of Zen's invitation to wake up—to wake up to our lives right here and now.

Being awake is a practice that requires cultivation. It seems we humans don't come by it naturally. We so easily become prisoners of our thoughts, opinions, judgments, and points of view, all of which water the seeds of divisiveness and duality, pitting me against you and us against the world. The principle practice that Zen offers us so we may see through this divisiveness and duality is zazen. Who would have thought silent sitting could cultivate our innate capacity to wake up to our lives? Lucky for us, the Buddha did. In *shikantaza* (just sitting), we manifest that which defies conceptualization and strategizing. We and the universe sit and awaken together. A regular sitting practice is indispensable to waking up and we are the fortunate beneficiaries of more than 2,500 years of devoted Buddhist teachers, including those whose essays comprise this book, offering their instruction in zazen, in *shikantaza*, in the Buddha Way. I hope you will turn to them, as I have, to receive their generous teachings and be inspired by their example.

I have found that my own sitting practice, alone and together with my dharma sisters and brothers, is deepened by regularly immersing myself in the natural world that surrounds and supports us. I find I require the sustenance of the mountains and water of which Master Dogen wrote in his "Mountains and Water Sutra."(6)

Blending the metaphorical and concrete meanings of mountains and water, Master Dogen leads me to where I must retreat from time to time to remind me of who I am. The imperative to do this seems ever more urgent to me in today's chaotic world, but I realize that many in our Buddhist tradition have for millennia retreated to the natural world to revive their broken spirits and open their hearts. "Chan," the Chinese word from which the Japanese "Zen" is derived, literally means to bow before mountains and water.(7) Zen temples and monasteries in Japan were typically sited on a mountain with a powerful stream passing by. Japanese tea houses were mountain outposts that had entrances so small that one's sword had to be removed to gain entry. When one enters the tea house, or the mountain, it becomes a realm of no rulers, a realm of no ego.

The life-giving and life-sustaining mountains and water are not just a respite from a world of struggle and suffering, but offer us gentle teachings when we enter them fully. Master Dogen tells us, "Mountains belong to people who love them."(8) When we immerse ourselves in the natural world, wherever that may be, it's hard not to love it; it's hard not to feel the rightness of the world that we had so recently dismissed as wrong to the core. "When mountains love their master," Dogen writes, "such a virtuous sage or wise person enters the mountains."(9) The mountains confer on us their love and wisdom and in so doing, Master Dogen tells us, "The sages and wise people extend their virtue."(10) We become the voice of the mountain and the mountain becomes our soul. It is reciprocal. Together we awaken. The water, too, opens our eyes. Come see, says Master Dogen: "Even in a drop of water innumerable buddha lands appear."(11) We make the aliveness of water, the aliveness of the Buddha Way, our own. "Where buddha ancestors reach," Dogen reassures us, "water never fails to appear. Because of this, buddha ancestors always take up water and make it their body and mind, make it their thought."(12) The natural world offers us a chance to transcend our illusion of separateness and come to understand something about our lives that we may not be able to articulate but which we feel most deeply. The mountains and water teach us to open our hearts without fear because we are none other than them: powerful, resilient, flexible and unknowable. We wake up to who we are.

Does it seem too facile to suggest that waking up to our lives can be the answer to the overwhelming suffering in the world today? To be sure, waking up is not about blissing out on one's zafu or only roaming through the wilderness. Waking up calls us to the life of the bodhisattva, the one who takes compassionate care of the world and its many beings. May we all do what is in our power to reduce suffering and act from the realization that we are not separate from all that is. As we engage wholeheartedly and often broken-heartedly with a world at war, may we also remember to cultivate peace within. It would be hard to find a better spokesperson for this than His Holiness the Dalai Lama, who conveyed this sentiment with beautiful simplicity in his keynote address at the University of California, San Diego commencement: "You have the opportunity and also the responsibility to create a better world, peaceful and a happier world. In order to do that, we must first have inner peace. World peace must be achieved through inner peace and not through weapon."(13)

Notes

1. Wumen Huikai and Koun Yamada, trans., *The Gateless Gate: The Classic Book of Zen Koans* (Somerville, MA: Wisdom Publications, 2004).

2. Red Pine, *The Diamond Sutra* (Berkeley, CA: Counterpoint, 2001).

3. Shunryu Suzuki, *Zen Mind, Beginner's Mind* (Boulder, CO: Shambhala Publications, 2011), 1.

4. Suzuki, *Zen Mind, Beginner's Mind*, 1.

5. Shohaku Okumura, *Realizing Genjokoan* (Somerville, MA: Wisdom Publications, 2010), 47.

6. Kazuaki Tanahashi, ed., *Moon in a Dewdrop: Writings of Zen Master Dogen* (New York: North Point Press, 1985), 97.

7. Carl Bielefeldt, *On the Spiritual Discourses of the Mountains and the Water*, www.thezensite.com/ZenTeachings/Dogen_Teachings/Shobogenzo/013sansuiKyo.pdf.

8. Tanahashi, *Moon in a Dewdrop*, 105.

9. Tanahashi, *Moon in a Dewdrop*, 105.

10. Tanahashi, *Moon in a Dewdrop*, 105.

11. Tanahashi, *Moon in a Dewdrop*, 103.

12. Tanahashi, *Moon in a Dewdrop*, 103.
13. Tenzin Monlam, "Inner Peace, Not Weapons to Achieve World Peace," quoting a talk given at University of California San Diego, June 18, 2017, by the Dalai Lama, www.phayul.com/news/tools/print.aspx?id=39168&t=1.

Myoshin Kate McCandless is the co-guiding teacher of Mountain Rain Zen Community in Vancouver, British Columbia, Canada. She received dharma transmission in the lineage of Shunryu Suzuki Roshi from her teacher Zoketsu Norman Fischer in 2011. She began Soto Zen practice in Japan with Shohaku Okumura, and has done residential practice at Green Gulch and Tassajara Zen Mountain Zen Mountain Center, as well as Great Vow Monastery. She has worked as an organic farmer, a teacher of English, a translator, and a hospice/bereavement counselor. Myoshin has contributed to the anthologies *Seeds of Change: A Collection of Zen Teachings* (Temple Ground Press, 2014) and *The Hidden Lamp: Stories from Twenty-Five Centuries of Awakened Women* (Wisdom, 2013), and has translated the haiku poetry of Mitsu Suzuki in *A White Tea Bowl: One Hundred Haiku from a Century of Life* (Ronsdale Press, 2014).

Beings are Numberless: When Bodhisattvas Get Discouraged

Myoshin Kate McCandless

> To live in this world
>
> you must be able
> to do three things:
> to love what is mortal;
> to hold it
>
> against your bones knowing
> your own life depends on it;
> and, when the time comes to let it go,
> to let it go.
>
> —Mary Oliver, from "In Blackwater Woods"[1]

I worry about plankton. I worry about albatrosses. I worry about the oceans. When I was young we learned in school that the ocean was a limitless resource that could feed the world. This claim can no longer be made. I worry about the people living in refugee camps around the world who are not getting enough to eat. I worry about the children, and what kind of world we'll be leaving them. I'm sure I'm in good company in my worry. Probably you have many worries, too. I once heard my Zen teacher, Zoketsu Norman Fischer, read a very long poem about worry. It took him more than ten minutes to list all the things he worries about, and he still wasn't finished.

• • • • •

In May of 2016, Michael, my partner and coteacher, and I guided a group of twenty Zen practitioners on a three-week trip to Japan. Before the group arrived, we spent two days wandering the narrow back streets of Kyoto, attending an annual international photography festival called Kyotographie. The fifteen venues, from ultramodern galleries, to ancient Zen temples, to beautiful old *machiya*, traditional merchant homes, added ambiance to the exhibitions. The theme for the 2016 festival was the circle of life: "A Circle is the ultimate system, the perfect emblem. Tracing the birth, life and death of all nature's creations, everything connects—intersecting, expanding, creating powerful patterns, showing us the fragility and beauty of our existence."[2] The images still haunt me, stir me, worry me. I invite you to come with us.

Plankton: a microcosmic aquatic world of floating, drifting lifeforms: bacteria, algae, archaea, protozoa, tiny jellies, and crustacean larvae. In the enlarged backlit photos of Christian Sardet at the Kyoto Municipal Museum, they are stunningly beautiful. Spined, filamentous, segmented, diaphanous, iridescent. Plankton provide food directly for sea creatures from other planktonic forms to the largest being on earth, the great blue whale, and indirectly to many forms of fish, sea mammals, birds, and humans. Phytoplankton, one-celled plants capable of photosynthesis, produce half of the oxygen we breathe. Like the great forests, they serve as the lungs of the earth.

Plankton are in trouble. They multiply or "bloom" in cycles dependent on an intricate balance of conditions including water temperature and acidity. As CO_2 levels rise in the oceans, acidity falls, causing some types of plankton to be unable to form their calcium shells, and others to produce nonviable eggs. If plankton populations crash, or blooms occur in new locations, or at altered times, the entire food chain is affected.[3]

Albatrosses are in trouble, too. The next Kyotographie venue we find is the Kondaya Genbei Kurogura, the "black storehouse" in the rear of the premises of a tenth-generation obi (kimono sash) merchant. The storehouse is plastered in black mortar, beautifully restored as a gallery space. Walking down the dark entrance hall, we see portrait after portrait of albatross chick corpses, lying in the sand of the Pacific island of Midway—at the center of each desiccated body a jumble of multicolored plastic flotsam: bottle caps, string, fragments, ringed by matted feathers, beaks, and bones. The parent birds skimmed the plastic junk from the surface of the ocean and fed their chicks until their stomachs could hold no more and they died of starvation. The photographer, Chris Jordan, was drawn to Midway to make a pilgrimage of witness. He writes, "I see it as a message, like a kind of poem, coming from Earth herself, a message that is not easy to receive because it is so shocking and sad."(4) As we walk down the hallway, stopping before each portrait, tears stream down my face. This is a whole body/mind/heart response.

Albatrosses are long-lived, but are slow breeders, producing only one chick annually or biennially, and not beginning to breed until they are three to four or even as old as fifteen. They are severely threatened by entanglement in fishing lines, invasive species, oil spills—and plastic debris.(5) Of the twenty-two species of albatrosses in the world, eight are classified by the International Union for Conservation of Nature as critically endangered or endangered, and the rest as vulnerable or near-threatened.(6)

We step into the round body of the storehouse, darkened, except for glowing lamps created by designer and artist Jurgen Lehl, who lived for forty years on the Okinawan island of Ishigaki. He made these lamps of plastic debris found on his daily beach walks.

> Sometimes, to my delight, I happen on an old glass float, but mostly, what I find is ugly plastic debris . . . pieces of styrene foam, plastic bottle caps, detergent receptacles, cheap toys, and so on. Some of this trash is Japanese and some has drifted ashore from other Asian countries. Whenever I find it, I pick it up, but the next day I find more.
>
> Eventually I came up with the idea of collecting all this trash, sorting it by color, and creating something with it. I wanted people to know . . . so much trash washes ashore. I can fabricate things with it. The other day, when traveling, I had a chance to visit the beach at Yonaguni. While walking in the sand, I had the oddest feeling something was not right. Thrusting my hand into the sand, I scooped some up to inspect it and got a shock. Mixed in with the sand, were countless particles of plastic, about the same size as the sand grains. It looked like a beautiful beach from afar, but this is

what it had become. We human beings had done this. It was the end of civilization . . . the thought struck me with real force. . . . If I can do something to make people aware of this, now is the time to act. . . . I consider this my last job in life.(7)

Jurgen Lehl died September 23, 2014, in an accident on the island he loved. The lamps glowing in the black storehouse are remarkably suggestive of plankton drifting in the dark seas.

Plastic does not biodegrade; it only breaks down into smaller and smaller particles. Scientists do not yet know the consequences of plankton ingesting these infinitesimal particles of plastic.(8) We humans have only been using plastic since the 1950s, and yet by 2014 international scientists "determined that 5.25 trillion particles of 'plastic smog' surface pollution—weighing in at 269,000 tons—pollute our oceans worldwide."(9) It is carried on ocean currents, accumulating in five massive gyres, and dispersing like smoke in the air. Today scientists scramble to research the effects of plastic pollution on marine ecosystems, and NGOs strive to educate the public, so that we can take individual and collective measures to mitigate and halt the damage. There are those who say, what's all this concern about albatrosses? Don't you care about humans? Some species just can't compete. Survival of the fittest—that's the way evolution works. And plankton will adapt—they've been around for millions of years. Or we'll engineer microbes that can digest plastic. Don't worry! But these images bring the message home: our fate is not separate from the fate of plankton and albatrosses.

· · · · ·

Continuing along the narrow streets of Kyoto, we come to the Mumeisha, a 107-year-old former fabric merchant's *machiya* residence. We remove our shoes in the stone-paved entryway, and step up into the former showroom. The exhibit here is called "Exile: 1945 to Today," the work of photographers from Magnum, the world's most prestigious photographic agency. One of the photographers, Larry Towell, writes, "Land makes people what they are. Of that I am sure. If they lose it, they forfeit their solvency and a little bit of their souls, which they will spend the rest of their lives trying to regain."(10)

We pass the courtyard garden, and into the dimly lit residential wing, a long tatami-floored room opening onto the inner garden at one end, flanked by shoji screens. Down the middle of the room is a long, narrow platform, with black, reflective plexiglass sides. The upper surface is lit from below, illuminating photos mounted on wood blocks of different sizes, each bearing an image of displaced men, women, and children in locations all over the world, from every decade since World War II. As you move slowly through the exhibit, pick up each block with both hands, as though holding a precious tea bowl, or as though you were a helpless god, witnessing the consequences of human greed, hatred, and ignorance. Look carefully, feeling your breath, your body, your response, then turn the block around to read the caption: the year, the place, the people. Syrians, French, Germans, Palestinians, Ethiopians, Guatemalans, men, women, the very young, the very old. Raise each block up with a silent prayer before placing it back.

It's becoming more and more evident that climate change, and ecological disruption contribute to political, economic and social instability. The fate of plankton and albatrosses is not separate from that of displaced people. "Look carefully with unaverted eyes: they are not somewhere far off beyond our realm of concern; they are our reality as well."(11)

• • • • •

We continue, zig-zagging through the back-streets of Kyoto, arriving on a wide thoroughfare at the Horikawa Oike Gallery, part of a public facility supporting school arts programs. The show is called "The First Hour," by French photographer, Thierry Bouet. We enter through a narrow aperture into a large white circular room, surrounded by larger-than-life-sized images of faces of infants within minutes of their birth. They look a little mashed and wrinkled, with traces of vernix, that waxy substance that protects the skin in the womb and lubricates the baby as it passes through the birth canal. They are so newly alive! I wonder what kind of world this will be when they are my age, sixty-five years from now. I can't help but worry about that.

Zen Teachings In Challenging Times

· · · · ·

In Buddhist practice, we balance compassion with equanimity, so an excess of worry would suggest an imbalance, or an attachment to outcome, wanting things to be other than they are. But it's hard not to worry about the great harm we humans are doing to each other, this planet and the other beings that cohabit it. The bodhisattva vows we chant daily commit us to saving numberless beings, ending inexhaustible delusions, entering boundless dharma gates, and embodying the unsurpassable Buddha way. How could we not be utterly humbled and daunted by such aspirations? Even bodhisattvas become discouraged sometimes.

The classic Mahayana Buddhist archetype of the bodhisattva is a being who eschews the personal enlightenment of the arhat, and opts to stay in the world of *samsara* helping other beings, until all beings are free from suffering. I have come to feel that the bodhisattva is one who deeply realizes that awakening can only occur within a matrix of interconnection with other beings. When we consciously set forth on the path of the bodhisattva, we vow not to turn away from suffering. We know that the roots of our own suffering are completely intertwined with the suffering of all other beings.

This is a radical commitment to make in a culture that conditions us in so many ways *to* turn away, to distract ourselves with the many baubles of consumer culture, with food, mind-altering substances, work, sex, Netflix, social media . . . . The news media bombard us with images and information of a scope and quantity unprecedented in human history. How can we apprentice bodhisattvas not be overwhelmed and paralyzed in the face of such magnitude?

> This earth will grow cold,
> a star among stars
>   and one of the smallest,
> a gilded mote on blue velvet—
>   I mean *this*, our great earth.
> This earth will grow cold one day,
> not like a block of ice
> or a dead cloud even
> but like an empty walnut it will roll along
>   in pitch-black space . . .
> You must grieve for this right now

> —you have to feel this sorrow now—
> for the world must be loved this much
> if you're going to say "I lived"...
> —Nazim Hikmet, from "On Living"(12)

The ancient sages could not possibly have imagined the world we live in today, but they were well-acquainted with the kinds of human suffering that still concern us: famine, disease, natural disasters; the dislocations, losses and damages of war; the harms of human cruelty and injustice. The wisdom traditions of the East recognized that world systems are born, rise, fall, and come to an end. And yet the bodhisattva does not use that long view as a rationale for indifference.

Vimalakirti, the great legendary layman sage and teacher has some encouragement to offer us. He is said to have lived at the time of the Buddha and been renowned for the depths of his understanding. In the *Vimalakirti Sutra*, he is depicted lying ill in his home, as the Buddha tries to persuade first his disciples, and then various bodhisattvas to pay a call on Vimalakirti and see how he is. One after another they protest, each giving an account of an incident when he was teaching the dharma and Vimalakirti came along and completely showed him up with the power of his insight and skill. Each one is too intimidated to call on Vimalakirti. Finally, Manjushri, the bodhisattva of wisdom, agrees, despite his own hesitancy.

Manjushri asks Vimalakirti about his illness, just like we do when a friend is ill: How are you doing? How long have you been sick? What's the treatment? How's it going? What's the prognosis? But Vimalakirti gives an unexpected answer. He declares that his illness is born of human ignorance and craving, that he is ill because all beings are ill. When all beings are free from suffering, his illness will be healed. Because bodhisattvas enter this realm of birth and death, they suffer illness.

How do we, as apprentice bodhisattvas, undertake to care for all beings? When Manjushri asks Vimalakirti how a bodhisattva should regard living beings, he replies, "As the wise view the moon in the water, or a face or form seen in a mirror; as shimmers of heat in a torrid season, as the echo that follows a cry, as clouds in the sky, as foam on the water, bubbles on the water, as a thing no firmer that the trunk of the plantain, no longer lasting than a flash of lightning."(13)

But Manjushri is puzzled. If we regard living beings in this way, how can we treat them with lovingkindness? I've been asked this question by Zen practitioners, particularly those who are parents. "Am I supposed to be so nonattached that I don't care about my child? How can I not care?" T. S. Eliot, after the horrors of World War I, the despair of his postwar poems, and his subsequent conversion to Anglicanism, cried out:

> Blessed sister, holy mother, spirit of the fountain, spirit of the garden,
> Suffer us to mock ourselves with falsehood.
> Teach us to care and not to care.
> Teach us to sit still.
> —From "Ash Wednesday"(14)

He was seeking for how to actualize his newfound faith, just as we do when we come to dharma practice.

• • • • •

Vimalakirti teaches us how to care with the love of a bodhisattva:

> He treats living beings with a love that never despairs, seeing that all is empty and without ego; treats them with the love of bestowal of the Dharma, never stinting in its gifts; treats them with the love of observance of the precepts, training those who break them to do better; treats them with the love of forbearance, guarding both others and self; treats them with the love of assiduousness, shouldering all beings as its burden; treats them with the love of meditation, unaffected by taste; treats them with the love of wisdom, which always knows the right time; treats them with the love of expedient means, with manifestations suited to every occasion.
>
> He treats them with a love that hides nothing, proceeding with the purity of an upright mind; treats them with the love of a deeply searching mind, one free of irrelevant motion; treats them with a love that is unerring, innocent of falsity and sham; treats them with a love full of peace and delight,

for through it they gain the delight of the Buddha. Such is the love of the bodhisattva.(15)

Vimalakirti is reminding Manjushri, as we all need reminding, of the bodhisattva's toolkit of practices, the paramitas: generosity, morality/ethics, patience, energy, meditative concentration, wisdom, and skillful means, as well as the *brahma viharas* (noble abodes): loving-kindness and compassion, joy and equanimity. We need to cultivate all these qualities and capacities, because they support and balance each other, when our practice gets off-kilter.

Vimilakirti tells us that to follow the Buddha way the bodhisattva must be able to live in all realms of human experience, to feel the entire gamut of human emotions, without becoming ensnared in self-clinging. He assures us that "the seeds of enlightenment are the body and the six senses; greed, aversion and ignorance; the five hindrances. The lotus does not grow on the upland plain; the lotus grows in the mud and mire of a damp low-lying place."(16) This very life, here and now, is the ground of our awakening. Feet rooted in the earth, heart as wide as the world, mind boundless.

In a passage I find deeply moving Manjushri asks Vimalakirti, "How should a bodhisattva go about comforting and instructing another bodhisattva who is ill?"

Vimalakirti replies,

> Tell him about the impermanence of the body, but do not tell him to despise or turn away from the body. Tell him about the sufferings of the body, but do not tell him to strive for nirvana. Tell him that the body is without ego, but urge him to teach and guide living beings. Tell him of the emptiness of the body, but do not tell him of its final extinction. Tell him to repent of former offenses, but do not tell him to consign them to the past. Tell him to use his own illness as a means of sympathizing with the illness of others . . . . Tell him to recall the good fortune he has won through religious practice, to concentrate on a life of purity, and not to give way to gloom or worry. He should cultivate constant diligence, striving to become a king of physicians who can heal the ailments of the assembly. This is how a bodhisattva should comfort and instruct a bodhisattva who is ill so as to make him feel happy.(17)

This is what we must do for each other as good bodhisattva companions, we must give comfort and encouragement.

• • • • •

You might wonder why I've used examples from a photography festival in a distant country to frame this discussion of how to do the bodhisattva's work of saving all beings. I could just as easily have talked about the events and issues that have been very present in my awareness in recent months: the hurricanes that devastated the Caribbean; the record-breaking wildfires that raged here in British Columbia during the summer, and continued in northern California even in October; the opioid epidemic claiming thousands of lives; the ongoing racism, violence, and hatred in the United States; the thousands of asylum seekers who have poured across the Canadian border from the U.S., some having lived there for years, now fearful of being deported, others having traveled thousands of miles, from Africa, to Europe, to South America, and the U.S.A., aiming for Canada as a place of refuge, which it may or may not turn out to be.

When events are hot and current in the news, we often limit our exposure to those images and stories. Not because we don't care, but out of fear of being disabled by caring, or fear of being numbed into disconnection. Sometimes it takes stepping aside from our everyday to-do list and receiving the work of an artist, poet, photographer, or musician to jolt us awake—body, heart, and mind at once. That's why I wanted to pay tribute to the bodhisattva work of the Kyotographie photographers. Others right now are making poetry, art, and plans for action in response to this year's events. Some are sitting in stillness, practicing full awareness of body, heart and mind, not turning away.

> My heart is moved by all I cannot save:
> so much has been destroyed
> I have to cast my lot with those
> who age after age, perversely,
> with no extraordinary power
> reconstitute the world.
> —Adrienne Rich, from "Natural Resources"[18]

• • • • •

Each of us will respond to the world around us in a different way. We are the arms of the thousand-armed Kanzeon (Kuanyin), bodhisattva of compassion, she who hears the cries of the world. Each hand has an eye in the center of its palm, to see the suffering of numberless beings, and each hand has a different tool with which to respond. This past year at our Zen center, we had a series of twenty-minute talks by sangha members about how they take their practice into the world. We called them ZED talks (Zen Engaged Dharma), and each one was different: teaching mindfulness in an inner-city school, engaging in activism: antipipeline, antihighway, probicycle; teaching nature awareness to children; supporting sustainable forestry in Hawaii for fine hardwoods used in guitar making; cultivating wholesome workplace communication; making art that weaves community building and activism together. We found the ZED talks inspiring and encouraging. In these troubled times, it's too easy to succumb to the bleak narratives of the news media, and fail to see the courage, integrity, and beauty with which people in our own communities and everywhere are working to reconstitute the world. We do this work through the way of action and the way of nonaction, with the wisdom to know when to act and speak, and when to be still. Never underestimate the gift of a quiet, calm mind in times of fear and struggle.

When we are overwhelmed by all we cannot save, we can take heart in our good companions on the Way, and be reminded of the obvious, that no one can save the world, or awaken, alone. We are not helpless gods, we are humans embodied on and of this earth. And though we often do not believe it, we are never helpless. Our help lies in Buddha, Dharma, and—hardest to remember—Sangha, the numberless beings we vow to save.

Notes

1. Mary Oliver, *American Primitive* (New York: Little, Brown, 1983), 82.
2. L. Reyboz and Y. Nakanishi, *Kyotographie 2016 Catalogue* (Kyoto: Kyotographie, 2016), 3.
3. Alanna Mitchell, *Seasick: The Global Ocean in Crisis* (Toronto: McLelland & Stewart, 2009), 69.
4. Reyboz and Nakanishi, *Kyotographie 2016*, 103.
5. Christopher Perrin, ed., *The Firefly Encyclopedia of Birds* (Richmond Hill, Ontario: Firefly Books, 2003), 66–67.
6. International Union for Conservation of Nature, *The IUCN Redlist of Endangered Species*, www.iucnredlist.org, 2017.
7. Reyboz and Nakanishi, *Kyotographie 2016*, 104
8. Five Gyres Institute, *5 Gyres*, www.5gyres.org, 2017.
9. Alan Weisman, "Polymers Are Forever," *Orion Magazine*, May 2007, 19.
10. Reyboz and Nakanishi, *Kyotographie 2016*, 105.
11. Reyboz and Nakanishi, *Kyotographie 2016*, 139.
12. Nazim Hikmet, *Poems of Nazim Hikmet*, trans. R. Blasing and M. K. Blasing (New York: Persea, 2002), 133–34.
13. Burton Watson, trans., *The Vimalakirti Sutra* (New York: Columbia University Press, 1997), 83.
14. T. S. Eliot, *Collected Poems, 1909–1962* (New York: Harcourt, Brace & World, 1963), 95.
15. Watson, *The Vimalakirti Sutra*, 84–85.
16. Watson, *The Vimalakirti Sutra*, 95.
17. Watson, *The Vimalakirti Sutra*, 67–68.
18. Adrienne Rich, *The Dream of a Common Language* (New York: W. W. Norton, 1978), 67.

Tenku Ruff trained in Zen monasteries in Japan and North America. She ordained as a Soto Zen priest under Tessai Yamamoto Roshi, abbot of Kannonji Temple in Morioka, Japan, and received dharma transmission in the same lineage. On *Rohatsu* 2012 Tenku completed the Shikoku eighty-eight-temple pilgrimage, dedicating the merit to patients who died from cancer in her hospital and to victims of the 2011 Great East Japan earthquake and tsunami. Tenku holds a master of divinity degree from Maitripa College and she is also a board-certified chaplain. Tenku has strong interests in teaching, all facets and disciplines of ethics, and inter-Buddhist/interfaith collaboration, education, and support.

Karkinos: The True Crab
Tenku Ruff

In Zen temples, as we come to the close of the day sitting in deep, still evening silence, one monk arises from zazen, moves silently toward the *moppan*, a wooden sounding block, and strikes it four times. The sharp, clear clack fills the hall, fills our bodies, and wakes us up. The monk calls out:

> May I respectfully remind you:
> Great is the matter of birth and death.
> All is impermanent, quickly passing.
> Wake up! Wake up!
> Do not squander your life!

At the end of zazen, at the end of the day, the call gives us a sense of solemn urgency. It calls us out of end-of-the-day wandering and brings us back to the present moment. We will soon go to sleep, or perhaps we will brush our teeth and return to zazen. For how long?

This moment is one of my favorite parts of the day. The *moppan* and the chanting that follows sound so true, so beautiful, so poignant. In deep winter, as our breath clouds the zendo, it is even more so.

Every night when we go to sleep, we die. And every morning, we awaken. The *moppan* reminds us never to become complacent, even in sleep, even as we wake up. Each moment is life and death.

As urgent as the great matter is though, complacency always hovers around our peripheral vision, like sleep, Facebook, or low grumblings about inconsequential slights. Contemplation of our own death staves off this complacency and imbues us with the truth of impermanence. The Buddha taught monks to cultivate mindfulness by meditating with corpses on the charnel grounds. My teacher encourages people to do zazen in the cemetery, especially at night, when darkness hides ghosts, animals, and falling leaves equally. In the modern world, we don't get many opportunities to witness death. The closest I have come is through my work as an end-of-life-care chaplain.

As a chaplain, I have sat with countless people as they prepare to leave this precious human life. Sometimes we talk about what they are going through. Sometimes, we sit in silence. Sometimes we do zazen together. Sometimes, people are in great pain or fear, and I hold their hand or press my palm to their shoulder, allowing them to be exactly as they are, exactly in that moment. Complacency does not come easily when contemplating death. Impending death, like the sound of the *moppan*, imparts a strong sense of urgency.

Oncology is the area in which I feel most at home as a chaplain. Cancer is a mystical, cryptic illness. Cancer is not even one thing, but many illnesses, huddled tightly under one umbrella. Often, I call it an existential illness because it raises so many unanswerable questions. Why me? What did I do? What did I not do? Why did this happen? How come my brother Bob smokes two packs a day and I've never smoked, but I'm the one who got lung cancer? Is God/the Universe/Allah punishing me? Will the cancer come back? (When?) Where am I going? Is death the end? Does anything really matter? These types of questions are the sea in which Zen priests swim freely.

When I worked on the oncology floor of a large hospital, deaths occurred nearly every day. Even so, it is surprising how rare it is to be present at the moment of death. Sometimes deaths come suddenly and catch us unprepared. In the hospital, especially on hospice, death often comes very, very slowly. Families get tired and hungry, yet they're afraid that the one hour when they leave for a quick lunch in a nearby restaurant will be the exact hour that their loved one dies. Often, it happens exactly in this way.

I have supported innumerable patients and families through the trajectory of cancer. Three of four of my grandparents died of cancer. My parents have both had cancer. In the hospital I meet the people who return, rather than the ones who do not, so my perspective is a bit skewed, but I know what the word "cancer" feels like to most who hear it. Even though about two-thirds of the people who get cancer will not die from it, the word "cancer" evokes deep fear. When people hear "cancer" they hear "death."

Recently, I heard the word "cancer" in relation to myself. I didn't hear it out loud, because, like the word "death," people avoid saying it. What I heard was the word "biopsy" and that I needed to have one. Inside my head, I heard "death."

I had gone to the hospital for a yearly mammogram, which my doctor recommended and I had resisted. Mammograms are unpleasant and their efficacy is disputed. After having my breasts pulled, pushed, and painfully pressed into a cold metal machine, the tech directed me to another room for a breast ultrasound, which I also grumbled about. I lay on the exam table, nervously studying the tech's face for nonverbal clues. There were none. I tried talking with her, joking a bit, and attempted to draw out information on what she saw. She was kind, but told me she was not allowed to share anything.

Next, the tech escorted me into the doctor's office. I felt a bit annoyed, thinking about the injustice of being subject to an examination I didn't want, being scared for no reason, and wasting time, money, and medical resources. I am generally healthy and a low risk for breast cancer. It is impossible to say "no" though, when "What if?" hovers around the edges of the room.

To my great surprise, my doctor recommended a breast biopsy. I pushed back. She showed me my ultrasound and the area in question. I saw a blur indistinguishable from any other blur in the picture. My mind couldn't take it in. I wanted to cry and felt silly for the urge to do so. I flipped into professional mode and asked intelligent questions in a direct voice. Finally, I sighed, looked into the doctor's eyes, asked her to put her papers down. "What does your gut say?" I asked.

"Benign," she answered firmly and immediately.

"Then why are we doing this?" I pushed.

"Because of the chance it isn't."

"What's the risk of not doing it?"

"You could have cancer," she responded.

That ended the conversation. The chance was small, but I could have cancer. And if so, I might not start treatment fast enough and the cancer could spread until it became untreatable. I could die.

Why should death be such a scary thing, when no living being is exempt from it? I have faced death in my zazen practice. I have met death with patients and families. I have intentionally cultivated awareness of death. Indeed, I often remark that hospice work is a Buddhist three-for-one bargain—sickness, old-age, and death under one roof. Honestly, I am not afraid of death. I have experienced the great profundity and mystery of the moment of death. As one Zen teacher once told me, "It has a quality not unlike *sesshin*."

The moment of death is deeply profound. The moment of death teaches us something neither describable in words nor understood with our thinking mind. The moment of death is the sharp "Wake up!" of the *moppan* and the deep stillness of a winter evening zendo, intertwined.

When facing death or sitting zazen, it is important to drop what we know and return to not-knowing, over and over. The absolute truth lives in the moment of not-knowing; knowing tends to come from our ego-self and is not good for much. Becoming comfortable with not knowing is the path to a deeper, warmer, belly awareness of what truly is.

At Hosshinji Monastery, Harada Sekkei Roshi told us, "If you understand something, then throw it away. If you don't understand, then throw that away. Throw away anything you have understood. If you think, 'I understand,' you are still hanging on to the concept of 'understand.' Let go of understanding. And then let go of letting go."

We humans constantly think we know something. Yet, it is often in the precise moment that we think "Aha! I understand!" that complacency comes creeping in from the sides. Complacency prevents depth in our practice, but we don't realize we have fallen into the trap until the sharp, clear sound of the *moppan* calls us back to the present moment.

> Clack! Clack! Clack!
> Let me respectfully remind you . . .

Learning how cancer works in the body, understanding prognostication, consulting with doctors and nurses, and sitting with people through their journeys may have led me to a sideways inkling that I understood cancer, at least on some level. I do not. The thing I most appreciate about cancer is its inability to be known.

    Biopsy. [Clack!]
    Let me respectfully remind you . . .

When I first started chaplaincy, the head of oncology told me never to judge the way patients and families respond to cancer because you never know how you'll react when it happens to you. She always thought she would be strongly against aggressive treatment, but when her time came, to her utter astonishment, she heard herself calling out, "I'll do anything, just don't let me die!" Similarly, Zen masters have whispered, "I don't want to die!" to students gathered around, waiting for one last drop of wisdom. We may think we understand death, but when the actual moment comes, there's no telling what we might do. Until death actually arrives, it is an idea.

There is a Chinese story about a man who loved dragons. He loved dragons so much that he collected them—dragon figurines, dragon tapestries, dragon paintings. People heard of his love for dragons and often brought him additions to his collection. Word spread, until an actual dragon heard about him. Full of excitement, the dragon traveled from afar to visit the man. When it arrived, the dragon put its eye up to the window and gazed upon the wonders inside. At about this time, the man looked up, saw the true dragon looking in at him and promptly fainted from fear. Dogen Zenji references this story in "Fukanzazengi," when he tells us to devote our energies "to the way of direct pointing at the real." "Please, honored followers of Zen, long accustomed to groping for the elephant," he implores, "do not doubt the True Dragon."[1]

In my case, the True Crab, not the True Dragon, showed up. In *The Emperor of All Maladies: A Biography of Cancer*, Siddhartha Mukherjee tells us that Hippocrates first named the disease we know as cancer around 400 BCE, choosing *karkinos*, the Greek word for crab. The tumor reminded Hippocrates "of a crab dug in the sand with its legs spread in a circle."[2] Though I have collected stories and information about cancer for years, when the eye of the True Crab stared me down, I felt afraid. I cried. I needed a long hug.

The only thing we know for sure is our direct experience, in the present moment. In the present moment, there is no separation between what we think of as "us" and the world around us. We are fully connected. This is why in Zen practice we return to now, over and over. In the present moment, there is no searching for something else, or better, or different. There is only the fullness and ease of what is—direct pointing at the real. In this case, the direct experience of having a biopsy in no way reflected my ideas of what a biopsy might be like. I did not expect to be awake, or to be scared. I don't know that I had much of an idea at all of what would happen, only that is was something I wanted to avoid, like going to the dentist, or war.

I did not have cancer. The results of the biopsy came back benign. Cancer-free. Does this mean I still do not know cancer? I do not know cancer, but my understanding has widened. I have taken my place in the line of people who know the direct experience of being afraid to hear the results of a biopsy.

To think that I understand cancer is a mistake. To think I do not understand cancer is a mistake. We must throw away our ideas of "understand" or "not understand" and return to our direct experience. Breathe. Idea-of-cancer. Fear. Calm. Pain. No-pain. No-cancer. Breathe. Then we must let go of all of this and rest in what is.

Cancer cells are mutated, distorted versions of the same cells that perform vital functions in our bodies. Cancer cells regularly arise and our body destroys them before they become a problem. We never know about these. There will always be some cells in our bodies that are mutated, with the potential to become cancerous. Thus, cancer is always with us, whether we think about it or not. Our cells are constantly changing and the potential for cancer is built into our genomes. So as we evolve, cancer also evolves. Cancer is within all of us, changing with us, as all things in the universe are with us, constantly changing.

In "Yuibutsu-yobutsu" (Only Buddha, Together Buddha) Dogen Zenji teaches, "There is life in death, and there is death in life. There is death that is always in death; there is life that is always in life. This is not contrived by humans willfully, but Dharma comes to be like this."[3] There are mutated cells in healthy bodies and healthy cells in cancer bodies. There is cancer that is always cancer; there is not-cancer that is always not-cancer. This is not contrived by humans willfully, but Dharma comes to be like this.

Healthy. [Clack!] Cancer. [Clack!] Impermanence. [Clack!]

How can we combine the urgency of cancer with the physical ability of not-cancer? The best time to cultivate meditative stability is when the body can be still and when our greatest concern is that the babysitter might eat the leftovers we were saving for ourselves. The time to practice is right now, in this moment, whether we have (active) cancer or not. If we have cancer, there's no choice but to practice. If we do not have cancer, there's no choice but to practice. When we wake up to the fact that life and death—that cancer and not-cancer—are not separate, and there is no line in the sand separating us from the holy abyss, the only thing to do is practice, wholeheartedly, without judgment, and without complacency.

> May I respectfully remind you:
> Great is the matter of birth and death.
> All is impermanent, quickly passing.
> Wake up! Wake up!
> Do not squander your life!

A close friend of mine died of colon cancer several years ago. Though we lived on different coasts, I was able to visit him one week before he died. He was in great pain, but lucid and able to speak deep truths. He was not afraid. A long-term Buddhist practitioner with a daily practice, my friend was also an academic. In the past he and I had many discussions about the role of academic study in Buddhist practice. My friend felt academic learning was an end in itself. I differed. I felt that the purpose of Buddhist academic study is to point us in the right practice direction.

In his last week, as I sat on my friend's couch, he wanted to tell me something vital. He leaned in and spoke with great urgency. "Do you see all of these books?" he said, gesturing to the vast library surrounding the room. His eyes focused sharply on me, kind and intense. "All I care about now is my practice. When I wake up, all day long, when I go to sleep, and all through night—all I want to do is practice."

My friend had the great fortune, as the moment of death approached, to have both great urgency and great meditative stability. He knew what to do and he did it. He still had terrible pain, he was devastated to leave his young child, and saying goodbye to his lovely, supportive, newly found wife was a torture. My friend was not pleased to be dying and it was not easy, but his twenty-year practice allowed him space for acceptance. It guided him over the difficult terrain. It comforted him in his letting go.

Though I have not let go, as we say euphemistically, it is something quite profound to witness—true, beautiful, and poignant. A chaplain colleague once reflected that she had been working at the hospital for a few years and had yet to be present at the moment of death. "How do you do it?" she asked.

"When I was a child," I answered, "I loved shooting stars. I still love shooting stars. Seeing one inspires such wonder and profundity. Yet, they don't happen very often. So, I slept backwards in my bed in order to press my face to the window, falling asleep while looking at the sky." In the same way, the last moments of a person's fleeting life are so full of beauty and wonder, I try to be there when it happens. I check in with the nurses or sit silently in the room. I have learned the subtle signs, both spiritual and physical, of a body coming to its departure. The moment of death is a great teacher and I do all that I can to be present for its teaching.

What death most has to teach us is how to live our lives. It teaches how to become fully present to everyday wonder and great beauty, and pain. It teaches us compassion. It teaches us to be fully present. It motivates us out of complacency and gives us appreciation for our fighting children. Death is in every moment of life—in the most profound shooting star and the most ordinary cup of tea. There is life in death, and there is death in life. This is the gift of the Dharma. And when the True Crab comes, who knows what we will do; who knows how it will be?

> Do not squander your life! [Clack]

I once had a 107-year-old patient whom I loved deeply. As I prepared to leave her room for the last time she looked just beyond me, out the window, and beamed. Pink crabapple blossoms swayed against a clear, blue spring sky. She turned her head back, looked into my eyes and said, "It's all so beautiful! Love your family. Love everyone. Love it all. It's so beautiful." I smiled and said, "I love you." She responded, "Thank you. I needed that."

> Four and fifty years
> I've hung the sky with stars.
> Now I leap through—
> What shattering!
> —Dogen Zenji[4]

Notes

1. Dogen Zenji, "Fukanzazengi," Soto Zen Text Project, *Soto School Scriptures for Daily Services and Practice* (Tokyo: Sotoshu Shumucho, 2001), 84. Available at http://www.zen-deshimaru.com/en/zen/fukanzazengi-eihei-dogen-unabridged-english-translation.

2. Siddhartha Muhkerjee, *The Emperor of all Maladies* (New York: Scribner, 2010), 47.

3. Dogen Zenji, "Yuibutsu-yobutsu," Shobogenzo, trans. in Hee-Jin Kim, *Eihei Dogen: Mystical Realist* (Somerville, MA: Wisdom, 2004), 175.

4. Lucien Stark, Takashi Ikemoto, and Taigan Takayama, *Zen Poems of China and Japan* (New York: Grove Press, 1973), 63.

V

Nen nen ju shin ki, Nen nen fu ri shin

This very moment arises from Mind,
this very moment itself is Mind

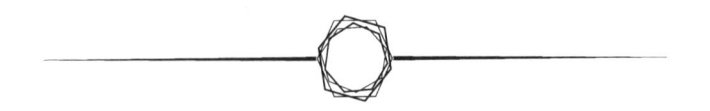

Myo-O Marilyn Habermas-Scher is affiliated with Hokyoji Zen Practice Community in Eitzen, Minnesota, where she received dharma transmission from Dokai Ron Georgesen in 2012 in the lineage of Dainin Katagiri Roshi, who was her root teacher. She spent her younger years as a professional choreographer and dancer, and she developed VoiceWork, a somatically based vocal approach while she was studying Zen with Ho-jo san. Since 2007 she has worked as an interfaith staff chaplain at the University of Minnesota Medical Center, M Health, in Minneapolis. Website: marilynmyo-o.com.

In Which This

Myo-O Marilyn Habermas-Scher

In March of 2009, my husband had a debilitating stroke, at the age of sixty-one. In the late spring of 2017, the "In which" phrases began to crowd the back of my mind. It was time to give voice to the struggle and practice of nine years of caregiving.

IN WHICH HIS SKIN IS GRAY, HIS CHEEKS ARE WAN, AND HE IS COUGHING

Upon returning from three weeks of retreat with my teacher at the winter practice period, I see that my husband is coughing a great deal. He's been ill while I was away.
"You don't look well," I say. "Please go see your doctor."
"No!" he shouts. "I am fine. Leave me alone!"

IN WHICH SHE BEGS HIM NOT TO GO UP NORTH TO THE WOODS

"I don't think you should go up north," I tell him.
"Leave me alone. Stay out of my business!" he retorts.
My husband is moving sharply around the kitchen, opening drawers and slamming the pantry door. He has transformed into a senior in high school; I have become his mother.
"Please rest up there," I caution.
"My guys will take care of me," he insists.
I am sure that there is a teaching story for this. Is it the one in which the professor goes to see the Zen master and the Zen master keeps pouring tea into his cup until it overflows?
This is often the human condition, is it not? We are filled with our strung-together thoughts and perceptions; our ears are filled

with wax, and our hearts are frozen. Knowing this, I attend to my thinking mind's desperate attempts to string this story together. As our beloved Zhaozhou taught us, "Conceiving is ill."

I am ill.

IN WHICH SHE HEARS FEET POUNDING UP THE STAIRS

In the late evening I am called to the county hospital, where I work as a chaplain, to meet an East Indian family. The father was being flown in by helicopter from North Dakota; he'd had a stroke while on a business trip. The doctors are saying that he will never return to normal. His wife is weeping, and his young adult daughters, one of whom is a physician, are crying out, "We will take him home with us!"

At 9 a.m. the next morning, as I lay sleeping the sleep of the just, I hear my daughter's feet pounding up the stairs. "Mom! Dad had a stroke! They took him by helicopter to Duluth!"

IN WHICH SHE SCREAMS, AND REALIZES THAT SHE IS THE MOM, WHO MUST NOT DO THAT

I scream.

Was I calm and equanimous at that moment? Was I the Kuanyin my daughter needed me to be? No, I was not. I watched the mental constructs called "My husband," "My life," "My future," "My stability," "My caution 'I knew he was ill and I begged him not to go up north with his guys'" fly apart like a meteor shower in my mind. Could I find steadiness by pulling all the pieces together? No, they would not pull together.

"Is this groundlessness?" the nun asked.

"Yes it is," was the master's reply.

It was also SHOCK.

Seeing the look on my twenty-six-year-old daughter's face, I understand: "Stop freaking out. You cannot get this in order. Knock it off. Be a mom."

IN WHICH SHE MEETS HER FUTURE DAUGHTER-IN-LAW "G" FOR THE FIRST TIME, AT THE BACK DOOR, AND IN WHICH "G" DRIVES US ALL TO DULUTH

Having screamed, and having woken up enough to stop doing that, I then greet "G" at our back door. "I am so glad to meet you" I say as I hug her in my sage-colored fleece bathrobe. "Would you please make us breakfast?" "G" is a Zen master. She is completely "one-doing." She is from New Jersey. She makes us breakfast, washes the dishes, and drives us all to the ICU at St. Mary's Hospital in Duluth where my husband has been brought in by helicopter.

I am calm in the car. I call my husband's family doctor and a neurologist he knows. "You sound so calm," one of them says.

Calm and shock are conditioned states. They arise when conditions come together, and they dissolve when those conditions change. Noting mental states: shock (frozen diaphragm), fear (frozen diaphragm plus racing mind plus attachment to both), agitation; aversion to getting what I don't want—this was suffering, exactly as Shakyamuni deconstructed it 2,500 years ago. The only instructions I can follow are: breathe in, breathe out, STAY AWAKE!

IN WHICH HIS SPEECH IS GARBLED

Arriving at the ICU, we are greeted by my dharma sister Judith, who had simply jumped in her car and driven to Duluth. She'd already checked out the doctors. My husband, decked out in hydration tubes, calls out, "G!" It is the first time he has met my daughter's partner as well. Later he forgets that I crawled into bed with him, underneath the tubes, and waited there for the six hours that it took Dr. Beaver, the neurologist, to come tell us what was going on. The right brainstem had been blocked, affecting my husband's speech, his swallowing, and the sensation of temperature on his left side and of pain on his right. He is not able to read well.

IN WHICH SHE HEARS THE STORY OF THE STROKE

He'd been sick when he arrived at the cabin with his four friends. His friends believed him when he told them that he'd be alright; he was the trained health practitioner among them. When the right side of his mouth began to droop, Dave got frightened and called the ambulance. He threw my husband over his back and into the station wagon. They met the ambulance on the highway outside of Ely, Minnesota. At the small community hospital, my husband, who holds a post-doc in neurology, diagnosed himself: "Right brainstem stroke." Friend Greg paced, pointing at his watch. "Get the helicopter. Take him to the trauma center!" The community hospital staff did this, eventually.

IN WHICH SHE RUMINATES ON HOW IT SHOULD HAVE GONE

"If I had been there, the ambulance would have been called the first time he tripped."

"If he had listened to me and not gone up north at all and gone to the doctor instead, this might not have happened. Or, it might have happened in Minneapolis, and he'd have gotten the stroke-modifying medication TPA in time."

The repeated "if, if, if. . ."—things were not the way they actually were but instead the way they should have been—became a recipe for resentment.

IN WHICH HE STANDS LIKE A NEWBORN FAWN

Day 2 in the ICU, my husband is no longer intubated. The physical therapists come in and stand him up. He looks just like a newborn fawn. He also leans to the right. He says that in a day or two, he'll go back to work.

Later, the hospitalist, who is in her sixties and has long gray hair, comes by and says to him, "You have pneumonia. I am giving you an antibiotic. Also, your cholesterol is high, and we're giving you a statin." She says, "I have your number, and this is what you need." He says, "I'm not taking a statin." But he did take it. He also took the antibiotic.

IN WHICH HER DAUGHTER SENDS HER TO HER ROOM

In settled stillness, the barely visible swirl of potential thought floats and undulates like the Milky Way, before it mysteriously arranges itself into words that we recognize.

We sit at the edge of the cliff, under the moon.

She realizes that her husband's finances are also swirling in unrecognizable patterns. At the same time, she confronts the pressure of cash outflow only. Overwhelmed, not wanting to feel overwhelmed, she shouts again—many bad words.

Her daughter says, "Mom, I am not going to help you with this until you calm down. Go to your room!"

IN WHICH HIS DAUGHTER TELLS HIM, "DAD, YOU ALMOST DIED"

A few weeks after leaving the Sister Kenny Acute Rehabilitation Unit, where my husband received physical, occupational, and speech therapy, we all visit his family practice physician of twenty years. She expresses amazement that he is able to sit up straight. His weight has dropped from 145 to 128 pounds. She explains why he must take a statin. He says that he plans to go back to work in a couple of weeks. In the car, on the way home, our daughter exclaims to him, "Dad! You almost died!" "I did?" he replies.

The Buddha's blinding flash of the obvious is laid out in the first of the Four Noble Truths. Life is replete with suffering. The first step in meeting suffering with wisdom is to recognize it, admit to it, and allow that suffering to be known. If no suffering is recognized, then there is no energy to pursue the other three Noble Truths. There is no insight, no transformation, no medicine, and no healing.

IN WHICH HIS TUMMY TUBE IS PLACED AND HE WANTS IT TAKEN OUT, IN WHICH IT COMES OUT BY ITSELF WHILE HE IS PICKING BEETS

Had my husband's stroke happened fifty years ago, he would have starved to death from being unable to swallow. He survives on five cans of Jevity, a tube-fed formula, a day. Although he has been told not to eat, he is determined to swallow and practices toward this end like a man with his hair on fire. Eleven months after the stroke, the tummy tube is taken out. Five months after that, his weight drops to 101 pounds. The doctor tells me, "He is really weak, but he doesn't think he is." The tummy tube is replaced. His weight creeps up to 118 pounds. One day, while he is pulling beets in the garden, it falls out. In the kitchen he holds up the end of the tube to me and asks, "Can you put this back in?" "That's above my pay grade," I say.

IN WHICH HE IS UNABLE TO SELF-REGULATE, IN WHICH HE REFUSES TO TAKE AN ANTIDEPRESSANT, AND IN WHICH HER CAR IS

WRECKED AND SHE TAKES ONE

Brain trauma leads to emotional lability. But instead of crying, my husband gets lost in anger and shouts.

I sit on the couch and hold a pillow. What is the practice for this? What would the Buddha do? "You have to be the Buddha now," my friend tells me. What other choice is there?

My husband and I make a visit to the hospital where I work, to meet with the physical medicine doctor I know there. Dr. "I" tells my husband, "I always order an antidepressant for men who've had a stroke and are cognitively intact but physically impaired. It makes the healing easier." My husband refuses to take one.

Rocking back and forth in *samsara* for months, for a year, for two years, brings me to my knees. The day after Thanksgiving, and two days before *Rohatsu*, the long winter retreat, I drive with our daughter to do an errand. A seventeen-year-old boy turns left on a flashing yellow arrow and hits my rear left bumper. The car is totaled. Our daughter is okay. I am also okay, except that *Rohatsu* has become a waterfall of tears.

My nervous system has been shredded and has lost its flexibility and responsiveness. I consider, "What would my ancestors have done?" I remember Hakuin's "soft butter" meditation. I counsel myself, "The ancestors used whatever worked." I find a skillful health practitioner and, finally, we settle on an antidepressant. I take it and, as promised, it fills in the gouges in the nerves and stops the exhaustion that comes from sobbing at the smallest provocation.

IN WHICH HER DOCTOR WRITES HER A NEW PRESCRIPTION, AND IN WHICH MASTER LIN WANTS TO SEE HER EVERY WEEK FOR QI GONG HEALING

Working overnight shifts at the county hospital sometimes requires driving downtown in the middle of night four times. This becomes impossible to sustain. The nurse practitioner who prescribed the antidepressant writes a new prescription: "No Overnight On-Call." This ends my job at the county hospital. Master Lin would never have said, "You are in rough shape. I am worried about you." Instead, he says, "Come to see me every week." I go to see him every week for three months.

IN WHICH, AFTER HE HAS BEEN BLEEDING FOR THREE MONTHS, IT IS DISCOVERED THAT HER HUSBAND HAS COLON CANCER

Four years after the stroke, and after bleeding for three months, the medical test scheduled can't be performed because he has a tumor. Surgery is done. He is lucky—no chemo.

But what about his eating sugary snacks every day? But what about his smoking sixty cigarettes in four days while up north with his friends? But what about his being untruthful about that?

IN WHICH SHE REALIZES THAT NOT BEING CODEPENDENT MEANS THAT HER HUSBAND CAN CHOOSE DEATH

> I care about you, but I cannot
> make your choices for you.
> —Practice phrase from the Divine Abodes

Except if I am trying to save "your" life, which is my life.

I remember walking along the gravel path that led to Taizoin, the famous six-hundred-year-old garden located on the grounds of Myoshinji in Kyoto. The small pine trees had been carefully pruned. I saw each pine needle, complete in itself. Breathing in, at that moment I knew: There is no obstruction. Breathing out, I knew: Each dharma is completely free to be itself. I had tears of joy.

I investigate my uncontrollable impulse to ensure that he will make responsible choices. Responsible choices mean those that I think will maintain his health. His insistence on the fiction that he could obtain sustainable nutrition by eating by mouth alone, even though his weight was at 101 pounds, had thrown me over the cliff. I call his brother and his best friend. I ask my husband, "Do you want to have a heart attack at your daughter's wedding? Is that what you want her to have as a wedding gift?"

I know about being codependent and about not being codependent, but really, did that include letting go when he was choosing death? I hit a wall and stop flailing. Yes, actually, he is completely free to make choices that may end his life.

My powerful Jewish-mother training is broken. This is freedom.

IN WHICH SHE CONSIDERS TWO OF THE SEVEN FACTORS OF ENLIGHTENMENT

Equanimity

I am the owner of my karma. My happiness and unhappiness depend upon my actions, not upon my wishes for myself.

Things are just as they are.

I care for you but cannot keep you from suffering.

I wish you happiness but cannot make your choices for you.

Investigation

First mind state observed: overwhelm and drowning.

Second mind state observed: grasping; the imperative to hold it all together.

Third mind state observed: panic.

Fourth mind state observed: aversion to panic.

And beneath this is found the cellularly held pattern of terror about, and protection from, annihilation.

In the first chapter of *The Holy Teaching of Vimalakirti*,[1] Shariputra says, "'As for me, O Brahma, I see this great earth, with its highs and lows, its thorns, its precipices, it peaks, and its abysses, as if it were entirely filled with ordure.' ... Thereupon the Lord touched the ground of this billion-world-galactic universe with his big toe, and suddenly it was transformed into a huge mass of precious gems."[2]

"The Buddha said, 'Sariputra, this Buddha-field is always thus pure, but the *Tathagata* makes it appear to be spoiled by many faults in order to bring about the maturity of inferior living beings.'"[3]

I return to my intention to investigate the *kleshas* that have been and are being exposed with the willingness to awaken to the breathtaking beauty that lies directly in the fabric of every one of these "In which she" stories.

Robert Thurman writes in the introduction to *The Holy Teaching of Vimalakirti*, "Our immediate reality is ultimate, cannot be escaped or negated and must be accepted as it is ... with no false hope of ever making it ultimate, since it is already so."[4]

IN WHICH SHE IS GRATEFUL AND UNDERSTANDS THAT WITHOUT PRACTICE AND UNDERSTANDING, SHE WOULD BE INSANE

The opportunity of purification of the heart–mind remains vivid and challenging. I wish it could be said that equanimity abounds and that compassion and wisdom manifest victory, that I am a shining example of the fruit of great effort. But I don't think so. Katagiri Roshi used to say, "Same old Katagiri's stinky nose, before enlightenment, after enlightenment." Thank God he said that! Devotion to the blossoming of Vimalakirti's teaching keeps me sane. Even if I do not know relief in the way I might hope to feel it, I still have doubtless faith that the most realistic track through this wilderness is the one laid out by our ancestors. They endlessly encourage me to "probe beneath the surface of apparent 'reality' in order to gain direct awareness of the ultimate reality of all things."(5)

Notes

1. Robert Thurman, *The Holy Teaching of Vimalakirti: A Mahayana Scripture* (University Park: Pennsylvania State University Press, 2000).
2. Thurman, *The Holy Teaching*, 18.
3. Thurman, *The Holy Teaching*, 19.
4. Thurman, *The Holy Teaching*, 3.
5. Thurman, *The Holy Teaching*, 3.

Shodo Spring is one of the many beings living in gratitude in/of the part of the Earth called North America. Her history includes birth in Ohio, meeting Zen with Dainin Katagiri, studying with Tenshin Anderson, and receiving ordination and transmission from Shohaku Okumura. Her practice has included pilgrimage, environmental activism, ceremony, and especially zazen. She has two daughters and four grandchildren, earns her livelihood as a psychotherapist, and practices farming as spiritual life. She is the author of *Take Up Your Life: Making Spirituality Work in the Real World* (Tuttle 1996), and is the founder of Mountains and Waters Alliance (mountainsandwatersalliance.org).

When the World Is On Fire: Reflections on These Times
Shodo Spring

Introduction: Not a Metaphor

The world is literally burning. Flooding. Shaking. Melting. Erupting. The news of summer and fall 2017 has included one disaster after another, in everyone's backyard, leaving our confidence in normalcy badly shaken.

The climate-caused weather events have put many of us into the state well known by others for years—decades—centuries. Uncertainty is a way of life; sickness, starvation, and cold or heat threaten. Which reminds me that there have been whole peoples who were at ease with uncertainty. We call them hunter-gatherers, and they have been able to live at ease in places most of us find inhospitable—the Kalahari Desert, the Arctic.(1) The ease comes from not expecting certainty, not demanding even personal survival.

Daniel Quinn writes about peoples who "live in the hands of the gods" versus those who attempt to take control of their surroundings.(2) We live in the latter, even though as Buddhists we are taught impermanence. Impermanence is not not just an idea.

Taking refuge is not an idea either—it has become a vivid reality, especially for those evicted from their homes by wildfires, floods, hurricanes, earthquakes, or wars. What's new for me is that people I know personally are now among the refugees. Most of them will be okay, at some level, mostly because we live in a rich country and it will spend its resources on them—particularly if they are white and middle-class. Because our country (and others) keep out desperate refugees in order to protect our own people from having to share. Because those who make decisions on our behalf operate from the mind of separation. Eventually the riches will be used up, and we will have to rely on our neighbors.

Conversations

The choice of Euro-American culture is still what it has been for a long time: to place our faith in our own ability to control nature. We replaced serfs with slaves, then with machines and chemicals—and have poisoned our food and depleted our soils, water, and air, which we regard as lifeless, as resources for human use. To live in this way, disconnected from everything around us, is a tragedy.

Thomas Berry puts it this way: "We are talking only to ourselves. We are not talking to the rivers, we are not listening to the wind and stars. We have broken the great conversation. By breaking that conversation we have shattered the universe. All the disasters that are happening now are a result of that spiritual autism."[3]

"We have shattered the universe." That is a strong statement. But the universe that consists of wholeness, of interrelation, of mutual cocreation—we shatter our experience of that universe, so it becomes ultimate reality but not lived reality.

The broken conversation includes breaking the conversation with each other. We blame each other, which escalates mutual blame makes it impossible to work together. It's easy enough to notice white supremacists blaming Muslims and calling violence on peaceful African American protesters. Yet environmentalists too have been separating into camps, accusing each other of being either complicit with the destruction or too aggressive. Those who agree on the situation but have different solutions (veganism versus holistic animal farming, for instance) seem to hate each other worst of all.

We find ourselves divided, alone. It's the dis-ease of the time. While the human assault on the natural world escalates. While almost none of us are talking with the rivers, trees, and mountains, or listening to them.

I'm learning, or trying to learn, to talk with them again. After two years of persistent effort, my habits have started to include asking for help from the hill. Noticing when I am out of communication.

Making offerings to a certain old tree stump at the north gate of the land and to the water spirits of the river, building an altar at the east gate where the creeks come together.

In the spring of 2015, I was pulling up weeds in the orchard, working with Justin Rowland, a Lakota person with a traditional upbringing. He suddenly said, "Those plants are very strong over here." Then he added, "They communicate with each other." Was my attempt to remove the weeds making them stronger?

I had assumed that if I worked hard enough I could eradicate the problem plants. It never occurred to me that, just as humans form defenses against outside assaults, the plant groups were strengthening themselves against my assault. To think of them as conscious—it changed everything. The question becomes: Can I pull up weeds and also be in conversation with them? If being in conversation comes first, how can I take care of this land—my accepted responsibility—and its many "invasive" plants and animals? How can I not be a victim of plant, animal, and insect bullies?

A Dream

I had a dream in which there were a hundred people living at my seventeen-acre farm. Although we could possibly feed ourselves by intensive farming plus foraging the woods, there wasn't enough food to carry us through the winter and spring until harvest. (Nor were there enough deer, squirrels, and rabbits.) It was completely obvious that it would be unfair to favor my own family—four of them were in the dream—and that the only fair thing would be to draw lots for who got the food—who survived. There was no question of my drawing those lots; the hard physical work would require strength I don't have (said the dream).

I woke shaking. The dream has stayed with me for over a year now. About the children, and one daughter and her husband, there was only grief and faint hope. And yes, in waking life I did bargain with myself about whether I had skills that would be needed, that would get me into the survival lottery. My other daughter's family, my niece and nephew, and others I loved—they were simply absent from the dream—I had no idea whether they were alive or dead.

In the dream, people were thoughtful and respectful, a community working together to find a way to survive. No preference was given for wealth (my ownership of the farm) or status.

I actually think something like this will happen, only it will be harder: there will also be bands of hungry people coming from the cities; some will join us, some will have guns and will be willing to kill in order to eat. It might not happen; I don't know when if it does, and I may never be ready.

The separate self wants to continue. Always. I may as well be kind to that urge in myself and in others.

Refuge and Impermanence

There are the Four Seals of Buddhism: impermanence, suffering, no-self, nirvana. Not accepting impermanence and no-self leads to suffering. Accepting them leads to nirvana. I wonder how this relates to Quinn's "living in the hands of the gods." Quinn's image is from before civilization saved humans from constant uncertainty. In that earlier time, death was not an unusual thing or a disaster. I imagine it did not hurt any less personally, but the sense of outrage or unfairness might have been different. Since the change, humans have sought refuge in our own power, in our structures, in our ability to store grain—instead of in the offerings of the earth, the kindness of the universe. After eight thousand years of agriculture, it's hard to imagine what that would be like.

Where is refuge? Shohaku Okumura said to me once, in the early days when I was still obsessed with enlightenment, "Enlightenment means you have nothing at all that you can rely on."[4] I take refuge in this teaching: there is nothing to rely on. I take refuge in Buddha, in the body of Buddha which is the whole universe. I take refuge in Sangha, the community of beings in the Way.

I don't take refuge in money, or in status, or in material possessions, or in structures of civilization, or in economic transactions. No, however hard times may be, the refuge will be in reality and in community—in the hands of the gods.

Vowing to Free All Beings

Practice is more than refuge. Practice includes the four vows:

> Beings are numberless, I vow to free them.
> Delusions are inexhaustible, I vow to end them.

Dharma gates are boundless, I vow to enter them.
Buddha's way is unsurpassable, I vow to become it.

Every time we chant a sutra, we offer the energy of that chanting. Sometimes that offering includes these words: "We aspire to turn the Dharma wheel unceasingly and to free the world from every tragedy of war, epidemic, natural disaster and starvation." I've chanted those words so often they're ingrained in my skull. For a long time I never thought about them. Now they seem penetratingly brilliant. War—Syrian civil war, Israel-Palestine conflict, possible U.S. war with Iraq or with North Korea, genocide against the Rohingya, against Red Nations and other indigenous peoples (for centuries); the low-level wars waged against protesters of many kinds, people labeled terrorists and hit with freezing water, rubber bullets, tear gas, arrests, and accusations. Epidemics—after disasters destroy infrastructure, cholera often follows. Natural disaster is in our face as I write: hurricanes and typhoons, floods, earthquakes, mudslides (Sierra Leone, August 2017, 500 dead and 3000 displaced), drought, wildfires around the world. Starvation—yes, we can numb ourselves to the people starving everywhere, but with droughts there will be more starvation right here. Which is why people are cruel to refugees: they fear their own starvation, and they lack a bigger picture.

We chant "to free the world" but Zen practice has nothing to do with escape. Zen practice understands that there is no escape. It looks straight at the tragedy in the world, and points to freedom—whatever that means. It is not specific, except for not looking away.

At the 2016 Soto Zen priests' conference, Hogen Bays gave a short talk titled "Nothing Is Amiss: The Foundation for Social Action." That names our situation. Nothing is amiss. The world does not need our fixing. Actually the idea of fixing (correcting, healing, saving) is an absurdity based on the mistake that there is something outside of us, or that we are outside of the rest of the universe.

Nothing is wrong. Everything is holy, the entire world is the temple, offered for our practice. And yet there is injustice, murder, disaster, oppression, every kind of horror we can imagine or not. How do we practice in this world as it is?

A Personal Story

As a child, I found refuge in the natural world, in the wildest places I could find. My strongest memories from that time are of the spring when I found the wild iris, and the years of returning again and again looking for them, until finally I had memorized their location, and knew they bloomed in May. Later there were hours at the local nature preserve: scrambling up a cliff above the creek, not sure how I would get down, very carefully finding each handhold and step. There's a decade full of discoveries, one after another—a grassy hillside I hadn't known before, the late afternoon sun reflecting on the creek, waves breaking onto the beach in a storm, the lake's glassy quiet the morning after.

Those explorations were the life of my childhood years, the holy action that sustained me, the intimacy I knew. In those lonely years, that is how the support of all beings showed itself to me. And I hated people, in general, for every road and every bit of litter intruding on my refuge. As I learned to make my way in the world, for a long time that way included undiagnosed depression. Even though my life was secure in every physical way.

At age thirty-five, I wandered into the Minnesota Zen Meditation Center and found something in zazen. I didn't even know I was looking. Three years later, in my first long *sesshin*, the world opened up. No longer was it only woods and waters that offered themselves to me. The internal walls started to crumble, and I could imagine meeting other people with the intimacy once reserved for rocks and wildflowers. The next journey of discovery began. Very gradually, sangha became essential. Sangha was the place where the remains of those walls simply were part of me, without shame or horror, and I could allow them to crumble at their own pace. Very gradually I also learned to allow others their own ruins and incompleteness.

Thirty years later I had fully entered the container of Zen, zazen, sangha. There was a ceremony called ordination—literally "home leaving." It's hard to say what that ceremony was, but looking back it seemed to me that I was finally moving in the direction I had always intended. The power of ceremony should not be underestimated. From a home in delusion, I moved into the homeless state, toward a home that might be found in zazen and vow.

Near the end of formal priest training, sitting in practice period, I was inundated with literal visions—mental pictures on the wall during zazen—of myself walking along the Keystone pipeline route. I sought counsel, prepared for a year, and then walked that route through the Great Plains with a few companions. Afterward, people asked what we had accomplished, and I had no answer. All I knew was that we were changed. We had brought our human, imperfect presence to a pending tragedy, we allowed the earth and sky to nourish us, and offered back what we could—one part of a vast movement to protect land and peoples. Much later the pipeline was canceled—briefly—and some people gave us credit. But cause and effect is not so literal. What was that about, and why did I have to do it?

The story I told myself about that walk was that it was a ceremony, a three-month, seventeen-hundred-mile ceremony, honoring and blessing the earth, receiving and giving to that which encompasses our lives. The imagery is not quite Buddhist: regarding earth and waters as sentient beings, conscious and intentional, is to invent a persona for them—as we invent for ourselves. I choose to make this mistake rather than the usual mistake of regarding them as insentient, inert, unwilling or unable to act. We make our own meanings, those of us who don't yet see clearly, and this meaning helps me, it helps my heart be open. In my story, the earth called, I didn't say no, and everything unfolded from there.

I live now in a semiwild place. The hill to the north is a sanctuary, a place that feels like magic, power, sacredness. Once someone was planning to build a house up there—right next to "my" land—ruining its wildness, desecrating its sacredness. After talking with zoning officials proved useless, I went out and walked on the hill, asking it for help, asking to protect itself. It seemed that I could hear the trees saying yes. Even the buckthorn, who must know that I plan to tear them up, seemed to give support. Then I waited. Two years later there is no house. The zoning has changed so that land seems to be protected. Although nothing is certain, my fear is gone.

For a long time—maybe this year—my life has been organized around a vow to stop climate change—without knowing what that can mean. In 2015, I created an organization, named Mountains and Waters Alliance, and think of it as an alliance of sentient beings committed to protect and restore the earth. Its members are more trees, bluffs, waterfalls and flowers than they are human beings—because asking humans is still hard for me. I include them in morning service, in the dedication of merit after chanting. I ask them for help, and I long to visit them more often.

This past June, walking on a mountain, talking with new beings, I was offered a teaching: There's nothing I need to do. The deep powers of the earth have it in their hands. It's not up to me.

It felt as if a heavy weight lifted off my shoulders. I returned home and was physically sick for a month—which may be a measure of how invested I was in my identity as activist. I'm moving slowly since then. It's as if every step I take has to be discovered, tested. What is my intention? If I think I'm saving the world, solving a problem, anything like that, it's a mistake. If I think I can sit idly at home, or even in the zendo, that might well be a mistake too: turning the Dharma wheel does not look like disengagement.

My story now is about making offerings to the earth, both ceremony and physical labor, and asking for help with everything. Absolutely everything, small and large, personal and world-wide.

Making Offerings

Cause and effect can't be known. We throw an action like a pebble into a pond, and watch the ripples. On the KXL there were a thousand pebbles, only one of them mine, cause and effect impossible to discern. Still, life itself impels us to act. We are the ripples, more than the pebbles. We are both.

How do we relate to the world around us? We offer ourselves, as intimately as possible, in whatever situation presents itself. To make an offering is to be alive to the other.

I went to testify at hearings on a pipeline, intended to run through northern Minnesota, through tribal lands, wild rice beds, and the clearest water in the state. The company building it has a reputation for accidents. My words won't make the difference. Why did I need to go? I needed to make that offering, to speak this Dharma in this context, with environmental activists and government officials and even pro-pipeline people.

Receiving What's Offered

We relate by receiving offerings too.

Once I found an aliveness in the woods. Now I find it in the untamed space called zazen—and in human community, and still also in woods, hills, starry skies, gardens and flowers and small beings. This receiving brings enormous gratitude, and also a desire to protect. I long to see humans relating to the natural world as part of it, as family, and not as something to use, dominate, or conquer. I want to share that this is a joyful and wonderful way to live.

I think that if we created a human society that lives this way, we would take care of the earth and walk back from the brink of climate catastrophe as well as from war, inequality, and oppression of all kinds. But that is to propose that an enlightened society could actually exist in the realm of illusion. Buddhist teaching wouldn't support focusing on such a society as a concrete goal. This is not quite the same as the way conventional wisdom opposes such a thought, saying human nature is selfish and violent. Those are not inherently Buddhist thoughts, but the ground of our own culture which is destroying a planet where humans lived for a hundred thousand years.

Closing Words

When we stop imagining that we are alone, life becomes possible. I am going to go out on a limb and say that to practice is to join the conversation, to live in the conversation with all beings—with wind and stars, rivers and mountains, prairies and woodlands. There we are never alone, never responsible for the whole outcome of any endeavor, never victim or even perpetrator. Here, we are simply and intimately part of the whole of life. Everything we meet breathes life into us and is, in turn, created by us. We become soft and fluid, our hearts open and alive. And our guidance in practice emerges of its own accord.

Notes

1. James Suzman, *Affluence without Abundance: The Disappearing World of the Bushmen* (New York: Bloomsbury, 2017). The book is a description of lifestyle of Kalahari Bushmen (San), including their adaptation to European invasion. The mention of the Arctic comes from observations and from conversations with Inupiaq elders in the NANA region of Alaska, during the winter of 1990–91.
2. Daniel Quinn, *Ishmael: An Adventure of the Mind and Spirit* (New York: Bantam, 1992), 240ff.
3. Thomas Berry, "Diagnosing Spiritual Sickness," http://natcath.org/NCR_Online/archives/081001/081001a.htm, para. 1.
4. Shohaku Okumura, personal communication, Hokyoji Zen Monastery, 1990s.

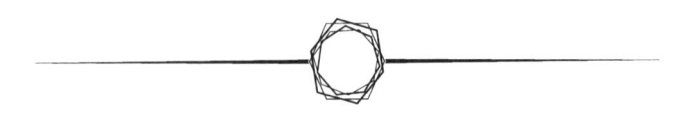

Sarah Dojin Emerson is head priest at the Stone Creek Zen Center. She lived and trained at different parts of the San Francisco Zen Center from 1996 to 2007. She ordained as a Zen Buddhist priest with Gaelyn Godwin, abbott of the Houston Zen Center, in 2007; and received dharma transmission in 2015. She lives with her husband, also a Zen priest, their kids, and a fluctuating number of animals in Sonoma County, California.

Birth and Death
Sarah Dojin Emerson

> This birth-and-death is the life of a buddha.
> —Dogen

Here's what I remember.

I am standing at the backdoor of my childhood home, our TV room. I turned twenty-two about a week before. I am watching my mother, who is lying on the folded-out sofa bed. This is the last day of her life.

A few months before this moment we found out she was terminal. The cancer she had had spread around her small intestine, there was "nothing more we could do." It was a great act of mercy on the part of her surgeon who took me aside and answered me directly (and it turns out accurately) when I asked, "How will she die exactly?" Because of where the cancer was, my mom would effectively die of starvation. "I know this is hard, but you should know, it's not a painful way to die. In fact, it's a natural shutting down of the body which will produce its own endorphins . . . ." How much time, did she think? "About two and a half months or so." And I felt two things: gratitude for this clarity, and then the sensation of stepping off a high cliff and falling.

I was falling through the space of something that "could never happen" happening. And while I was falling I felt a huge rift opening between my brother and my father and myself, who were occupying what we, on one side, imagined to be lives that had expansive futures in them and my mom, on the other, who no longer had the luxury of that kind of imagination. In my whole life up until that point, it felt like we were all walking on the same path, but now it felt like she was walking on a different one, living in a different category, where possibility and potential were no longer part of the view.

But in the moment I am remembering, when I am standing by the back door of the TV room that day she was dying, something happened, something opened. It was a moment of sudden grace where I understood, indelibly and thoroughly, that I was not apart from dying; that I too would definitely walk through this gate of death. True, my mom was doing it right now and I wasn't, and that was a big difference. But I definitely would someday, without a doubt. Death was not apart from my life. And this understanding, more like a whole body experience, gave me a way back in: to her, to our relationship, to the way we had always been together. And I lay down in the bed next to her and talked to her, and stayed there until she died a few hours later.

I was not yet a practitioner of Zen at this point in my life. My only encounter with Zen was a book my college boyfriend had handed me one day from a class he was taking. He said something like, "This guy is talking about the stuff you're always talking about." The book was *Zen Mind, Beginner's Mind* (and I now consider his comment to be the highest of compliments). But my mother's death, and this particular moment when I was not apart from it, were the essential seeds in my becoming a practitioner of Zen. In the months and years to come, I wandered around doing sort of normal, post–college graduation things: working a lot, saving my money, traveling, moving in with my boyfriend. But really all I was doing was seeking a way to reckon with the relationship between life and death. This longing eventually led me across the country to San Francisco, to close enough proximity to the San Francisco Zen Center, to a recognition that *this building* I had ridden by on my bike was the same place *that guy from that book* had lived—and finally one day led me through the door. Once inside, I heard and read things like "Birth and death are the great matter." That got my attention. And whole roomfuls of people together saying outrageous things like "Beings are numberless, I vow to save them." And I thought this might be the place to find a way to live with life and death, and how they live in one another . . . and how they live in me.

Nen nen ju shin ki, Nen nen fu ri shin
This very moment arises from Mind, this very moment itself is Mind   Emerson

• • • • •

Now it is ten years later. I am on my knees in a birthing tub that has been brought into the tiny cabin my husband and I are currently occupying at Tassajara Zen Mountain Center, where we have been living and practicing Zen for years. I am in labor. We are waiting for the birth of our first child.

In the days before our daughter was born I was often struck by how similar the days awaiting this birth were to the days awaiting my mother's death. The only difference really was the governing tone: great loss versus great anticipation. But the motions of my family were just the same. My Dad was around, puttering. Some medical checks by the midwives happened at home. Some work was accomplished, although with half of my attention. Food was cooked, movies were watched, slow hikes were taken. We were all anticipating something tremendous by spending time on the most basic tasks and simple pleasures. Rooting at home in the quiet and mundane, while waiting for the gateway of humanity to open and the Configuration of the Living to change. I was waiting for my whole world to change.

I understand, now, that my labor was fast and furious. But in that moment on my knees, a regular, linear sense of time was not available to me. As far as I could see, this had been going on a long time, and that was long enough. I vividly remember having another thoroughly embodied thought, which was: "On the next contraction I am going to push, and not stop pushing until this baby comes out. It doesn't matter if, in this process, I split in half and die. My husband will be a good father, and this child will have a good life without me." This realization was not of wanting death, but was a kind of openness to it, a willingness, it wasn't the worst thing I could imagine in that moment. Since then, this moment has taken on a more metaphoric tone in my mind's story, as an essential pivot of my life as a parent: the complete relinquishing of my own well-being as the central principle of my life, to someone else's well-being, namely this child's, taking that central place. But at the time, in all honesty, I just wanted the pain to end. And death did not seem like an impossible option.

I remember the next day, holding my precious daughter in my arms with great joy, and saying, "I can't believe anyone voluntarily ever has a second child!" And then I watched the memory of the pain of birth fade week after week: evolutionary amnesia. It took a couple of years for the memory to be fully eclipsed by the joys of our daughter, but eventually it was. And a curiosity about bringing more life into our family began to flicker into our consciousnesses, and we started to think about "number two."

• • • • •

And now it is four and a half years later again. I am in a high-tech hospital in Boston where our second daughter was born hours before. I am moving down what is called The Hall of Hope (which later we could only refer to as "The F-ing Hall of Hope"), which leads to the NICU. There are images of tiny, tiny babies, and then photos of them later in life as thriving kids and teenagers. Our baby has a good chance, we're told. She's a lot bigger and more developed ... and we are here in this place of medical miracles. But I am also soon to be understanding that my younger daughter does not have much time to live. She was born eight weeks early, healthy in many ways, in her sweet pinkness, in the tight waves of blond already on her head, but not in her lungs. She never cried after surfing out on a gush of fluid. Although they have tried to drain the fluid from her lungs, and use a special ventilator that shuffles the air in gently; although they have called in neonatal pulmonary experts from the Children's Hospital, her oxygen level has been below 20 percent for over an hour. I have worked in enough medical environments to have an understanding of what this does to a human brain. When I take it all in and eventually ask, "So, are we letting her go?" The doctor pauses, breathes, and says "We never make that kind of decision without consulting everyone, and everyone working with your daughter agrees ... that would be the best thing to do." And so I said ok then, we need some time alone with our child. And, now here is the pivotal memory: the understanding that this is not what I expected, it's not at all what I want; but my daughter's life is going to be very brief, and if I don't get with that program, I am going to miss it. So I got with that program, and I didn't miss it.

And now I am holding her, and telling her things about life, the stuff I wished for her, nothing fancy: about how it is to fall asleep in a boat on a mooring in the sunshine, and the sound of crickets at night, about what it feels like to run barefoot on a dock, how she might have taken crayons and drawn all over the walls of her big sister's room just to drive her nuts. And I am singing "The Secret of Life" to her, for some reason that song. We have called our family, asked them to come and to bring our older daughter so she can meet her sister. And she comes, with my father and brother, my stepmom and sister-in-law and my nephew. My four-year-old holds her baby sister, as I hold them both in my arms and think, "These are my girls." And with that thought comes another thought, a certainty that this is the only time I will think this, that another child is coming someday, but it won't be a girl. This arrived in my mind in that moment like a fact.

And later we are letting them take the tubes out. And her tiny, uncomplicated, pure little heart keeps beating for a long time, even without much oxygen. She is resting now in her Daddy's arms. I have to use the bathroom, which makes me laugh out loud. How could I have to pee while my daughter is dying?! But I do, and so I do, and her sweet heart slows to a stop by the time I return.

• • • • •

> In birth there is nothing but birth and in death there is nothing but death. Accordingly, when birth comes, face and actualize birth, and when death comes, face and actualize death. Do not avoid them or desire them.
> —Dogen

Between each of these moments, and many since then, I have lived a lot of human experiences. Some have certainly included inconsolable wailing, being reduced to a pile on the floor in pain, and the sincere longing for a specialized team of women to come and keen outside my house. But there were also these moments I describe above that shine through, and that share in common a resounding taste, smell, sound, and flavor of a quiet neutrality: that death has its place in life, it has a belonging that I would not have expected if I had been imagining, and not living, these moments.

No matter what I might have thought in the abstract, when the gate of birth-and-death opens in my life, the tone is quiet, everydayness is amplified, and the normalcy of death's presence is almost alarming in its familiarity. When death arrives, it's just what's happening, among the sandwiches and March Madness on the TV somewhere nearby, and jokes and tears, and love.

> This birth-and-death is the life of a buddha. If you try to exclude it you will lose the life of a buddha. If you cling to it, trying to remain in it, you will also lose the life of a buddha, and what remains will be the mere form of a buddha. Only when you don't avoid birth-and-death or long for it, do you enter a buddha's mind.
> However, do not analyze or speak about it. Just set aside your body and mind, forget about them, and throw them into the house of the buddha; then all is done by the buddha.
> —Dogen

The first moment I describe above, the moment that felt like a moment of grace, I understand now as a moment of freedom, where the strain of trying to separate things that are naturally and fully integrated, like life and death, dropped away. Death wasn't apart from my life, my life wasn't apart from death; and in that moment, I didn't have to exert the effort required to convince myself that they were not connected to one another. It was a moment free from the strain of dualism. It was, in fact, a moment of grace. But the habit energy of a dualistic approach to everything was still very strong in me. And so when I came to Zen practice, I came to it with a solidly dualistic conception: to get *me* on one side of a barrier of equanimity, and *the feelings that cause me pain* (as if they had a life apart from me) on the other. Once this plan was accomplished, I would no longer be pained by the mortal condition of myself or others. This, I imagined was what it meant to be to become "fearless" in the face of death.

I didn't have a very broad understanding of Zen, but I did have a strong image of a "Zen person," and an imagined reality to go along with it. A "Zen person" was unflappable, steady, immovable, unswayed by feelings. If they had feelings at all, they were mere flower petals drifting by on a river of equanimity. The world and its relentless imposition of impermanence could not hurt them. And my intention was to *get* this state of being! I intended to become so "Zen," so "equanimous," that people I love dying, and the idea of losing my own life, would no longer bother me. Zen practice would be a devotion that would pare away my involvement in the pain of this world. In different ways, I strived for this for many years, and with great effort.

But fortunately, really from the beginning of my practice, the teachings of my human life were weaving in with the Dharma, and were working on me below the surface of my conscious intentions. Instead of becoming less involved with the world as I practiced, I was becoming more available to it. Instead of feeling fewer emotional responses to the world around me, the more I practiced, the more I was aware of how intensely I felt, all the time. And then there were these people around me, these other sincere Zen practitioners, who somehow seeped their way into my heart, before I even noticed and tried to fend them off. And love asserted itself in my life again as a condition of my being, not an option for me to choose or not choose. I vividly remember, in those first years at Tassajara, watching color returning to my world, which had gone gray with grief in the years before. I discovered, at least for myself, that equanimity is a state full of feeling. And the fearlessness I was seeking in the face of my pain, takes a very different form from numbness or indifference: one where the amount of freedom available in any moment is directly proportional to the lack of resistance I can muster to what is arising, even when what's arising sucks, even when death arrives.

Practice, and all of this, worked together to wear down my dualistic habits, not entirely, but consistently enough so that by the time our second daughter came into the world for her brief life, new habit grooves had been laid down in my being, so that my body-heart-mind knew, in a way my conscious mind still did not, that the freedom from suffering I sought would not be found in turning away from what is happening, but turning wholly toward it. The path of turning toward was available that morning that she came and went so potently, but so quickly. Our second daughter was conceived within days of my ordination as a Soto Zen priest. The teaching of her short, Moon-face-Buddha (a Buddha who lives for one day) life, has lived in me for the whole of my life as a priest; teaching me over and over about the nonduality of birth-and-death, not as some beautiful, abstract concept, but as simply a lived reality, one I make efforts to keep showing up for.

I think it's my life in practice that has allowed me to open enough to fully see that, even with the great tides of grief and pain that have followed the death of people I love, whenever death has arrived in front of me, she has shown herself to not be a vicious reaper of loved ones, but a familiar aspect of their lives, and of my life. Death is something written in, down to the bottom, right from birth. But even holding and understanding this, practice has also brought me to accept that in all moments, I am a human being, with a human heart, who loves what she loves, and doesn't want to be separated from those people and things. I have made peace with my human heart and the pain and joy it feels. So at this point in my practice, "fearlessness in the face of death" looks like this: I grieve immensely when people I love (and even some that I don't know) die. It's just my human response, which is also often something that just happens to be arising in the moment in front of me. So, although the forms it takes doesn't look anything like what I expected, I have to confess something pretty tabooed in Zen, where we strive to not have any gaining idea: that I got what I came (and keep coming) for.

Dogen Zenji, founder of Soto Zen in the thirteenth century, wrote a fascicle entitled "Birth and Death." The same kanji that Dogen used in this title were used to translate the term "*Samsara*" into Chinese. *Samsara*: this realm of desire and suffering that is our home, this place of constant arising and ceasing. The first sentence of the fascicle, "This birth-and-death is the life of a buddha," could also be translated: "*Samsara* is the life of the Buddha." I have spent many years turning this short piece of writing, and I find it to be an excellent guide. It's Dogen's offering to his fellow human beings who want to practice the way of Zen about how to orient one's self in the tides of arising and ceasing that are our world. Sometimes what is arising and ceasing is a thought so petty it barely registers in our consciousness, and sometimes it's the arriving or departing of an actual human life. In either case, in any case, the teaching Dogen offers is the same: to engage completely, to allow the fullness of what's happening to happen fully. For me to answer the question of how practice has supported in me in times of struggle and challenge, it is the teaching over and over of the intimacy and completeness Dogen points to in "Birth and Death," that to be truly and willingly intimate with what's at hand is a life of freedom and fearlessness. To turn fully toward, and to fully feel and experience the whole of what is there to be felt and experienced is the life of the Buddha.

> Just understand that birth-and-death itself is nirvana. There is nothing such as birth and death to be avoided; there is nothing such as nirvana to be sought. Only when you realize this are you free from birth and death.
> —Dogen

Note

The epigraph and quotations within the essay are all from Kazuaki Tanahashi and Arnold Kotler, trans., "Shoji: Birth and Death," in Moon in a Dewdrop: Writings of Zen Master Dogen, ed. Kazuaki Tanahashi (New York: North Point Press, 1985), 74–75.

Heiku Jaime McLeod is a priest and teacher at Treetop Zen Center in Oakland, Maine, and a volunteer chaplain at Bates College. She is a member of the White Plum Asanga, the Soto Zen Buddhist Association, and the Zen Peacemaker Order. Heiku makes her living as an editor and journalist, and currently works in higher education publishing and as a contributing editor for *Buddhadharma: The Practitioner's Quarterly*. She believes practice requires compassionate activity in the world and strives to point to the possibility of awakened living in the realms of work, love, and home. Heiku lives in Lewiston, Maine, with her wife, Melissa, and their two children.

Picking and Choosing
Heiku Jaime McLeod

Years ago, when I was a newspaper reporter working on what I thought would be just another quirky human interest feature, I found myself sitting across a worn wooden dining-room table from the first Zen Buddhist priest I'd ever met. Her shaved head and robes made her seem exotic, and there was something undeniably sphinx-like in her demeanor, but her warmth and geniality, coupled with her easy, generous laugh, set me at ease.

"What led you to this," I asked, gesturing around the temple, to everything and nothing in particular.

She paused, considering the question for a long while before answering. Finally, she replied, "I was looking for peace of mind." In a world where the law of impermanence leaves us with nothing to hold onto, she said, "If your peace of mind depends on your loved ones not dying, or you not dying, you're in trouble." True peace, she told me, is not dependent on external conditions. Even in our dying breath, we always have everything we need.

I didn't know much at all about Buddhism, and what I thought I knew, from high school and college world religion surveys, had been badly distorted. But as someone with, as one of my health-care providers once put it, "an extensive trauma history," as well as a familial predisposition to depression, anxiety, and alcoholism, I knew—with more certainty than I'd ever known anything before—I wanted that kind of peace. And if practicing Zen could give me that, then I supposed I would have to start practicing Zen.

I felt less certain, however, about how exactly sitting around on a little black cushion and chanting a bunch of words I didn't understand was supposed to impart the peace of mind I so desperately craved. And when I finally began to get an inkling, I couldn't help but feel skeptical. The crux of this dissonance could be summed up in the opening lines of "On Trust in the Heart," a famous poem by Jianzhi Sengcan, the third patriarch of Zen in China, which appears in the service books of many Zen centers:

> The perfect way is only difficult for those who pick and choose.
>
> Do not like, do not dislike; all will then be clear.
>
> Make a hairbreadth difference and heaven and earth are set apart.
>
> If you want the truth to stand clear before you, never be for or against.
>
> The struggle between for and against is the mind's worst disease.

Even farther back, we can see the outlines of this teaching right in Shakyamuni Buddha's Four Noble Truths, one of the earliest and most basic teachings he offered after his enlightenment experience under the Bodhi tree.

First, there is *dukkha*—that is, discomfort and discontent, or as some translate it, suffering. We never have enough of what we want; we jealously guard what we do have, desperately, futilely, trying to keep it; and we're always getting more and more of what we don't want.

Second, the cause of that discomfort and discontent is our own clinging and aversion.

Third, there is a way out of this discomfort and discontent. We don't have to endure it forever.

And fourth, the way out is to ardently train our minds to let go of our clinging and aversion by practicing the Buddha's Eightfold Path.

In other words, "Do not like, do not dislike; all will then be clear."

That promise, that we can be free from suffering, is Buddhism's major draw. It's so simple, and yet sounds too good to be true, as though Shakyamuni took a marketing class from Zig Ziglar. "Be free from suffering in eight simple steps! No money down! Act now!" Who wouldn't want to at least look into it?

For me, though, as compelling as that promise was, I also felt some unease with it. Let go of my preferences? And then what? Let the world descend into chaos? Wash my hands of my commitment to social justice, of my heartfelt desire to see an end to poverty, war, sexism, racial inequality, or the despoilment of our planet? So what if kids in developing countries—hell, kids in our own country—are eating garbage or breathing toxic fumes? As long as I have inner peace, that's all that matters, right?

My feelings echoed the words of the Rev. Dr. Martin Luther King, Jr., "There are certain things in our nation and in the world [to] which I am proud to be maladjusted." If starting down the Buddhist path meant not caring—if it meant learning to become adjusted to horror and injustice—I wasn't sure I wanted any part of it.

And, indeed, there have been Buddhists throughout history who succumbed to just such pernicious quietism, of retreating from the world and refusing to sully their hands with material concerns. But, to my thinking, this interpretation of the teachings misses the mark.

The environmental activist, author, and Buddhist scholar Joanna Macy hit upon this very difficulty in a 2014 dialogue with members of the Buddhist Peace Fellowship:

> Western Buddhists... are very suspicious of attachment. They feel they need to be detached ... so don't get upset about racism, or injustice, or the poison in the rivers, because that... means you're too attached. This causes some difficulty for me, because I'm attached. I think one of the problems with Westernized Buddhists is premature equanimity. When the Buddha said "don't be attached," he meant don't be attached to the ego.(1)

Macy is among a growing number of "engaged Buddhists," practitioners who, prompted by teachings on compassion and the direct realization that all beings are inextricably interconnected, engage in social action as a form of practice. To me, that's just as it should be. My root teacher, Peter Seishin Wohl, has always insisted the term "engaged Buddhism" is redundant. To practice the Buddha Way, he always said, is to be engaged, intimately, with the world and all of its suffering beings.

So I cringe when I hear the aim of Buddhism described as "detachment." I prefer the term "nonattachment," which doesn't conjure the same connotations of being aloof or disinterested—of being "checked out"—that detachment does. Waking up is not about checking out. It's about checking in, fearlessly facing what's in front of us without denial, without our habitual storylines, and without retreating to the safety of our fantasy worlds or addictions.

This idea shows up in the second case of *The Blue Cliff Record*, which both quotes and expands upon "On Trust in the Heart."

> Chao-chou, teaching the assembly, said, "The Ultimate Path is without difficulty; just avoid picking and choosing. As soon as there are words spoken, 'this is picking and choosing, this is clarity.' This old monk does not abide within clarity; do you still preserve anything or not?"
>
> At that time a certain monk asked, "Since you do not abide within clarity, what do you preserve?"
>
> Chao-chou replied, "I don't know either."
>
> The monk said, "Since you don't know, Teacher, why do you nevertheless say that you do not abide within clarity?"
>
> Chao-chou said, "It is enough to ask about the matter; bow and withdraw."(2)

Many of us come to Zen because we crave clarity in an uncertain world, but Chao-chou understood that to abide within clarity would mean clinging to an idealized state called "clarity," rather than being present right here and now. This open, accepting state of mind is often referred to by Zen teachers, ancient and modern, as "not knowing." Far from the "not knowing" of ignorance, this "not knowing" means letting go of what we think we know—of what our grasping, clinging egos think we or others need—and attending to what is.

It doesn't mean we can't use the wisdom we've gained from experience. And it doesn't mean we won't have preferences. As long as we are human beings who live and breathe, we will always have preferences. (I, for one, have a strong preference for breathing.) It means we don't have to be hemmed in by what we know or what we want. It means we stay open to possibilities and present to reality, even when things don't go quite how we think they should.

Several years ago, the award-winning journalist Ben Sherwood interviewed dozens of people who had survived life threatening situations—plane crashes, shipwrecks, concentration camps. The resulting book, *The Survivor's Club*, was an exploration into whether his subjects had any unifying strategies or personal qualities the rest of us could learn from. One of the most poignant takeaways for me was that several survivors attributed their continued existence to their ability to accept the reality of what happened to them. Survivor after survivor shared stories of others who might also have escaped with their lives had they not fallen apart in the crucial moments or hours after the precipitating crisis, unable to process and integrate the new, painful reality they suddenly inhabited.

One of those survivors was Tim Sears, a thirty-one-year-old Michigander who fell overboard from a cruise ship into the Gulf of Mexico. Sears survived alone at sea for more than twelve hours before he was rescued by a Maltese copper freighter. Of Sears's ordeal, Sherwood writes:

> He didn't cry out to God, asking why this was happening. Instead, he accepted the new reality and dealt with it. Well, I'm here, he told himself. If I'm going to get out of this situation, I need to keep maintaining and be strong and get through it until at least daylight.(3)

One might assume positive thinking would be crucial to maintaining the will to survive, but some of Sherwood's interviewees suggested otherwise. Paul Barney, a shipwreck survivor who nearly froze to death clinging to a life raft in the frigid Baltic Sea, recalled a fellow passenger he dubbed "Mr. Positive," who was "quite a vociferous character."

> "'We're going to be saved,' he would say. 'They're coming for us. It won't be long.'" Sometime before dawn, Mr. Positive fell silent, succumbing to the cold. "Sadly, his positivity ran out . . . . He was let down too often. And that would have taken a toll on him quite a lot . . . raising his hopes and hav-

ing them dashed time and time again . . . would have really stripped him of his energy."(4)

Sherwood associates this effect with the so-called Stockdale Paradox, named for Admiral James Stockdale, the highest ranking American prisoner of war during the Vietnam conflict. When writer Jim Collins asked Stockdale which of his fellow POWs perished first, the admiral replied, "Oh, that's easy. The optimists." He went on to explain that they "were the ones who said, 'We're going to be out by Christmas.' And Christmas would come and Christmas would go. And then Thanksgiving, and then it would be Christmas again. And they died of a broken heart."(5)

But isn't cultivating equanimity in the face of difficult circumstances the same thing as positive thinking? After all, in another case from *The Blue Cliff Record*, Master Yun Men Weyan famously said, "Every day is a good day." To understand Master Yun Men's pronouncement as promoting Pollyannaism—as a forebear of Pangloss's "All is for the best in this, the best of all possible worlds"— is to take his words out of context, though. To help clarify this point, here is the case in its entirety:

> Yun Men said, "I don't ask you about before the fifteenth day; try to say something about after the fifteenth day."
> Yun Men himself answered for everyone, "Every day is a good day."(6)

In the lunar calendar, the fifteenth day of the month falls around the time of the full moon. And the full moon is a traditional symbol of enlightenment and clarity. In asking the assembly to "say something about after the fifteenth day," Yun Men was challenging them to bring forth an expression of their awakening. His "Every day is a good day" wasn't the pronouncement of a man wearing rose-colored glasses, but a reminder that every day, every instant, offers us an opportunity to awaken. That, in fact, there is no other time in which we can awaken.

Too often, in some of the sexier books about Zen, the dropping away of body and mind and the emergence of our original face can sound like some kind of spiritual jackpot. If we just keep pumping quarters into the meditation slot machine, someday we might hit it big. But enlightenment is not a state we reach once and for all. Enlightenment is a daily vow, a daily struggle, to maintain equanimity even in the midst of the joys and sorrows of our fragile human existence—even when our hearts are broken, and they will break if we're paying attention—and to use that equanimity to help us work for the benefit of all beings.

It's not that Sherwood's survivors felt no emotion about their situations, or that they sat placidly, in perfect samadhi, amid the twisted wreckage that had, not long before, been sailing gracefully through the raging sea or the sky above. I'd bet not one of them was "detached." Each of them fought tooth and nail against adversity—injury, illness, exposure, hunger, thirst, and fear of never being found—doing whatever needed to be done to ensure their survival. Pushing aside the inevitable despair and self-pity that each of us is so familiar with at times, they kept their heads clear and their eyes on dealing with whatever necessity was in front of them, finding water or shelter, seeking a way out, or signaling for rescue. Instead of panicking, they simply did the next thing that needed to be done until they were safe.

This metaphor can easily be extended to any situation we find ourselves in. Whether we're trying to overcome an addiction or a neurotic tendency, achieve a personal goal, or are standing up to confront environmental devastation or systemic oppression, we must start from a place of what the Insight Meditation teacher Tara Brach calls "radical acceptance." This acceptance doesn't mean we give up on improving ourselves or our world. It doesn't mean we decide everything is fine just the way it is, so let's open another box of Twinkies and binge-watch the next season of our favorite Netflix show. And it doesn't mean we're free to float in eternal bliss on a lotus petal in some heavenly being realm we've created in our own minds, either.

Letting go of like and dislike means we don't wait for some ideal future situation to begin working toward the change we want to see in the world, or in ourselves. Because that future will never come. We only ever have right now, so we have to start from who and where we are. Like a good doctor, if we want to heal ourselves, our fellow beings, and our world, we have to start by looking deeply at and acknowledging the sickness and its causes. A doctor doesn't wait until the patient is well to begin healing her. As paradoxical as it may seem, if we want to bring about what could be, we must begin by embracing and accepting what is. If we try to push painful realities away, to separate from them, to retreat into the comfortable certainty of our likes and dislikes, we'll never be able to see clearly what needs to be done. Our egos will be in the way.

When we are able to practice true acceptance and intimacy with every aspect of our lives, we may even experience moments of genuine transcendence—not mere dissociation, crass sentimentality, or bypassing—right within our darkest hours. Remember Tim Sears? Sherwood writes:

> Tim even managed to take time to marvel at nature's beauty. Indeed the most memorable experience of the entire ordeal, he says, came when "all of a sudden everything around me for as far as I could see were bright green little fish jumping." He stopped swimming just to look. "It was like, wow, this is amazing." At that precise moment, he thought, there was no place else in the world you could see such a stunning sight. "It was beautiful."(7)

Sears's story has echoes of an old Zen story, made famous in the last century by Paul Reps and Nyogen Senzaki:

> A man traveling across a field encountered a tiger. He fled, the tiger after him. Coming to a precipice, he caught hold of the root of a wild vine and swung himself down over the edge. The tiger sniffed at him from above. Trembling, the man looked down to where, far below, another tiger was waiting to eat him. Only the vine sustained him. Two mice, one white and one black, little by little started to gnaw away at the vine. The man saw a luscious strawberry near him. Grasping the vine with one hand, he plucked the strawberry with the other. How sweet it tasted!(8)

Zen practitioners don't need to reside in a fantasy world, pretending everything is OK, even as the sky is literally falling. We simply do the next right thing, one step after another, tending to whatever needs to be tended to, letting go of whatever weighs us down.

Notes

1. Richard Eskow, "Don't Just Sit There, Do Something," Tricycle, November 10, 2014, tricycle.org/trikedaily/dont-just-sit-there-do-something/.
2. Thomas Cleary and J. C. Cleary, *The Blue Cliff Record* (Boulder, CO: Shambhala Publications, 1977), 10.
3. Ben Sherwood, *The Survivors Club* (New York: Grand Central Publishing, 2009), 211.
4. Sherwood, *The Survivors Club*, 41.
5. Sherwood, *The Survivors Club*, 41–42.
6. Cleary and Cleary, *The Blue Cliff Record*, 37.
7. Sherwood, *The Survivors Club*, 212.
8. Paul Reps and Nyogen Senzaki, *Zen Flesh, Zen Bones* (New York: Anchor/Doubleday, 1958), 22–23.

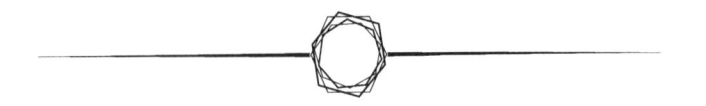

Eido Frances Carney is the teacher and abbess at Olympia Zen Center in Washington. Transmitted by Niho Tetsumei Roshi at Entusji in Japan in 1997, she promotes the teachings of Zen priest-poet Ryokan. She is the founder of Temple Ground Press, editor of *Receiving the Marrow: Teachings on Dogen by Soto Zen Women Priests*, and author of *Kakurenbo, or the Whereabouts of Zen Priest Ryokan*.

Can Kanzeon Bodhisattva Laugh?
Eido Frances Carney

There were days in our small city after the presidential election of 2016 when as many as two hundred people waited in line at the pharmacy for a prescription. In our fairly large hospital, when a friend needed to be admitted, she had twenty-nine people ahead of her in need of a bed. This was not funny. Medical practitioners agreed that the stress of the election had exacerbated illnesses, and the sheer numbers of patients waiting for treatment overwhelmed the clinics. Were these illnesses an unconscious response to the cultural conflicts, an existential dilemma that we were experiencing? Had we some control over our physical response to the election? People seemed to be acting out a psychologically detached suicide through illness, just as Hamlet explores the possibility of his demise at his own hand, or, he asks, whether it is better to simply be impassive in the suffering that life metes upon us.

> To be, or not to be, that is the question:
> Whether 'tis nobler in the mind to suffer
> The slings and arrows of outrageous fortune,
> Or to take Arms against a Sea of troubles,
> And by opposing end them: to die, to sleep
> No more; and by a sleep, to say we end
> The heart-ache, and the thousand natural shocks
> That Flesh is heir to? (1)

It is well to remember that while short of three million votes, a portion of the population celebrated the election; there was plenty of snarky laughter there. Their candidate won. Yet many on the majority side of the election were dashed against the rocks and unable to think what could be done in response. No jokes to be heard. This was not entirely because of a single person placed into power, but the potential disintegration of numerous compassionate protection policies that were hard won and put in place were now at stake: the climate, the environment, women's rights, civil rights, immigration, health care, the economy, and constitutional integrity itself. Very few took a *que sera, sera* approach. I, myself, was beset by a flurry of questions which I could not settle in answer or action. Which cause could I take on and could it have a positive effect? Should I become active in the political arena? Or would it be better to quietly maintain practice and know that zazen makes a positive, primary change in us and in the culture around us? But does this change occur in the world even if others are not practicing but rather acting against the public good? Is practice powerful enough to change history? Am I so deeply focused that I cannot be swayed by political power and circumstance? How is anger in response to the election seeping into my daily activities? Am I spending too much time on useless destructive news? Am I purposely listening to voices that invoke an angry response? Is the political arena a reality? Should I absent myself from the politics of our nation? Where is the balance of practice in relation to the movement of world politics and international relations? Is my daily life truly affected by the government? Am I responsible to speak out when I see the poor and the homeless mistreated? What is it that I should do in response to unethical legislation? How shall I respond to misstatements and lying by my government and its leaders? What should I do? What is my responsibility?

Surely Kanzeon, the Bodhisattva of Compassion, in listening to the cries of suffering, listens to the cries of Hamlet as well as the rest of us. Hamlet remains the epitome of great existential angst; he asks ultimate questions. My questions were just a sample of those that surged through me. Yet, even as I aimed toward balance, laughter and a lighthearted response to events that were naturally funny seemed a necessary element to lift us, and to help many of our sangha who were also tossed about by what we perceived to be our country's untimely demise. I thought about the visage of the Kanzeon statues, often depicted with deeply serious appearance because someone who is weeping from sorrow and loss could not appeal to someone who is laughing. Just not appropriate. Yet someone who is laughing is not necessarily someone who is without suffering. Simply, that for that moment, suffering is relieved as laughter changes how we see the world. I wondered if Kanzeon Bodhisattva could laugh.

Of course, it was never my aim to answer these questions for anyone else, nor could I entirely answer for myself; rather, my aim has been, as it has also been the sangha's aim, to practice with our best effort in muddy waters and sustain a healthy spiritual life with the right ingredient of humor. The political questions that disturbed us were, and continue to be, disconcerting and full of dis-ease, and if dis-ease is not tempered with understanding and steady practice and necessary lightheartedness at appropriate times, it can bring about illness in us. We know that conflict and anger are a poison, and dwelling in anger is not helpful, or useful, or wise.

Kurt Vonnegut writes in *Palm Sunday: An Autobiographical Collage*:

> It's hard to tell if this is a happy and natural response to particular moments in life, or if this seeming insanity rises from the array of challenges—the burgeoning human worldwide poverty and displacement, the unspeakably monumental problems. It doesn't go by me that the challenges and the opportunities before us are too much to encompass and so I laugh while dangling on the precipice of tears. Yet the laughter is delicious and I refuse to give over to the dark side. Laughs are exactly as honorable as tears. Laughter and tears are both responses to frustration and exhaustion, to the futility of thinking and striving anymore. I myself prefer to laugh, since there is less cleaning up to do afterward.(2)

The Stephen Colbert Show, so I am told by an expat, is the single most popular program on television in Europe right now. In conversation with this friend, we agree that laughter is saving us from tipping over into fury, and if other nations are laughing at us from abroad and not just with us, more power to them. They see our country in a way that we do not as we are caught in our tomfoolery and juvenility and arrested in incivility and destructiveness. Colbert is at once brilliant and cruel and we laugh in the intricate

Zen Teachings In Challenging Times

complexities of humor, a piece of us gritting our teeth and a piece glad that the arrow is hitting its mark. We are relieved as we laugh out loud at his exaggerated insights into the childish maneuvers of our politicians and lawmakers. We know that what is happening on the wider sphere is not funny yet through raw humor we allow a painful truth to be told.

It's clear that teachers are doing their best to help themselves and others stand in the middle of a burning world. And yet, without laughter we are doomed. Is it that we may take ourselves a little too seriously? Or is it that through laughter, we manage to bear the pain and suffering, "the slings and arrows of outrageous fortune." There isn't a lot funny about Hamlet—although thinking there might be takes us right to the Monty Python edge of humor.

Honest to goodness, the practice of Zen, if it is to do what it promises, must have the experience of laughter, the mercy of lightheartedness in its essence and core underpinnings at the very heart of the moment of Awakening. The thousand armed Bodhisattva of Compassion must be holding a comedy play in one of her helping hands. Isn't it Shunryu Suzuki Roshi who said we shouldn't take ourselves too seriously. So, while we have many, many serious issues to deal with, given the challenge of our times, if we are not able to laugh, we are doomed. And this laughter need not be only politically motivated, but we owe it to ourselves to stand higher than the compelling grip of narcissistic illness that is the emphasis of our news and public discourse.

Alan Watts believed that laughter is a form of meditation. His video on Youtube[3] has him laughing for a sustained two and a half minutes. Then he quiets himself and asks, "How did that feel?" and "Who are you now?" He mentions a Zen master who said that we might be better off inducing laughter in ourselves each morning rather than sitting on a cushion falling asleep.

One of my first questions to Inoue Kando Roshi, a teacher of *Shobogenzo* in Japan was, "Did Dogen Zenji ever laugh?" Much of *Shobogenzo* is starkly serious and I couldn't find amusement in the eye of the great Zen master between the lines of the text. Kando Roshi was taken aback, "Well, of course he laughed," he answered. But it takes some doing to see where that takes place in a cultural context and in a translated text. Nevertheless, it seems to me a necessary component to the character of any Zen practitioner and particularly to the founder of Soto Zen. As the founder goes, so go the students. As the teachings go, so go the followers.

When Dogen Zenji tells us to "study the Self" he is talking about the big Self, the awakened Self and he teaches us to forget the small self and the self of any kind and simply allow the myriad things to come forward to awaken us. There is no doubt that this awakened teaching is the central point of our practice. But if we were to simply disregard the workings of the small self, the everyday self, the psychological self, the self that is experiencing disturbance, we would be ignoring an aspect of what it means to spiritually mature. We cannot leave behind what we are feeling. We must acknowledge the totality of our whole being.

For most of us, although we may have deep experiences on the cushion, we still have to "grow up," as Ken Wilbur puts it.[4] We must mature psychologically as well as spiritually. Growing up means to study the workings of the psychological mind and examine how the prejudices, wounds, afflictions, disappointments, betrayals, losses, grief, attachments—all of "the slings and arrows of outrageous fortune" that have been hurled against us—have affected us, are still operating in us, constitute our karmic patterns, are the mechanism of cause and effect, and we must come to terms with them and take responsibility for our participation in the full spectrum of life. There is no greater nor more urgent work than to come to bald, raw honesty and look squarely at ourselves in the mirror. And, our work in that process is to not carry accumulated suffering like the clanging weight of Jacob Marley's chains. The cosmic joke is on us, after all, that we are treading water in the deep well of existential abyss and we imagine we are trapped. Yet no situation is more useful than to see through the paradox and discover where true meaning lies.

Kobun Chino Otogawa Roshi encouraged his students to get up close to their problems. He taught that when we encounter someone who disturbs us or makes us angry, we should get close to that person and not try to escape from the situation. This is our point of practice, the center of practice, the heart of practice, he said. He often stressed this and his students listened patiently and tried to fulfill his teaching. But one week while Kobun Roshi was away, Dainin Katagiri Roshi came to teach. People had all kinds of questions for

Katagiri Roshi, but one student who had been mulling over Kobun Roshi's teachings asked Katagiri Roshi: "I have someone at work who drives me crazy. Every time I go near him I get so angry and I fall into a rage inside myself. What should I do?" Katagiri Roshi looked at the man totally nonplussed and simply declared: "Stay away from that man!" Poor Katagiri Roshi: uncontrollable laughter went on for at least ten minutes.

Walking away is one way and it has wisdom and merit. Another is to get up close and study the mind, study what is going on in us, and study any reaction of dislike, resentment, abhorrence, or disorienting emotion. Flexibility is called for and the ability to laugh at ourselves that we would stubbornly hold to only one answer. Sometimes walk away; sometimes stick close. Every situation calls for its own response. Zen practice does not suggest that we should abandon our intelligence or our public voice, which must give an appropriate response to seriously damaging and hurtful actions that are taking place in our country. There are many unethical and corrupt happenings and we should be free to point them out. We have a moral obligation to be intelligent, says Lionel Trilling.(5) For Zen practitioners, the question is whether or not we stand on the firm ground of seasoned practice, that we respond with clarity and confidence at the bedrock of our training, and that our arguments are vested in the history and foundations of justice and equality. At the same time, laughter is a deeply intelligent and humanly necessary response. Laughter does not preclude getting up close, but rather it assists us to abandon self righteousness, a fixed stance, a false strictness, and helps us dodge "the slings and arrows of outrageous fortune." All the while remembering that some sufferings can only be met with crying anguish or profound silence.

The deep wisdom in such up close practice is not easy, but its merit is exemplary particularly given the obvious fact that the current world situation is not going to disappear any day soon. Problems of one kind or another are always with us. There are those who believe that we are at the end stages of empire, given our hubristic hegemony in past decades, and thus we can only expect the disintegration of culture, ethics, education, and relationship to other nations. This may well be the case, but in Zen, we just keep practicing regardless of the conditions or state of the union. Our task is always to make the most of the moment, to continue to bear witness, to grow from all situations, and to make every effort to live in enlightenment. And Awakening contains the ultimate laughter. Ryokan in a poem uses the metaphor of the moon in the mind of Awakening:

> Who among the moon viewers tonight will have the prize?
>
> Who will reflect the clearest moon in the lake of his mind?
>
> Surely you all know of that riverside moon viewing of long ago
>
> When Fugan alone, the rest lagging, ran beyond the flesh
>
> And of Yakkyo who moon inspired cracked a laugh on a hilltop. (6)

Mind opens. Yakkyo laughs. The natural response of seeing through, of getting up close to letting mind be Mind. All falls away and suffering is washed clean in the cosmic opening. Like the clarity of the monk hanging onto a weak branch on the side of a cliff. A tiger above, a tiger below, he sees a piece of fruit growing beside him: "Ah the strawberry, tastes so sweet." The total existential moment from which we can't escape. Life and death in the balance. And yet, laughter deep and fulfilling.

The discriminating mind is faster than the speed of light. The mind that entertains anger is a habit that flashes on and off as quickly as thoughts come and go. But such thoughts also linger and etch their way into the body like field mice making nests in a car engine. Silent and stealthy they pick up nuts and leaves and form little nests in the warmth of the heater or on the struts that hold the engine. Before we know it, like field mice, we've got a habitual lair, made of our collections, gathering more and more information to stuff into a dark corner to prove why we should be angry.

This is the process that can be studied in the quiet recesses in which we hide discriminating thoughts. Up close, we can examine this process. Notice the points that are provoked and tempted into reactivity when we turn on the news; observe the heat of anger that begins to burn. But also notice how the heat is dissipated when we just stand back and watch. We can't both react and investigate at the same time. Notice how reaction diminishes when we are on the lookout and observing. Notice how noticing slows down the triggers that provoke old connections and habits of storage of thoughts and ideas. See how notions settle into the nest, with bits and pieces of torment trying to root us in dissatisfaction. Where did the anger come from? How have we let it settle in? What roots, like deep weeds, is it enforcing in the soil of the mind? Do we have a warm spot to house our anger, a spot that we will not admit nor let go? Can we follow the path of the field mouse forming the nest? Can we avoid rejecting it until we see how it moves and settles? Can we find out where it lives? Can we see the dark side of ourselves as humans who make mental nests of not so nice ideas? Can we not turn away from this study of ourselves in order to pretend that we are perfect? Often we cut off the investigation because we don't want to think that we are petty, mean, and intolerant. We all are to some degree. It's part of being human. The real question is whether we can root this out and transform ourselves and polish the character such that we can live in a fruitful way with good relations regardless of the flavor of our politics and the condition of our leaders.

We don't get something for nothing. Life is work and at some point we ought embrace the joy of it. We must tend to the practice of making every effort to live in enlightenment. When we make this choice, little by little we are lifted from the pit of rage, frustration, discouragement, and all the other apparent forces that seem to drag us into an internal, self perpetuated war. When we read the newspaper, we can translate what we read into our understanding of Dharma. What does this mean? It means when we read about an earthquake, for instance, with people trapped under buildings, unless we ourselves can go immediately to that place and help lift bricks out of the way to free the people, we can immediately stand on faith and keep the mind of Kanzeon, the Bodhisattva of Compassion, the one who hears the cries of suffering, opens the heart of compassion to listen. As we chant in the *Lotus Sutra*, "constant mindfulness of Sound-Observer, the one who can extinguish the woes of existence," we join in the dynamic compassionate action right where we are. Kanzeon is alive and working in the world when we turn to the Bodhisattva of Compassion to lift and extinguish the suffering around us. Laughter that does not disregard nor render suffering superficial can bring joy to the moment and unify us. The illness of our times must not win the day. We can elevate and strengthen the mind of practice to include all of existence in the light of dharma. We can all be saved from the worst dilemmas even the dilemma of our own dark cubbyholes and nests. Morning Mind is Kanzeon! Evening Mind is Kanzeon, This very moment arises from Mind. This very moment itself is Mind. Mind hears it all. Kanzeon hears the cries of suffering. Kanzeon hears the cries of laughter.

Notes

1. William Shakespeare, *The Complete Works* (Baltimore, MD: Penguin, 1969).
2. Kurt Vonnegut, *Palm Sunday: An Autobiographical Collage* (New York, NY: Dial Press, 1981).
3. Alan Watts, *The Laughing Meditation* www.youtube.com/watch?v=06dWxtT1KNY.
4. Ken Wilbur, *Integral Meditation: Mindfulness as a Way to Grow Up, Wake Up, and Show Up in Your Life* (Boulder, CO: Shambhala, 2016).
5. Lionel Trilling, *The Moral Obligation to Be Intelligent: Selected Essays* (New York: Farrar, Straus and Giroux, 2000).
6. Daigu Ryokan, *The Zen Poems of Ryokan*, trans. Nobuyuki Yuasa (Princeton, NJ: Princeton University Press, 1981).

Chants

Enmei Jikku Kannon Gyo

Kanzeon! Namu Butsu
Kanzeon! At one with Buddha
Yo Butsu u in, Yo Butsu u en
Related to all Buddhas in cause and effect
Buppo so en
Our true nature is
Jo raku ga jo
Eternal, joyous, selfless, pure
Cho nen Kanzeon
Morning mind is Kanzeon
Bo nen Kanzeon
Evening mind is Kanzeon
Nen nen ju shin ki
This very moment arises from Mind
Nen nen fu ri shin
This very moment itself is Mind

Heart of Great Perfect Wisdom Sutra

Avalokiteshvara Bodhisattva, when deeply practicing prajna paramita, clearly saw that all five aggregates are empty and thus relieved all suffering. Shariputra, form does not differ from emptiness, emptiness does not differ from form. Form itself is emptiness, emptiness itself form. Sensations, perceptions, formations, and consciousness are also like this. Shariputra, all dharmas are marked by emptiness; they neither increase nor decrease. Therefore, given emptiness, there is no form, no sensation, no perception, no formation, no consciousness; no eyes, no ears, no nose, no tongue, no body no mind; no sight, no sound, no smell, no taste, no touch, no object of mind; no realm of sight . . . no realm of mind consciousness. There is neither ignorance nor extinction of ignorance . . . neither old age and death, nor extinction of old age and death; no suffering, no cause, no cessation, no path; no knowledge and no attainment. With nothing to attain, a bodhisattva relies on prajna paramita, and thus the mind is without hindrance. Without hindrance, there is no fear. Far beyond all inverted views, one realizes nirvana. All buddhas of past, present, and future rely on prajna paramita and thereby attain unsurpassed, complete, perfect enlightenment. Therefore, know the prajna paramita as the great miraculous mantra, the great bright mantra, the supreme mantra, the incomparable mantra, which removes all suffering and is true, not false. Therefore we proclaim the prajna paramita mantra, the mantra that says: "Gate Gate Paragate Parasamgate Bodhi Svaha."

Hymn to the Perfection of Wisdom

Homage to the Perfection of Wisdom, the Lovely, the Holy. The Perfection of Wisdom gives light. Unstained, the entire world cannot stain her, she is a source of light, and from everyone in the triple world she removes darkness. Most excellent are her works. She brings light so that all fear and distress may be forsaken, and disperses the gloom and darkness of delusion. She herself is an organ of vision, she has a clear knowledge of being of all Dharmas, for she does not stray away from it. The Perfection of Wisdom of the Buddhas sets in motion the Wheel of Dharma.

Glossary

Ananda was one of the ten great disciples of the Buddha and became the Buddha's personal attendant. He is known for having an extraordinary memory for retaining the Buddha's discourses. Ananda, more than any other, advocated for women and the recognition of the women's monastic order.

Avalokiteshvara (also known as Kanzeon in Japanese, and Kuanyin in Chinese) is the Bodhisattva of Compassion, who hears the cries of suffering throughout the world and helps to extinguish the woes of existence.

Bodhicitta is a Sanskrit word that refers to the awakened mind or the mind of enlightenment. It also refers to the seed of awakening that is nurtured by the intention to practice and the actualization of practice in the heart of compassion.

Bodhidharma, circa 470–543 CE, was the twenty-eighth Indian patriarch after the Buddha and the first Chinese patriarch of Ch'an, or Zen.

Bodhisattva refers to an enlightened being, a helper who practices virtue, resides in the nature of compassion and wisdom, and assists other beings in the steps toward liberation. The bodhisattva promises to remain as a helper to alleviate suffering and foregoes nirvana until all beings are awakened. "Bodhisattva" can also mean a personification of Buddha Nature.

Bodhi-Mind is the mind of wisdom awakened in the unity of subject and object, and realization of the essential nature of emptiness of all existence. The awakened mind also refers to realization and insight of the four noble truths.

Brahma vihara is a term referring to the divine states of dwelling. The meditator practices four states of mind that overcome ill will, and these states are radiated in the four directions. The four comprise limitless kindness toward all beings, limitless compassion toward the suffering, limitless joy for those who have overcome suffering, and limitless equanimity toward all beings, friends or enemies. These are perfect virtues necessary to a bodhisattva to bring others to liberation.

Buddha dharma, in Zen, is the ungraspable truth, which rests in the enlightenment experience of Shakyamuni Buddha, and which we too grasp in our experience of awakening. It is not transmitted orally or through texts, but rather is realized in the direct experience of enlightenment.

Buddhahood is the matter of realizing the actuality of perfect enlightenment, which is the birthright of all human beings.

Buddha nature is the true and eternal nature of all sentient life. This means that through appropriate spiritual practice all sentient life may experience the realization of enlightenment and buddhahood

Dharma has numerous meanings: that which is the underlying nature of the world; the teachings or the law of universal truth; all living phenomena; the ethical rules of behavior for Buddhist practitioners; a reflection of the content of the human mind.

Dharmakaya, in Mahayana Buddhism, is one of "three bodies" that express the absolute dynamic of a buddha: the Dharmakaya (transcendent reality), Sambhogakaya (the enjoyment of truth), and Nirmanakaya (the earthly body of transformation). Dharmakaya is essentially the true spiritual nature of Buddha, beyond duality and without characteristics.

Dukkha means suffering and is a mark of existence and is central to the Buddha's teachings of the Four Noble Truths and can be extinguished by the practice of the Eightfold Path.

Eightfold Path is the practice that leads to release from suffering and is the fourth step in the Four Noble Truths. The Eightfold Path comprises (1) perfect view, (2) perfect resolve, (3) perfect speech, (4) perfect conduct, (5) perfect livelihood, (6) perfect effort, (7) perfect mindfulness, (8) perfect concentration.

Emptiness in Buddhism is the truth that inherent existence is dependently originated in all its causes and conditions, even in the principle of causality. Emptiness is therefore pure mind, the mind of enlightenment.

Four Noble Truths constitute the Buddha's basic teaching; they are (1) the truth of suffering in life, (2) the truth that cravings or appetites are the cause of suffering, (3) the truth that suffering can be extinguished, and (4) the truth that following the Eightfold Path can lead to the end of suffering.

Fukanzazengi is a work written by the founder of Soto Zen in Japan, Eihei Dogen; it iterates the essential fundamentals of Zazen, seated meditation.

Gassho is a gesture of unity and supplication made with the hands, holding them palm-to-palm and upright in front of the body and away from the face. It is a sign of courtesy and greeting between Buddhists, and is used formally in religious ceremony as a sign of reverence.

Genzo-e is a special study retreat to investigate the teachings of Eihei Dogen.

Jizo, also known in Sanskrit as Kshitigarbha, and in China as Ti-ts'ang, is a bodhisattva celebrated in folk belief as one who saves us from hell realms and is the helper to deceased children. Jizo also protects travelers. Jizo may be portrayed in a male or a female form.

Juzu, or *ojuzu* or *mala* beads are prayer beads (usually 18, 21, 27, 54, or 108 beads) used for counting the number of chants, mantras, or prostrations in honor of the Buddha.

Jukai is the granting and receiving of precepts in ceremony in which one officially becomes a Buddhist. The candidate vows to uphold the Buddha, the Dharma, and the Sangha, to avoid all evil, to practice good, to save all beings, and to follow the Buddha way.

Kanzeon. See Avalokiteshvara.

Kensho is a Japanese word that means "seeing one's nature." Sometimes this is synonymous with *satori*, which means the experience of awakening or enlightenment. It is the experience that cannot be explained or grasped conceptually as it is beyond duality and beyond seeing oneself as a self. *Kensho* also implies an "opening" experience that is still to be deepened through continual practice.

Kesa or ***okesa*** is a large patchwork robe, most often made of humble cloth, that is worn by Zen priests for zazen and ceremonies. During other occasions, the *rakusu*, or little robe, will be worn. At a special celebration, more elaborate robes made of richer cloth may be worn.

Klesha refers to a mental state that leads to unwholesome actions. *Kleshas* might include anger, jealousy, fear, depression, anxiety, or any negative emotion. Greed, anger, and ignorance are *kleshas*, and are known as the Three Poisons, which are the root of all other *kleshas*.

Koan is a paradoxical teaching, phrase, or brief narrative used in Zen training to direct the mind toward the nature of ultimate reality. A koan cannot be answered or understood through reason, but requires an insight or intuitive leap that takes one beyond logical mentation to another level of understanding.

Kuanyin, the Goddess of Compassion. See Avalokiteshvara.

Lotus Sutra is a discourse of the Buddha that was delivered toward the end of his public life and that contains the complete teachings of the Buddha. In this sutra, the Buddha is not a historical figure, but rather a transcendent Nature, which is available to everyone such that they themselves can awaken to their own True Nature and become a Buddha themselves.

Mahapajapati was the stepmother of the Buddha. She raised him after his mother died in his infancy. Later she became the leader of the women's monastic order rescuing thousands of women from all over India who, for cultural reasons, had been exiled from their towns and condemned by their families.

Mahaprajnaparamita is a term referring to the Heart Sutra, one of the most important sutras in Mahayana Buddhism. The sutra is chanted frequently in Zen because it expresses the teaching of emptiness and its inherent and immediate experience.

Mala. See *Juzu*.

Manjushri, in Japanese known as Monju, is a bodhisattva known as "one who is noble and gentle." Manjushri is the Bodhisattva of Wisdom that dispels the darkness of ignorance.

Mudra is a way of holding the hands or the body in a symbolic gesture to indicate an aspect of the Buddha. In Buddhist iconography, particular gestures of the hands refer to such aspects as protection, care of the sutras, supreme wisdom, concentration, fearlessness, and other spiritual expressions.

Nirvana, in Zen, is synonymous with Buddha nature or with prajna, wisdom. When one has attained prajna, that is, awakening into one's true nature, then one lives in the state of nirvana, which is not separate from this existence. Nirvana is the state of living one's true nature as a human being.

Oryoki refers, first, to the nesting bowls that one receives during ordination and which will be the only religious "property" of a Zen monk along with the robe. Today, lay people also receive *oryoki* bowls. The term also refers simply to the one bowl that the Buddha's followers used for their begging rounds and meals. A third meaning is the meal-taking ceremony in which practitioners eat in silence and handle the bowls in a formal, ceremonial way. The word *oryoki* in Japanese means "holding just enough" which implies that one eats without greed and takes just enough to meet the body's need for nutrition and energy for the work one is doing.

Rakusu means "little robe" and refers to a rectangular religious article worn by priests, monks, and lay people to symbolize the patchwork robe of Shakyamuni Buddha. The *rakusu* is made of cloth and is conferred on someone who receives the Precepts and is initiated into Buddhism.

Rohatsu, in Japanese, literally means the "eighth day of the twelfth month"; it refers to a weeklong *sesshin* leading up the "eighth day," when the Buddha, having spent the whole night in meditation, looked up, saw the morning star, and attained enlightenment.

Samsara, in Mahayana Buddhism, refers to the phenomenal world and is equivalent to nirvana. That is, the true nature of the phenomenal world is emptiness and is therefore the same as nirvana, or freedom from attachment to delusion, or oneness with the Absolute.

Sangha is one of the Three Treasures: Buddha, Dharma, and Sangha. The sangha is the Buddhist community of practitioners. In a monastery, or in the original Buddhist community, "sangha" may refer only to those who are practicing monks, whereas in a wider sense, it includes all who are equally practicing together.

Satori (see also *Kensho*) may be synonymous with *kensho*, but is often referred to as the Buddha's or the matriarchal/patriarchal ancestors' great awakening, while *kensho* is an initial beginning awakening or enlightenment experience.

Sesshin means to "gather or collect the heart-mind." It is a time of intense zazen with the whole heart-mind engaged fully in practice. In a monastery, *sesshin* may occur several times a month, lasting one week at a time. In Zen centers, *sesshin* may be less frequent, but the intention of full engagement of the heart-mind in Zazen is the same.

Shariputra was one of the ten great disciples of the Buddha who was known for his great wisdom. It is said that he died just a few months prior to the Buddha's death.

Shikantaza derives from three Japanese roots: *shikan* meaning

Glossary

"only this," *ta* meaning "precisely," and *za* meaning "to sit." It means to forego techniques of meditation and instead, to practice what is called zazen: a state of attentive, bright awareness, and being present to everything equally without directing the mind toward any particular object.

Shravaka is a student in search of enlightenment, who can experience this only by "hearing" the Buddha's teachings and realizing the essence of the Four Noble Truths. The *shravaka* is one who has nirvana as an ultimate goal.

Shugyo refers to deep, focused, mind-body training that engages right effort and mindfulness in activity, such as zazen, that leads to liberation. While monastic training is referred to as *shugyo*, all activity of a Zen practitioner, whether monk or layperson, is undertaken mindfully. The work of a householder or a business person can lead to the experience of awakening when the activities of daily life are not frivolous, but are spiritual activities in their true context as the means to liberation.

Shuso is a traditional, rotating position in the Zen training monastery in which the candidate chosen by the abbess or abbot, fulfills the role of modeling or leading practice for the sangha. The appointment may last from three months to one year. The appointment culminates in a *Shuso Hossen* ceremony in which the *shuso's* understanding and maturing in the Dharma is tested by the Sangha in a Dharma question-and-answer exchange.

Skanda, when used in the plural, refers to a collection of traits or aggregates that form what we might call the human personality. The *skandas* include form, feeling, perception, thoughts, and consciousness. These aggregates by themselves are impermanent, empty, and without essence. Nevertheless, they are the cause or the object of attraction to appetite, longing, or desire, which brings about suffering. As there is no true abiding "self" there is no real personality or ego to be found and thus, the "ego self" is an illusion.

Sutra is a teaching, perhaps a parable or allegory, based on faith or philosophy, which derives directly from the Buddha. The sutras are prose texts that always begin with the words, "Thus have I heard." The words are ascribed to Ananda, whose excellent memory allowed them to be transcribed immediately after the death of the Buddha.

Tathagata (pronounced ta-ta-ga-ta) is one of the names of the Buddha and means "thus come, thus gone, thus perfected." The term points toward one who has attained complete perfect enlightenment.

Tonglen means "receiving and sending" and is a Tibetan meditation practice in which the in-breath receives and recognizes the suffering of oneself and others, and the out-breath extends compassion, loving-kindness, and *bodhicitta* into the world, thus transforming oneself and the suffering of others.

Upekkha or **Upeksha** refers to an important Buddhist virtue, that of having a mind that is independent of either joy or suffering, and that is lifted above distinctions. It is a state of equilibrium.

Vinaya translates as the "Basket of Discipline," which contains the rules and regulations governing the community of monks and nuns and which in essence regulates the moral, ethical, and spiritual aspects of the daily life of those who live under the monastic *Vinaya* rule.

Zazen is the term used to refer to seated attentiveness in an actively present state, attentive to each passing moment, without focusing on any particular object or thought. This practice is also called *shikantaza*, or "just sitting," which is the practice of being one's true self, or Buddha nature.

Zen simply means meditation. Today the word has taken on many other connotations, some of them implying an in-group or faddish connection. Zen, however, is a sacred practice that begins with zazen, meditation. It is inappropriate to use the word "Zen" in frivolous or banal contexts. Za means to sit and zen means to meditate. There is no Zen without zazen.

Glossary

Zendo is a hall or room set aside for the practice of Zazen. While monasteries have formal designs for the arrangement of monks and practitioners, a less formal zendo may be set up in a home or office, embracing the practice of zazen in daily life.

Acknowledgments

While we were putting the book together, some of us were traveling, teaching, celebrating the arrival of grandchildren, or mourning deaths; some of us were ill, or had to take time out for surgery, or were supporting family members and friends who were going through such passages. Many lives are woven into the text of these pages, much experience, and much wisdom.

The editor, Eido Frances Carney, and the copy editor, Maura High, are very grateful to all the contributors to this volume, for their essays, their patience in working with us through the sometimes bumpy process of production, and for their work in the wider sangha.

If it was a matter of consistency, style, conformity to the best publication standards, it was Maura's job to see that it was taken care of. Eido did the work of conceiving of this project and the book's title and aim. She reached out to the women Zen teachers who could contribute, and coordinated her editorial work with the practical and organizational tasks undertaken by the copy editor.

Fletcher Ward of Straight Light Studio designed the book and moved through all the stages of shaping each page and the intricacies of design elements that produce a polished text. Except for *Teachings on Dogen*, Fletcher has designed all of our books, and Temple Ground is very proud of the elegance, warmth of style, and handsomeness of design on the written page.

And, thanks to the contributors and those who support them, seen and unseen, known and unknown, we now have a book for the world.

Books by Temple Ground Press

Receiving the Marrow: Teachings on Dogen by Soto Zen Women Priests, Edited by Eido Frances Carney, 2012.

Kakurenbo Or the Whereabouts of Zen Priest Ryokan, Eido Frances Carney with translation of Ryokan's poems by Nobuyuki Yuasa with permission from Princeton University Press, 2013.

Seeds of Virtue, Seeds of Change, A Collection of Zen Teachings, Edited by Jikyo Cheryl Wolfer, 2014.

Spanish Edition:
Kakurenbo seguir el rastro del sacerdote Zen Ryokan, Eido Frances Carney, Translated by El Centro Zen de Mexico A.R., La Comunidad Budhista Zen Jardin de Luz Madrid, 2016.

The Eightfold Path, Edited by Jikyo Cheryl Wolfer, Introduction by Byakuren Judith Ragir, 2016.

Zen Teachings in Challenging Times, Introduction by Patricia Dai-En Bennage, 2018.

Forthcoming:
Zen Teachings for Our Times, Enji Boissevain, 2019.

Available online or at your independent bookstore.

Made in the USA
Columbia, SC
06 June 2020